Conjured Bodies

Conjured Bodies

Queer Racialization in
Contemporary Latinidad

LAURA GRAPPO

University of Texas Press ◆ *Austin*

Requests for permission to reproduce material from this work should be sent to:
Permissions
University of Texas Press
P.O. Box 7819
Austin, TX 78713-7819
utpress.utexas.edu/rp-form

♾ The paper used in this book meets the minimum requirements of
ANSI/NISO Z39.48-1992 (R1997) (Permanence of Paper).

Library of Congress Cataloging-in-Publication Data
Names: Grappo, Laura, author.
Title: Conjured bodies : queer racialization in contemporary Latinidad / Laura
    Grappo.
Other titles: Queer racialization in contemporary Latinidad
Description: First edition. | Austin : University of Texas Press, 2022. | Includes
    bibliographical references and index.
Identifiers:
    LCCN 2021054499
    ISBN 978-1-4773-2519-3 (cloth)
    ISBN 978-1-4773-2520-9 (paperback)
    ISBN 978-1-4773-2521-6 (PDF)
    ISBN 978-1-4773-2522-3 (ePub)
Subjects: LCSH: Latin Americans—Press coverage—United States—Case studies. |
    Latin Americans—Ethnic identity—Press coverage—United States—Case
    studies. | Latin Americans—Race identity—Press coverage—United States—
    Case studies. | Hispanic American gays—Press coverage—United States—Case
    studies. | Latin Americans—Press coverage—Political aspects—United States. |
    Latin Americans—United States—Social conditions.
Classification: LCC E184.875 G73 2022 | DDC 305.868/073—dc23/eng/20211214
LC record available at https://lccn.loc.gov/2021054499

doi:10.7560/325193

For Megan

Contents

Acknowledgments

This book has been a long time in the making but truly came into fruition during my time at Wesleyan University in the Department of American Studies. I am grateful to my colleagues there, past and present. I would like to thank Matt Garrett, Tricia Hill, Indira Karamcheti, Liza McAlister, Joel Pfister, and Amy Tang for their colleagueship and support. I am especially grateful to Margot Weiss for her guidance, mentorship, and time spent with my writing, and to J. Kēhaulani Kauanui for her scholarly generosity and encouragement. I also would like to thank the members of the Wesleyan University Center for the Humanities fall 2017 seminar Rethinking Necropolitics for their feedback on early versions of this project.

When I completed my undergraduate degree at Wesleyan all of those years ago, I could hardly have imagined that I would have ended up back at the place that set me on a path toward academic life. I am thankful to Christina Crosby, my undergraduate advisor and for these past few years my colleague, for her years of support and kindness. I feel certain that I would not be where I am today without her.

I am grateful to Kerry Webb at the University of Texas Press for her assistance in shepherding the manuscript through the review process, and to Andrew Hnatow for his assistance with image permissions. I would also like to thank the readers and editors at *Latino Studies*, who provided feedback on portions of chapter 1. Earlier versions of chapter 1 and chapter 4 were also presented at the American Studies Association in 2016 and 2018, and the Berkshire Conference of Women Historians in 2014. I would like to thank all of the panelists and participants who engaged with my work in these settings.

I would not have been able to complete this project without the guidance of my advisors in the graduate program of American studies at Yale University. I thank Hazel Carby, Joanne Meyerowitz, Alicia Schmidt Camacho, Paul Gilroy, and Matt Jacobsen for their inspiring courses, ideas, and encouragement. I am grateful to friends, classmates, and colleagues at Yale University, particularly Susie Woo and G. Melissa García, for their friendship and support as we moved through the program together. During this time, an earlier version of the book was supported by the Ford Foundation Dissertation Fellowship; I will always appreciate the funding provided during that critical year. I am grateful to the Mellon Mays Fellowship Program for their support during my undergraduate years.

I would also like to thank my colleagues in the American Studies Department at Dickinson College for supporting my work and early career. I would like to thank my wonderful students at Dickinson College and Wesleyan University for many hours of invigorating conversation and debate.

Last but not least, I would like to thank my extended family, both far and near, for their encouragement, support, and sense of humor throughout this long process. My kids, Rocco and Luz, have kept everything in perspective—I want to thank them for their endless questions, countless distractions, and many long walks in the woods, talking about everything under the sun. Most of all, I have to thank my partner, Megan Glick, without whom this book would not exist. Your fierce intellect, generosity of spirit, and ability to crack me up have been the grounding center to my life. Thank you for everything and thank you for all the things. This book is dedicated to you.

Conjured Bodies

"The browning of America": Conjured Bodies and Queer Racialization

On July 30, 2018, a lengthy article written by *Vox*'s cofounder and editor-at-large, Ezra Klein, appeared online under the title "White Threat in a Browning America."[1] Addressing the rise of the Trump administration and the role of racial tensions in US electoral decision-making, the article carefully cites academic studies from diverse fields in order to explain how demographic changes have given rise to racial anxiety among whites across class backgrounds. This anxiety, Klein observes, continues to fracture the possibility of multiracial coalitions, a problem all the more alarming as the nation's ethnoracial diversity continues to multiply. Although similar tensions can be found in earlier time periods, Klein cites the consecutive occurrence of the first Black US presidency and the expansion of the Latinx[2] population as a uniquely threatening combination.

To be sure, Klein's argument is not particularly novel; dozens of similar articles could be found throughout the public sphere in the months and years following Trump's victory. These pieces all tell a similar story. They are generally left leaning, while cautiously acknowledging the very real pain that many working-class whites feel regarding their own economic prospects and those of the nation. They ask the chicken-or-egg question about racial tension and economic decline. They tell us in a surprised and saddened tone that the United States has not made as much progress as "we" would have thought likely only a few years ago, when the Obamas moved into the White House. Perhaps most importantly, they cite an impending "browning of America," or a future so heavily impacted by the growth of Latinxs that the nation becomes a "minority-majority" state. In Klein's piece, this final point is illustrated through an accompanying two-second GIF of an empty US map that quickly fills with brown heads falling from the sky (fig. 0.1). Stylistically rendered in monochromatic tans and browns, the GIF works in

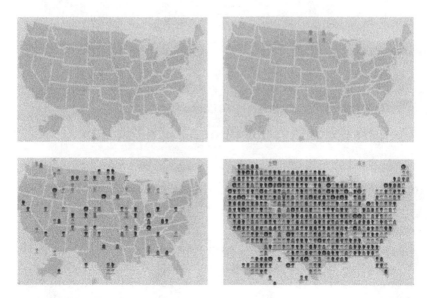

Figure 0.1. Time-lapse progression of a two-second GIF. From Ezra Klein, "White Threat in a Browning America," *Vox*, July 30, 2018.

concert with the "facts" provided in the piece, and quite literally gives credence to fears of a browning nation. Looking at the GIF, it is not hard to imagine it appearing in a more politically conservative context.

Indeed, since its emergence in the 1990s, the phrase "the browning of America" has been utilized across the political spectrum. While certain aspects of the narrative may differ, the specifics are often the same. Time and again, we are told about gaps between median ages (fifty-eight for whites, twenty-nine for Asian Americans, twenty-seven for African Americans, and eleven for Latinxs), about white deaths outpacing white births, and about the US Census Bureau's declaration that "non-Hispanic whites" are the only population currently in decline. Presented in charts, graphs, and tables, this data relies upon explicit racial categorizations (e.g., Hispanic, Black, and so on) or speaks more loosely of "minorities" versus "whites." Of course, what these narratives do not and cannot reference is any actual data on the very thing they seek to describe—"the browning of America"—as there is, officially, no "brown" racial or ethnic designation.

This contradiction—the fact that Latinxs are widely portrayed as a dangerous "browning" force on the one hand, and that there is no real way to measure brownness according to normative data categories on the other—raises several questions: What does it mean that the bulk of public discourse surrounding the nation's racial futurity relies upon a misnomer? What does it mean for "Latinx" and "brown" to act as synonyms in political discourse? What does this interchangeability mean when it is used to describe a matter of great national distress? Have we simply not noticed this incongruity because of the conceptual ambiguity already present within the term "Latinx," which is at times imagined to be a race, an ethnicity, or both?

In an era of intensified precarity for Latinx subjects, the insidious narrative of America's browning is not simply a question of semantics. Since the successful rise of the Trump campaign, anti-Latinx sentiment has become emboldened across the United States. As a nation, we have witnessed the reduction of refugee admissions, the increased policing and arrest of undocumented immigrants for what Lisa Marie Cacho has called "de facto status crimes" (i.e., crimes of existence),[3] the cancellation of the Deferred Action for Childhood Arrivals (DACA) program, the reduction of Temporary Protected Status (TPS) for persons from Central America and the Caribbean, and the separate incarceration of parents and children at the border in detention centers where detainees of all ages are not provided access to basic physical necessities. To put the matter a different way, every day Latinx people are differentially deported, incarcerated, and mistreated on the basis of national heritage. But it is also their general "brownness"—whatever this means—that imperils them in the first place.

Conjured Bodies is a book about the political use value of the conceptual ambiguity present within Latinidad. Through a series of case studies that deconstruct representations of Latinx identities and positionalities in the mainstream media, I document how Latinidad's malleability and vagueness allow it to be marshaled and deployed for other purposes. Like the problem of the concept of "browning," these representations have direct consequences for the lives of Latinx people. At the same time, they also have broader implications for the negotiation of race, gender, sexuality, and inequality in the contemporary United States. The title of the book thus refers to the processes by which Latinidad is "conjured," or called forth in particular times and places, for diverse and seemingly unrelated political purposes. In this context, "conjuring" indicates a kind of projected fantasy.

In the following case studies, I examine the ways in which the ambiguity surrounding the categorization of Latinidad—as a race, an ethnicity, or a combination thereof—produces a useable and transferable semiotics of difference that relies upon recurring but mutable tropes of gender and sexual difference. I call this phenomenon the "queer racialization of Latinidad" to indicate a process of mirroring that takes place between ambiguities present within the concepts of "queer" and "Latinx" and that in turn allows for a mystification of inter- and intrapopulational inequalities. Each case study revolves around one or more Latinx figures who have received considerable attention in the mainstream media, including the San Antonio Four, a group of queer Latina women (Elizabeth Ramirez, Kristie Mayhugh, Cassandra Rivera, and Ana Vasquez) wrongfully incarcerated and then exonerated for child sexual abuse; Lorena (Gallo) Bobbitt, an Ecuadorian immigrant who made headlines for cutting off her white American husband's penis after years of abuse; Aaron Hernandez, a professional football player who committed suicide at the age of twenty-seven following a severe case of concussion-induced chronic traumatic encephalopathy (CTE); and, finally, the pop singer Kali Uchis and the professional baseball players Vladimir Guerrero and Sammy Sosa, whose racial identities have been sources of public controversy. Throughout *Conjured Bodies*, I argue that the representation of these individuals has profound consequences for the conceptualization and treatment of Latinx peoples and communities.[4]

While the book's case studies are divergent in many ways and span a wide range of sociopolitical issues, they also share an important core feature. Namely, they highlight how Latinidad is deployed to manipulate contemporary US narratives of racialization and to distract from the realities of inequitable political, social, and economic circumstances. In other words, I argue that when Latinx figures enter the national public forum, the narratives surrounding them often work to cover over other, more significant issues. Thus, each chapter analyzes one or more conjured stories about Latinidad and, in doing so, reveals how Latinx ambiguity is marshaled to obfuscate particular cultural fears or anxieties, to reentrench normative positions, and to mystify existing inequalities.

Section I. Latinx Ambiguity as Queer Racialization

While the politics of ethnoracial identification are always complicated, they are especially so in the case of "Latinx," precisely because there is no consistent bureaucratic opinion or statistical designation, to say nothing of the debates that exist within Latinx communities on these issues and that continue to impact how Latinxs respond to demographic surveys. As Clara E. Rodríguez observes, a "shifting, context-dependent experience is at the core of many Latinos' life in the United States. . . . For many Latinos, race is primarily cultural; multiple identities are a normal state of affairs; and 'racial mixture' is subject to many different, sometimes fluctuating, definitions."[5]

Thus at times, "Latinx" may signify a race, an ethnicity, or both, and, increasingly, individuals considered to be "white" are asked to identify as "Hispanic" or "non-Hispanic."[6]

Scholars such as Cristina Mora, Arlene Dávila, Mérida Rúa, and Suzanne Oboler have explained the myriad reasons that these ambiguous designations take place, ranging from civil-rights-era activism and the necessity of inter-ethnic and interracial coalitions to changes in the postindustrial economy that led to the rise of ethnoracial niche marketing and to the production of a feedback loop between governmental census categories and diverse communities' abilities to be economically and politically recognizable.[7] Dating to the 1960s, this consolidation is understood to have fully congealed by the 1990s around the term "Hispanic." Importantly, this occurs during the same years in which the phrase "the browning of America" becomes deployed.

Within the realm of Latinx studies, there is a long tradition of celebrating conceptual multiplicity. As Isabel Molina-Guzmán describes, Latinidad "may embody multiple simultaneous ethnic and racial affiliations . . . providing for a more flexible performance of identity that does not always cohere to commonsense biological definitions of ethnicity or phenotypic definitions of race."[8] For decades, field-defining scholars, including Gloria Anzaldúa, Cherríe Moraga, Maria Figueroa, and Alicia Arrizón, among others, have argued that Latinidad is empowered through (rather than hindered by) its indefinability.[9] Asserting that because concrete methods of racialization are often associated with practices of specification, hierarchization, separation, and disenfranchisement, these scholars suggest that the ambiguities afforded by Latinidad are potentially liberatory. For example, in her path-breaking work *Borderlands / La Frontera* (1987), Anzaldúa describes a revolutionary "new *mestiza* consciousness . . . a consciousness of the Borderlands" that transcends the "clash of cultures" and that is defined by a "tolerance for contradictions, a tolerance for ambiguity."[10] "The work of *mestiza* consciousness," she observes, lies in a

> massive uprooting of dualistic thinking. . . . [A]s a *mestiza* I have no country, my homeland cast me out; yet all countries are mine because I am every woman's sister or potential lover. (As a lesbian, I have no race, my own people disclaim me; but I am all races because there is the queer of me in all races.) . . . I am an act of kneading, of uniting and joining that not only has produced both a creature of darkness and a creature of light, but also a creature that questions the definitions of light and dark and gives them new meanings.[11]

Here, Anzaldúa points to the ways in which freedom lies in the disruption of existing binaries and draws an analogy with queerness that has since become commonplace.

Throughout the field of Latinx studies, this analogy is made both with respect to conceptual similarities and with respect to the literal enactment of identity and lived material reality. Thus, while Antonio Viego has argued that Latinidad "queers ethnicity and race" by challenging normative dichotomies of difference and "the logic by which ethnicity/race can be posed as a binary pair," Juana María Rodríguez suggests that there is a fundamental connection between Latinx and queer embodiment.[12] For Rodríguez, "the colorful extravagances of *Latinidad* and the flaming gestures of queer fabulousness are ways to counteract demands for corporeal conformity, to refuse to alter our bodies and our movements for the sake of social comfort others take in their invented forms of appropriateness."[13]

At the same time, scholars including José Estéban Muñoz, Hiram Pérez, Leticia Alvarado, and Deb Vargas have moved toward an even more expansive conceptualization of identity through the lens of "brownness."[14] In his foundational essays on this issue, Muñoz asserts the importance of moving beyond frameworks that understand "racial or ethnic difference as solely cultural," toward an approach that foregrounds "the ways in which various historically coherent groups 'feel' differently and navigate the material world on a different emotional register."[15] Describing the difference between "visual ethnic recognition" and affective belonging, he observes that "one can feel very Brown and perhaps not register as Brown as the dark-skinned person standing next to one who is involved in the endeavor of trying to feel white."[16] Drawing from this work, Alvarado notes that the "instability [of Latinidad] as a performative site for the doing of racialized subjectivity" implies "the lack of a proper singular subject that centers the antinormative sensibility at the core of brownness," while Pérez suggests that we might look to trauma as a "constitutive force in relation to group identity."[17]

In contrast to these approaches, this book is concerned with the ways in which ambiguity and a lack of specificity with respect to Latinidad do not always promote radical ends but instead often serve to help those already in power, precisely because such uncertainty can be manipulated to occlude or mystify. In other words, I demonstrate that in attempting to break away from pejorative racial designations and the confinements of traditional markers of identity, we also forgo the differentiating specificities that are necessary to understand how oppression operates. When "brownness" can be anything and everything, it follows a neoliberal logic of progress through inclusion.

At the same time, it covers over intercommunal inequalities and differences in a way that mirrors less politically radical deployments of brownness.

Yet even as I diverge from arguments that advocate for an ever-expanding identitarian paradigm, I am nonetheless indebted to this very same body of scholarship for its theorization of the connections between conceptualizations of Latinidad and queerness. Indeed, each of the case studies in *Conjured Bodies* demonstrates the centrality of gender and sexuality to manipulative deployments of Latinidad. Throughout the book, I illustrate how Latinidad is produced through a process of "queer racialization," a phrase that is intended to evoke both the peculiarity of Latinx as an ethnoracial signifier and the significance of the sex/gender/sexuality matrix to its strategic instrumentalization. Ultimately, I argue that dominant portrayals of Latinidad produce a transferable semiotics of difference that has critical implications for broader patterns of difference and inequality produced along axes of ethnicity, race, gender, and sexuality.

Section II. Conjuring as Paradigm

In utilizing the paradigm of "conjuring" to describe the manipulation and deployment of Latinidad, I situate my analyses alongside recent scholarship across the humanities and social sciences that foregrounds analytics of haunting, spectrality, and racialized social death. First staked out by Jacques Derrida in *Specters of Marx* (1993) and since referred to as the "spectral turn" in poststructuralist thought, the use of the "ghost" as a conceptual paradigm has significant implications for understanding practices of racialized denigration and dehumanization.[18] As Judith Butler has observed, processes of marginalization often involve a contradiction in terms that is best articulated through the spectral metaphor. The Other "cannot be mourned, because they are always already lost, or rather, never 'were.'" This "derealization . . . means that [they are] neither alive nor dead, but *interminably spectral*."[19]

Similarly, theorists such as Renée Bergland, Anne McClintock, Avery Gordon, David Marriott, and Dixa Ramírez have all pointed to the ways in which repressed histories of slavery, settler colonialism, and imperialism produce an ongoing "occult presence" of racialized violence.[20] Achille Mbembe and Lisa Marie Cacho have also considered the politics and thresholds of symbolic death for individuals who exist within societies that do not value their personhood. While Mbembe proposes the concept of "necropolitics" to articulate forms of haunting that relegate entire populations to an existence under the shadow of material and figurative "death-worlds," Cacho argues that racism in itself is a "killing abstraction . . . ensur[ing] that certain people will live an 'abstract existence.'"[21] Adjacent to these works, Cecilia Menjívar, Elana Zilberg, Susan Bibler Coutin, and Armando García have demonstrated the ways in which Latinx undocumented immigrants exist in an intermediary zone between citizen and subject, a space that García identifies as a form of life "without ontology."[22] Similarly, Luis D. León and Esther Peeren have deployed the term "ghost" to connote what Peeren describes as undocumented workers' "lack of social visibility, unobtrusiveness, enigmatic abilities, [and] uncertain status between life and death."[23]

In this book, I consider the ways in which the metaphor of conjuring is particularly useful when juxtaposed with Latinx studies scholarship that examines the hyperspectacularization of Latinx bodies in mass media representations. As scholars such as Frances Aparicio, Susana Chávez-Silverman, Isabel Molina-Guzmán, Angharad Valdivia, Norma Alarcón, Myra Mendible, William Calvos-Quiros, and Hiram Pérez have noted, Latinxs are often portrayed stereotypically and homogeneously. Made into "fetishized objects consumed within an economics of desire that obscures the social relationships of its producers," Latinxs become a site of overdetermination and ambivalence.[24] While Calvos-Quiros writes that Latinxs are often depicted as "social monsters that must be controlled, reeducated, segregated, or 'deported' into invisibility," Pérez observes that such hyperbolic stereotypes are "opportunistically and systematically deployed at times of crisis."[25]

While this conceptual monstrosity—fashioned through the production of racial and sexual alterity—may be understood to reverberate throughout a wide variety of discourses that surround nonwhite people of diverse backgrounds, there is also something uniquely important about its deployment in the case of Latinidad. After all, the most loathsome monsters are those without a proper name, shape, or location. Conceptually and politically, ambiguous monsters allow for the justification of heightened forms of surveillance, policing, and violence (hence the effectiveness of the phrase "the browning of America"). As Leo Chavez describes, portrayals of Latinxs often suggest that they "are not like previous immigrant groups, who ultimately became part of the nation." Rather, they are conceived of as "an invading force from south of the border that is bent on . . . destroying the American way of life through their unwillingness or inability to assimilate."[26] Chavez calls this the "Latino Threat Narrative," which, as he explains, relies upon the capacity of media spectacles to "transform a 'worldview'—that is, a taken-for-granted [likely fallacious] understanding of the world—into an objective force, one that is taken as 'truth.'"[27] Similarly, Molina-Guzmán reminds us that the circulation of meaning through the mass media plays a critical role in the reproduction of social and political inequality specifically around issues of race, ethnicity, and gender. . . . Consequently, news stories . . . are not an impartial reflection of the reality of US Latinos generally . . . but rather what Stuart Allan . . . defines as an "ideological construction of reality" or what John Fiske . . . described as a "sense of reality that is ideological." . . . [B]roadcast and print journalists [thus] transform texts into discourse, to transform words and images into stories that perform beyond the function of information.[28]

In addition to acknowledging the discursive biases that enter into the production of "news," *Conjured Bodies* is attentive to the ways in which meaning circulates within popular media. As Barbie Zelizer documents, though we often think about journalistic production in dichotomous terms—as "real news" versus "tabloid news"—these forms are often coproductive, and we do each a disservice by ignoring how and in what ways they rely upon each other.[29] Following from this premise, I use a broad range of media sources in order to fully understand how Latinx subjects are represented. As Laurie Ouellette observes,

To approach the study of media critically involves situating media within economic, political, cultural, and social contexts and addressing its relationship to capitalism, labor, citizenship, gender, race and class dynamics, inequalities, sexuality, globalization, and other issues that are both larger than media, and intertwined with the production, circulation, and use of media texts, images, sounds, spaces, artifacts, technologies, and discourses. Doing so is not a singular process, but rather a pluralistic and historical inquiry.[30]

Throughout the book, I demonstrate how and why these representations matter in the construction of norms, the boundaries of citizenship, and the imagination of which lives matter most, and which matter least.

I use the notion of "conjuring" in the book to interrogate the violence insinuated through the deployment of media representations of Latinidad, both as it pertains to Latinx subjects and as it extends to other minoritized subjects. As David Marriott and Adrián Pérez-Melgosa have argued, there is indeed a deep connection between practices of the *spectacularization* and the *spectralization* of the Other. According to Marriott, "racism is experienced as an encounter with a mirror image in which one sees one's double, one's simulacrum, one's ghostly semblance—a specter which you greet with frustration and impotence, because of its inseparable hold on one's life."[31] Further, he explains, because the "spectacle of black lives [is] consumed painlessly, virtually, teletechnologically" on a daily basis, we must ask how "the commodity value of black death-in-life" is a problem that is coproduced by real-world violence and its representation within the realm of popular culture.[32]

Similarly, in his study of fictional and documentary films covering inter-American migration, Pérez-Melgosa illustrates how the bodies of migrants are continually represented as "abused, extenuated, bruised, covered in scars, ravaged by illness, and eventually as ominous corpses."[33] For Pérez-Melgosa, these images represent a form of "low intensity necropolitics" that reproduces the notion that "those in power deploy death as the norm and life as a right that has to be continuously won over by individuals."[34] Tragically, he notes, these representations are found in films of diverse political backing, particularly those that seek to denounce the "human tragedy" of migration.[35] In this same vein, *Conjured Bodies* considers how it is the very existence of Latinidad's media spectacularization, rather than the overt political leanings of specific forms thereof, that occasion the opportunity for its ongoing manipulation and deployment.

Section III. Sites of Queer Racialization in Contemporary Latinidad

While it may be argued that any era is impacted by the lingering effects of those that have come before it—and thus, in a sense, all moments are "haunted"—*Conjured Bodies* calls attention to the ways in which the 1990s and early 2000s were significant periods in the production of Latinidad's queer racialization. Moving forward from this moment, *Conjured Bodies* identifies the ways in which much of the anti-Latinx discourse that has come to characterize the late 2010s can be traced back to key events and figures that emerged in the 1990s and have held the nation's curiosity in an ongoing fashion. Thus, while my central argument is not historical in nature, I am nonetheless concerned with the ideological traffic that continues to take place between these recent decades. For this reason, the chapters are organized in a loosely chronological fashion, even as they often examine figures and events that share overlapping spheres of time and space.

Chapter 1, "'This could be Satanic-related': Fantasies of Innocence and Criminalization in the Case of the San Antonio Four," explores the series of events that led to the fifteen-year wrongful incarceration of four queer Latina women for child sexual abuse during the course of so-called satanic rituals in San Antonio, Texas, in 1994. The chapter focuses on two narratives. First, it examines the documentary *Southwest of Salem: The Story of the San Antonio Four* (dir. Deborah Esquenazi), which premiered to critical acclaim at the 2016 Tribeca Film Festival. Investigative journalism associated with the documentary as well as the publicity that surrounded it became credited in the process of the four women's exoneration, which culminated in the same year as the film's release. By unpacking the relationship between the film and the cases levied against the women, this chapter addresses tensions that exist among narratives of innocence, criminal culpability, and the production of intersectional identities. In doing so, the chapter interrogates the pressures of normalizing discourses on frameworks of juridical exoneration, demonstrating how the intersection of queer and Latinx positionalities operated to produce a tragic conflict, requiring a measure of self-effacement in the name of vindication. This portion of the chapter also departs from other academic and popular interpretations of the film that have tended to understand it as a shining testament to the power of grassroots social justice activism. Instead, I demonstrate how the film mobilizes a narrative of homonormativity in order to garner public sympathy.

The second and related narrative examined in chapter 1 is the postincarceration experience of one of the four women, Ana Vasquez, who became a criminal justice reform advocate following her release. Specifically, I contextualize her participation in two organizations, the Innocence Project of Texas (dedicated to exonerating wrongfully incarcerated persons) and the Houston Forensic Science Center (an independent laboratory founded in response to corruption in the Houston Police Department's own forensic lab), alongside the growing presence of Latinx employees in US Customs and Border Protection at the US-Mexico border. In doing so, I consider the significance of the case of the San Antonio Four both to the legacy of homophobic law that has long characterized juridical culture in Texas and to the increasing militarization of the US-Mexico border, which has become an important source of revenue and employment for the state's residents. By contextualizing Vasquez's story alongside demographic changes in personnel at the Border Patrol, I demonstrate how the case of the Four represents the instrumentalization of Latinidad in the service of homonationalist rhetoric that promotes the state as a site of enfranchisement and justice for the "right" kinds of queer and Latinx people.

Chapter 2, "'A life is worth more than a penis': Lorena (Gallo) Bobbitt and the Domestication of Abuse," examines a case that ran concurrently with that of the San Antonio Four but attained a spectacular level of international notoriety. In 1994, Lorena Gallo, then Bobbitt, an Ecuadorian woman married to a white American man, John Wayne Bobbitt, was arrested for using a knife to cut off her husband's penis while he was intoxicated and asleep. While the Bobbitt trial really never left the American popular consciousness, it has also received renewed attention and a revised narrative in the era of the #MeToo movement. In January 2019, for example, Amazon released a high-budget, four-part docuseries entitled *Lorena*. Directed and produced by the Academy Award winner Jordan Peele, *Lorena* reframes the Bobbitt case in relation to the couple's history of domestic violence. Popular response to the documentary has revealed tremendous and newfound sympathy for Lorena, whose on-camera retrospective interviews narrate how years of physical, sexual, and psychological abuse pushed her to strike back against her husband's "weapon of choice."

Yet, at the time of the original trial, Lorena was portrayed and interpreted in a very different manner. Although she had testified to her husband's violent behavior, his actions were not understood as exculpatory evidence. Instead, such testimony was used to bolster a temporary insanity defense known as "irresistible impulse," which accrued meaning in the 1990s as the issue of spousal abuse became a matter of heightened public debate. Public opinion on the Bobbitt trial seemed to ebb and flow, both evoking and disavowing the rhetoric of feminism and the terms of Lorena's "cultural difference" in order to understand her actions.

Taking all of these factors into consideration, chapter 2 thinks about the relationship between perceptions of Lorena's ethnoracial identity on the one hand and the trajectory of normative white feminist anti-abuse activism on the other. While there is no doubt that Lorena's status as a racialized foreigner and non-US citizen was relevant in the unfolding of her trial, it is also the case that both popular and academic treatments have tended to focus on how her identity impacted her condemnation within the media and court proceedings. By contrast, I foreground the question of Lorena's potential relationship to whiteness alongside the aims of normative white feminism in order to understand the *lack* of severity in the court's sentencing decision. In other words, while existing assessments of Lorena's treatment in the public imaginary suggest that her ethnoracial difference provided the impetus for her arrest and condemnation, this chapter considers what it means that she received only forty-five days of institutionalization in a psychiatric hospital for a crime that had the potential to carry a twenty-year prison sentence.

By looking at the relationship among the rise of domestic violence awareness, the revision of immigration policy with respect to victims of abuse, and the emergence of legal defense strategies that foregrounded gender and cultural background, I demonstrate how Lorena's case became conjured to enable one of the first successful articulations of "battered woman syndrome" through the lens of her ethnoracial difference. Looking at the overlap in the timelines and rhetoric of US domestic violence policy and immigrant protection policy, chapter 2 illustrates how legal regulations surrounding the treatment of "battered immigrants" became a critical forum for debates about the protection of white US women. Chapter 2 thus grapples with the significance of Lorena's marginal whiteness, ambiguous citizenship status, and feminine gender presentation in the production of public sympathy toward her case and related domestic violence legislation, both in the 1990s and in the 2010s.

Chapter 3, "'A troubled, battered mind': The Queer Lives and Deaths of Aaron Hernandez, 1989–2017," turns toward a public figure whose professional and personal trajectories came to mark him as beyond redemption. Indeed, if chapter 2 offers a story of cultural, social, and legal transformation mobilized through the coordinates of Lorena's identity, and chapter 1 illustrates how adherence to standards of homonormativity and homonationalism elicit particular sympathies and disavowals, chapter 3 moves in a different direction, to demonstrate how projected ethnoracial, gender, and sexual ambiguities are mobilized within the arena of professional sports, with dire consequences for young men of color.

Born and raised in Bristol, Connecticut, Aaron Hernandez was a successful athlete from an early age and set several national high school records. In 2007, he was listed as the top tight-end recruit by Scout.com, and after agreeing to graduate a semester early in order to prepare for the fall season, he left home to join the University of Florida's team a month after his seventeenth birthday. Three years later, he was forced to leave college after a series of behavioral and academic controversies and was drafted by the New England Patriots in 2010. By 2013, at the age of twenty-three, he was removed from the team due to multiple allegations of murder that culminated in his arrest for the shooting of a friend, Odin Lloyd. In 2015, a jury found Hernandez guilty of murder in the first degree, and two years later, in 2017, he was found dead by his own hand in a prison cell at the Souza-Baranowski Correctional Center in Lancaster, Massachusetts.

Hernandez's suicide gave way to tremendous speculation about the state of his mental health and its relationship to the violent act that had landed him in prison in the first place. Not only did autopsies reveal that he suffered from an extremely advanced form of chronic traumatic encephalopathy (CTE) stemming from a lifetime of repetitive head injuries both on and off the field, but so too did information about his sexuality come to light in the days preceding and following his death. Though Hernandez had lived as an ostensibly straight man with his long-term girlfriend and their biological child, rumors about his sexual liaisons with other men surfaced in the wake of his incarceration. Two days before his death, he was publicly outed by a radio show host who joked derisively about his queer sexuality.

This chapter considers the narratives that surrounded Hernandez's ascent to fame in life and in death. It addresses how his racial, gender, and sexual identities constrained his achievements and produced a trajectory of athletic and financial success that became coterminous with a descent into criminalization, debility, and, ultimately, death. In order to do so, the chapter draws upon theories of necropower and debility to consider how the exploitation of men of color within the institution of professional football has served to reduce them to disposable bodies made to sustain and absorb endless corporeal damage.[36] By thinking through how race is used to mitigate definitions of "risk" surrounding CTE for football players alongside concurrent discourses that locate sexual identity as a form of bodily "truth," this chapter imagines Hernandez as a conjured figure whose fungibility is seemingly produced through an assent to the expectations of professional athletics. Moreover, I consider how the negative and denigrating publicity that continues to surround him even in his death at once manages to evoke tropes of anti-Blackness while also covering over the structural forms of violence accrued in a sport "dominated" by African American players. Ultimately, this chapter demonstrates how anti-Black racism can be mobilized in the absence of actual Black personhood through the queer racialization of Latinidad: indeed, Hernandez was of Italian American and Puerto Rican heritage, had an olive complexion, and was even mistakenly identified as "Hawaiian" in his criminal proceedings.

Building upon this argument, chapter 4, "'Who's going to tell Sammy Sosa he is Afro-Latino?': Transraciality and Panethnic Latinx Authenticity," considers how anti-Black sentiment circulates within multiracial Latinx populations and within US society more broadly. By bringing together several incidents and individuals rather than focusing on a singular "case," this chapter diverges from the previous three. In doing so, it addresses the stakes of Latinx identification in relation to two primary issues: (1) the rise of transraciality (or the idea that race can be understood as voluntary and mutable, comparable to the way that gender is conceived of by transgender people) and (2) criticism surrounding claims of Afro-Latinx identity and Latinx authenticity.

In the first instance, I demonstrate how, in addition to appropriating the rhetoric and identities of transgender people, the rising phenomenon of transracial identification is made possible through the conjuring of Latinidad, or through the utilization of ideological frames that cast Latinx identity as a fluid, quasi-ethnic, quasi-racial category. I do so by interrogating public conversations surrounding comparisons made between Rachel Dolezal (a Black-passing white woman revealed as a fraud in 2015, who has subsequently self-identified as "transracial") and Caitlyn Jenner (a former Olympic athlete whose gender transition was made public in the same month as the Dolezal scandal).

In the second instance, I explore how public discourse surrounding the claim to varying degrees of "Blackness" by and for Afro-Latinxs often revitalizes anti-Black sentiment while simultaneously rendering Afro-Latinx subjects invisible. By analyzing debates surrounding the ethnoracial identity, self-presentation, and public remarks of the Colombian American pop star Kali Uchis, I illustrate how flexible identifications with whiteness and Blackness have become central to the success of many Latinx musicians within the US entertainment industry. I then turn to controversies over the ethnoracial identities of the former professional baseball players Vladimir Guerrero and Sammy Sosa (both of Dominican heritage) in order to consider how anti-Blackness functions within a historically "white" sport. While Guerrero became an object of public interest once a teammate challenged his racial identification, Sosa has long received scrutiny for his possible use of skin lightening products.

Overall, the chapter considers the ways in which anti-Blackness is at once constitutive of Latinidad and produced through it by hegemonic ideologies. By thinking about how Latinx panethnicity can be used to ambiguate racial identity in general, and the Black/white dichotomy in particular, this chapter illustrates how anti-Blackness is often produced as a problem that is "exterior" to US race relations and how the confusion over Latinx multiraciality—itself a product of government systems of classification—is often used as a source of humor to make light of colorist hierarchies and to invalidate the saliency of race in the modern United States.

Importantly, the problems identified in chapter 4 operate against the theoretical move toward "brownness" made by Muñoz and others. While approaches to brownness often envision it as an alternative to more exclusionary models with clearer categories, I ask whether the concept may ultimately serve to advance many of the same problems identified throughout the course of the book, in which the ambiguity surrounding Latinidad becomes mobilized for questionable ends. For this reason, in the conclusion I circle back to the introduction to draw a parallel between the theoretical frame of brownness on the one hand and the ethnocentric, conservative rhetoric surrounding "the browning of America" on the other. Reflecting upon chapter 4's discussion of the rise of transracialism, I consider how the mirrored ambiguities present in the terms "queer" and "Latinx" may ultimately serve to limit rather than liberate, and to circumscribe rather than radicalize.

CHAPTER 1

"This could be Satanic-related": Fantasies of Innocence and Criminalization in the Case of the San Antonio Four

At the beginning of our trial, during jury selection, the attorneys talked about us being gay as if it were a disease, or something to be frightened of—that we were not human. If people there had not thought about [our sexuality] as an issue, at the end of jury selection, I'm sure they felt differently. In closing arguments [the prosecutor] stated that we are gay and the victims are female. . . . Being gay does not make us perverts or sick people . . . does not mean that we are going to hurt small children. . . . [W]e are normal and humane people just like heterosexuals.
CASSANDRA RIVERA, "FOUR LIVES LOST"

There is no vision of a collective, democratic public culture or of an ongoing engagement with contentious, cantankerous queer politics. Instead we have been administered a kind of political sedative—we get marriage and the military then we go home and cook dinner, forever. . . . This New Homonormativity comes equipped with a rhetorical recoding of key terms in the history of gay politics.
LISA DUGGAN, "THE NEW HOMONORMATIVITY: THE SEXUAL POLITICS OF NEOLIBERALISM"

In April 2016, the documentary *Southwest of Salem: The Story of the San Antonio Four* premiered to critical acclaim at the Tribeca Film Festival. The film explores the strange series of events that led to the fourteen-year wrongful incarceration of four queer Latina women for child sexual abuse during the course of "satanic rituals" in San Antonio, Texas.[1] Arrested in 1994, the four women—Elizabeth Ramirez (twenty-two), Kristie Mayhugh (twenty-one), Cassandra Rivera (nineteen), and Anna Vasquez (nineteen)—were charged with numerous crimes related to the sexual abuse of a child, allegedly perpetrated against two of Ramirez's nieces, ages seven and nine. While Ramirez was charged separately from and received a longer sentence than the other three, their cases were inextricably linked from the beginning. Throughout the trials, the question of the women's sexuality continually surfaced; that they were "lesbians" and "homosexuals" were matters of fact presented to prospective jurors in the conservative area of Bexar County, leading many to self-recuse. At several points in the trials, the prosecution referred to the women's "lifestyle" and sexual conduct as potentially contiguous with the types of child abuse described by the alleged victims.

Southwest of Salem reveals the force with which homophobia structured the women's trials as well as the case itself. It explores how the original allegations were coerced and fabricated by Ramirez's nieces' father, Javier Limon, a man whose advances Ramirez had rebuked on numerous occasions. It refutes the "scientific" evidence presented at the women's trials and offers other points of fact that verify their claim to innocence. Ultimately, it helped lead to the women's exoneration when the team working on the film successfully obtained and recorded the recantation of one of Ramirez's nieces' original testimonies. The significance of the film was articulated by the court in its decision, which cited the investigative work and publicity garnered by the documentary in its ruling.[2] Media coverage of the film was also overwhelmingly positive, leading to increased public concern for the fate of the women. Critics, journalists, and activists alike lauded the documentary for bringing the women's struggle to light, striking a blow for justice.[3] Even still, the film's disproportionate focus on one of the women (Vasquez), coupled with its hyperrepresentation of the women's familial lives, suggests the limits of compassion toward those who exist outside the boundaries of normativity.

This chapter unpacks the relationship between *Southwest of Salem* and the cases levied against the San Antonio Four in order to explore the tensions that exist among narratives of innocence, criminal culpability, and the production of intersectional identities. It examines the pressures of normalizing discourses on narratives of exoneration, demonstrating how the intersection of nonnormative sexual, gender, and racial positionalities produces a tragic paradox that requires a measure of self-effacement in the name of vindication. More specifically, it considers how the women's Latina identities impacted the court's understanding of their sexual and gender identities, how these intersections in turn culminated in their incarceration, and how *Southwest* works to recast their subjectivities in the context of ongoing political and cultural transformations.

This chapter is organized into five sections. Section I provides critical context on the "satanic panic" phenomenon of the 1980s and 1990s that led to the invocation of satanism during the women's trials. Section II examines the relationship between queer sexualities and Latinx identities in order to consider how the film raises questions about the constraints of existing frameworks of social justice and the reproduction of particular narratives of respectability. Section III considers the role of fantastic imagery in the mobilization of 1990s xenophobic attitudes toward the US-Mexico border, as well as the role that fantastic narratives played in the case of the Four. Section IV then explores how narrative choices and the concordant production of particular forms of silence in *Southwest* speak to broader contradictions surrounding the ongoing marginalization of queer Latinxs. Lastly, section V considers the significance of one of the Four's (Vasquez's) post-exoneration involvement in criminal justice reform within the contexts of lesbian and gay civil rights on the one hand and the expansion of the prison-military complex on the other. In doing so, I argue that current responses to the case and the documentary as social justice "victories" serve to obscure critical questions that remain unresolved about the case and, ultimately, to reframe and erase the discriminatory conditions that led to the women's wrongful incarceration in the first place. In this chapter, the phenomenon of queer racialization can be seen most clearly in the co-optation of the Four's exoneration by triumphant LGBTQ narratives as well as the normalization of Latinx imbrication within the carceral state.

Section I. "Satanic panic": Race, Sexuality, and Mass Paranoia

Elizabeth Ramirez, Kristie Mayhugh, Cassandra Rivera, and Anna Vasquez had been friends for many years. They were all from working-class Latinx backgrounds, and each struggled with her family's disapproval of her sexuality to differing degrees. Ramirez and Mayhugh had at one point been romantically involved, though at the time of the arrest, they were friends and roommates. Rivera and Vasquez were in a romantic relationship, raising Rivera's biological children from a previous relationship. At the time of their incarceration, Ramirez was pregnant, and she was subsequently forced to surrender the child. The events that led to the women's arrests began when police arrived at Ramirez's door in 1994 with allegations that she and her friends had sexually abused her sister's seven- and nine-year-old daughters. Ramirez was stunned by the accusation. Her nieces had spent time at her apartment and with her friends on many occasions. She wondered if the children's father (her sister's ex-boyfriend, Javier Limon) was behind the story. Limon's interest in Ramirez was publicly known. He had offered to marry her and had sent her several unrequited love letters, and she recalled having felt threatened by him. Limon's daughters' accusations occurred slightly after Ramirez rejected his marriage proposal, and it seemed possible he had concocted the story to punish her.[4]

From the beginning of the case, the girls' testimonies appeared strange and inconsistent. They claimed that they had been at Ramirez and Rivera's residence during a party, where the women used drugs, wielded a gun, and forced the girls to perform sexual acts as part of a satanic ritual. Yet each time the girls told their story, important aspects changed, from who was present at the party, to which woman held the gun. Explaining away these discrepancies, the prosecutors argued that "the girls were young children who could hardly be expected to keep facts straight."[5] Yet the accounts of the children alone did not convict the Four. Instead, physician testimony from Nancy Kellogg, head of pediatrics at the University of Texas Health Science Center at San Antonio, stated that she had seen signs of sexual abuse on one of the girls, which she linked both to satanic rituals and to lesbianism.[6] Kellogg was later forced to retract her findings; neither her theory of how the alleged abuse had occurred nor her identification of purported physical evidence followed prevailing medical knowledge.[7]

As this chapter demonstrates, the court's willingness to overlook the peculiarities present in the alleged victims' statements and to accept the dubious testimony surrounding satanism was clearly tied to the identities of the accused. Records of police and prosecutor questions reveal an intentional confusion over lesbianism itself (wherein the women were continually challenged about their friendships and whether they were in fact all sexually involved with one another) and over the distinction between queer sexuality and pedophilia.[8] Importantly, even as it became apparent that the courts would likely indict the women, all four maintained their innocence, refusing to take a plea bargain that would have resulted in reduced sentences. Had they done so, they could have admitted guilt, undergone sex offender treatment, and walked away from their lengthy incarceration.[9]

The bizarre nature of the alleged crime situates the case of the Four as part of the "satanic panic," a phrase that refers to a number of child sexual abuse cases, mostly in the 1980s and early 1990s, in which allegations of child abuse were connected to a belief in the occult and so-called "ritual satanic worship."[10] Although rumors of instances of satanic ritual abuse were unremittingly popular in the media during this period, the evidence for their actual existence remains implausible. By 1994, the National Center on Child Abuse and Neglect (NCCAN) had reports of over twelve thousand claims of satanic ritual child abuse across the nation. Yet, after collecting data from eleven thousand police personnel, psychiatric care workers, clinical social workers, and district attorneys, NCCAN found no credible evidence that any such abuse had ever taken place.[11] Scholarship that has dealt with the satanic panic phenomenon has largely interpreted it as a form of social hysteria, much like the ancient yet still resonant witch hunt narrative, which imagines deviant community members as outcasts and uses them as scapegoats.[12]

Several points of historical contextualization are necessary to understand how and why these charges were successful in their specific time and place. First was their disproportionate emergence within the context of the growing day-care industry, a business that signaled post-second-wave-feminist commitments to working outside the home and that came with commensurate social anxiety. Second was the broader surge in cultural conservatism, particularly the evangelical Christian third wave. Employing ancient Christian demonology rhetoric, this sect contends that literal demons are omnipresent in everyday life and can enter anyone who is insufficiently religious. Third-wave Christian literature asserts that particular behaviors (extramarital affairs, homosexuality, and pornography), especially forms of nonnormative sexuality, invite demonic possession. In this context, racial animus was also understood as a path to demonic possession, through the vehicle of intergenerational inheritance or through the racialization of non-Judeo-Christian religious traditions.[13]

At the same time, the feminist "sex wars" and larger issues of sex negativity emerged, catalyzing public debates about the prevalence of sexual violence. Writers such as Susan Brownmiller asserted that rape must be understood as a pervasive, endemic, and powerfully effective tool of social control.[14] As feminist work began to contend with the realities of child abuse and incest, heightened sensitivity to the often hidden nature of these types of violations led to the deployment of therapeutic techniques intended to reveal buried traumas. In particular, the contentious and now largely debunked practice of recovered-memory therapy became an emerging practice. Now more commonly known as "false memory syndrome," this technique provides a form of guided meditation or mild hypnosis in which a therapist leads clients to discover "repressed" memories of childhood abuse.[15] The most influential text of this sort was a self-help book entitled *The Courage to Heal: A Guide for Women Survivors of Child Sexual Abuse*, in which the authors inform readers,

> Often the knowledge you were abused starts with a tiny feeling, an intuition. It's important to trust that inner voice and work from there. Assume your feelings are valid. So far, no one we've talked to thought she might have been abused, and then later discovered that she hadn't been. The pro-

gression always goes the other way, from suspicion to confirmation. If you think you were abused and your life shows the symptoms, then you were.[16]

This call to belief, based upon the nebulous and precarious terrain of intuition, suspicion, and memory, develops from a feminist epistemology. In affirming the validity of women's own knowledge of their experiences—no matter how unclear, uncertain, or untethered to factual evidence they may be—recovered-memory therapy both legitimized women's affective experiences and challenged the institutional power of patriarchal legal, medical, and cultural authorities.

In the case of the satanic panic, psychotherapeutic intervention seemed especially suited to reveal deeply hidden experiences of ritualistically infused sexual abuse. As the psychiatrist Paul McHugh characterizes it, "psychotherapy came to be seen as a universal balm that in a mysterious way would better us by calling from some memory of inner ghosts and demons and exorcising them."[17] While the psychological excavation of such memories was intended to heal the patient by allowing her to come to terms with supposed childhood abuse, the practice of recovered memory was soon discredited. When the FBI investigated three hundred cases of repressed-memory satanic abuse in 1989, they were unable to verify any of them.[18] Further, most cases of satanic ritual child abuse were diagnosed by statistically few clinical psychologists, supporting the idea that some therapists might have implanted particular memories that patients then "discovered" during the course of treatment.[19] The practice of recovering memories resonated during the 1980s and early 1990s in part because of a broader popular cultural interest in satanism and the occult, which W. Scott Poole connects to societal unrest in the post-civil-rights and post-Vietnam eras. Poole writes, "While Satan had always been a primary site for the construction of American notions of innocence and of evil, by the 1980s the demonic had become a central cultural discourse, a social mechanism that worked on multiple levels of American religion and popular entertainment." This interest in the occult could be seen across popular media, including music, graphic novels, gaming, television, and film.[20]

Beyond the contributing factors that led to the general satanic panic (the growing day-care industry, the rise of conservative Christianity, feminist concerns over sexual abuse and the emergence of "repressed memories," and growing popular cultural interest in satanism and the occult), the case of the San Antonio Four must also be understood in relation to the HIV/AIDS crisis as well as public disputes over the US-Mexico border and growing concern over the rise of the Latinx population. These additional factors are especially important when considering the timeline of the satanic panic, which had mostly died down by the time of the four women's arrests in 1994, and which had already received significant scientific discrediting by the time the prosecution's expert witness testified to the likelihood of the abuse as "possibly satanic" in nature.[21]

Section II. "The larger issues at hand": Queer and Latinx Pathologization

While the HIV/AIDS crisis of the 1980s and early 1990s is most often associated with narratives of prejudice directed toward gay men, it is also the case that the deployment of homophobia by politicians, conservative activists, and the medical community spoke in generalized language about HIV/AIDS as a result of queer sex. As scholars have observed, the symbolic link between queer sexuality and AIDS could be seen widely in everything from the original naming of the disease as GRID, or gay-related immunodeficiency, to the Christian Right's rhetoric that framed the disease as a "threat" to "American families."[22] Thus the hysteria over queer bodies, debates about forms of social segregation, and forms of legal discrimination based upon nonnormative sexual identities as inherently predatory, pathological, and contagious, extended in both symbolic and literal ways to the broader queer population. Writing in 1987 during the early years of the epidemic, Paula Treichler called HIV/AIDS an "epidemic of signification" in which

> the social dimension [of the disease] is far more pervasive and central than we are accustomed to believing. Science is not the true material base generating our merely symbolic superstructure. Our social constructions of AIDS (in terms of global devastation, threat to civil rights, emblem of sex and death, the "gay plague," the postmodern condition, whatever) are based not upon objective, scientifically determined "reality" but upon what we are told about this reality: that is, upon *prior* social constructions routinely produced within the discourses of biomedical science. . . . There is a continuum, then, not a dichotomy, between popular and biomedical discourses . . . and these play out in language. . . . [S]cientific and medical discourses have traditions . . . [that] may disguise contradiction and irrationality.[23]

In this way, the HIV/AIDS epidemic concretized centuries-old beliefs in queer sexuality as deviant and dangerous, providing "proof" of God's disdain in the realm of religion, and of the consequences of trespassing "natural" relations in the realm of the medical sciences.[24] At the same time, other issues crystalized during the early 1990s that produced an intensified homophobic sentiment in the nation, including ongoing disputes about gays in the military and the early stirrings of the same-sex marriage campaigns and countercampaigns. Conservative pundits were also known to conflate gay identity with pedophilia and child molestation and to circulate strange stories that cast gay sex as immoral and monstrous.[25]

In the case of the Four, homophobia was not only present as part of larger American cultural and legal narratives but also pervasive within Latinx communities. As the work of scholars such as Gloria Anzaldúa, Carla Trujillo, and Cherríe Moraga make clear, the inhabitation of queer identity is often seen as a rejection of Latinx cultural and familial mandates. Anzaldúa cites lesbian sexuality as "the ultimate rebellion" for Latinxs; Trujillo argues that Chicana lesbians, through challenging Latinx cultural patterns of patriarchal control, may be understood as "*vendidas* [traitors] to the race, blasphemers to the Church, atrocities against nature"; and Moraga testifies to the self-hatred and cultural alienation Latinx queers may experience.[26] In part, these understandings suggest the limits of acceptable difference for minoritized and devalued populations, whose citizenship, always already liminal in nature, cannot afford a radical politics of sexual difference.

Historically, Latinxs in the United States have been cast in a homogenizing frame by dominant cultural representations, and have been understood as hypersexual and hyperfertile, attributes that have been used to justify forms of sexual violence and coercive measures of reproductive control. As William Calvo-Quirós writes, "Latina/os have been portrayed as lazy, noisy, welfare 'vampires,' hypersexual, and violent . . . as social monsters that must be controlled, reeducated, segregated, or 'deported' into invisibility."[27] Similarly, Jillian Hernandez notes that because "Latina bodies are read as out of control and used against the communities they 'represent' . . . efforts to counter those constructions in Latina/o communities [are] an internalization of technologies of discipline that center on policing women's bodies."[28] In this context, appeals toward normative sexual identity from within Latinx communities can be seen as a form of survival, even as it further marginalizes many of its constituents. For example, Hernandez observes that social outreach organizations often target and vilify "working class Latina girls pejoratively labeled 'chongas,'" deploying methods of empowerment that instruct them "to perform a very prescribed notion of gendered respectability—acting like 'ladies.'"[29] Hernandez further writes that while the rebellious sartorial style of the "chonga" girl renders her "hypervisible" within her own community and within the eyes of the state, she "is practically invisible in feminist or cultural studies scholarship," pointing to the difficulty of incorporating nonnormative intersectional identities into existing frameworks of feminist analysis.[30]

While Hernandez states that "chonga" is a fairly recent term, it also has older roots in the term "chusmería," described by José Esteban Muñoz as "a form of behavior that refuses standards of bourgeois comportment," and which produces the figure of the "chusma" as a stigmatized caste that may indicate poverty, proximity to Blackness, nonnormative gender or sexual identity, a lack of assimilation (or assimilability) to American ways of life, and/or an "excessive nationalism" evidenced by an "over-the-top" connection to one's country of origin.[31] Mobilizing these characteristics as an analytical frame for interpreting queer of color performance aesthetics, Muñoz argues for a "critical *chusmería*—a tactical refusal to keep things 'pristine' and binarized . . . a loud defiance of a rather fixed order."[32]

Building upon Muñoz's work, Deborah Vargas proposes the term "lo sucio" as a "Latino queer analytic" that elaborates on the concept of "*suciedad*—a Latino vernacular for dirty, nasty, and filthy."[33] Vargas situates *lo sucio* "in relation to contemporary neoliberal projects that disappear the most vulnerable and disenfranchised by cleaning up spaces and populations deemed dirty and wasteful: welfare moms, economically impoverished neighborhoods, and overcrowded rental dwellings," all of which signify a transgression of normative domestic relations, intimate ties, and forms of geospatial inhabitance.[34] Like Muñoz's understanding of critical *chusmería* as a fundamentally disruptive methodology, Vargas imagines *lo sucio* as a site of the "*potentiality* of sustainability and persistence for queer sex and sexuality" through the very excesses of "dirt," "filth," and "nonnormativity" that both appall and undermine the "neoliberal hetero- and homonormative" state.[35] Similarly, Muñoz mobilizes the concept of "potentiality" as central to queer existence, which he describes as "a mode of nonbeing that is eminent, a thing that is present but not actually existing in the present tense."[36]

Muñoz's and Vargas's theorizations operate against a broader politics of temporality within queer studies that tend to proffer—in the words of Lee Edelman—"no future," insofar as the notion of futurity is imbricated in heteronormative frameworks of (re)productivity.[37] Instead, they imagine queerness as empowered by a "not-here-yet" affective pulse and an ongoing reconfiguration of that which is cast as excess or waste by the hegemonic claims of the state. "To avoid being the loser in or being the loss of structural systems to normalize gender and sexuality," Vargas observes, "queerness learns to lag behind, opt out, and move around the promises known too well that were never intended for subjects of disenfranchisement."[38]

While powerful and compelling, such theorizations of queerness are problematized by the case of the San Antonio Four and the question of respectability that haunts their representation in *Southwest of Salem*. To be clear, the critique that follows is not intended to undermine the important work accomplished by the film or the profound significance of the extensive efforts that led to the Four's exoneration. Instead, I am interested in the ways in which narratives of justice and innocence require adherence to certain paradigms, foreclosing alternate interpretations and reframing sites of invisibility. Moreover, it is my hope and intention to further the conversation begun by the film, to move toward a more holistic version of justice.

Given the relative obscurity of their cases until the release of *Southwest* in 2016, little academic work exists on the women's experiences, the trials, or the documentary. Existing scholarly examinations understand the film in ways parallel to and complementary of progressive media accounts—that is, as delivering long-overdue justice to a group of women marked as Other by their racial, sexual, and gender identities. Such interpretations also affirm the film's director Deborah Esquenazi's own assessment of its impact as a "stunning victory, not only for the San Antonio Four, but for gay rights," proving "that even with no cultural capital, power, or resources, we can make great change."[39]

The cultural anthropologist Elvia Mendoza, who also worked on the film crew for *Southwest*, explains that by shedding light on "historically invisible formations of violence," filmmaking constitutes an important "methodology by which to engage [queer people of color's] experiences and trace their memories."[40] In particular, Mendoza describes how the production of *Southwest* enabled a "subversive research methodology" by providing paths of access to hidden information and a "more *meaningful* relationship" with her subjects. For Mendoza, the film's significance lies in its ability "to garner support for Anna, Cassie, Liz, and Kris, as well as a means by which to talk about the larger issues at hand."[41]

The literary scholar T. Jackie Cuevas echoes Mendoza's positive assessment of the documentary, highlighting the "crucial cultural work" performed by the film's representation of intersectional forms of discrimination that galvanized political and monetary backing for the women.[42] Cuevas further cites *Southwest* as an example of the necessity of "gender variant critique," defined as an extension of queer of color critique that foregrounds

the framework of women of color feminisms, to reconsider the relationships among gender, sexuality, race, and class, particularly when gender and intersecting categories become destabilized by gender variance. . . . [A] gender variant critique works toward extricating us from the regulatory social structures in which we are deeply imbricated. A gender variant approach provides an analytic tool for critiquing and potentially transforming those structures.[43]

In Cuevas's estimation, the film exemplifies the potentialities of a gender-variant critique by virtue of its representation of the women's corporeal self-fashioning, which does "not necessarily conform to heteronormative gendered expectations, or cis-heteronormativity."[44] To this point, Cuevas describes the women's appearances and provides a still image from the documentary that depicts a home-movie clip of Vasquez and Rivera kissing on the beach. In the scene that the still is taken from, Vasquez is seen wearing oversized clothing and a hairstyle typically understood as masculine, while Rivera appears normatively feminine (fig. 1.1a).

Yet while Cuevas understands this moment as an example of how the film pays homage to the women's gender and sexual nonconformity, it is also not insignificant that Vasquez's nonnormative, masculinized gender presentation is countered by Rivera's normative, feminine gender presentation. Further, this complementary representation portrays a moment of intimacy that is reflective of the film's broader construction of the women as monogamous and family oriented. In the minutes surrounding the still, the home video shows Rivera applying sunscreen to Vasquez (fig. 1.1b) and walking hand in hand with Rivera's children (fig. 1.1c), whom Vasquez helped to parent. Such representations can be found throughout *Southwest*, which intercuts footage and still photographs that depict the couple in traditional family settings and poses (e.g., fig. 1.1d).

Indeed, aside from the visuals presented of the women's personal style, the film's portrayal of their lives often operates to normalize their subjectivities. In the scenes that feature the home-movie footage from the beach, voice-overs of Rivera and Vasquez explain their relationship:

> RIVERA: We spent a lot of time together, and we ended up really caring for each other.
>
> VOICE (*speaking from off camera in home movie*): Get closer, guys, give a little kiss, there you go! [*The two kiss.*]
>
> RIVERA: She was just the one I was going to settle down with.
>
> VASQUEZ: I truly feel like Cass and I were one, were one together, you know? We fell in love, you know, and we moved in together, and we were living with the children, you know, and raising them. It was something I wasn't ready for, but I also took it on. I mean, you know, we were good, we were good to each other.

Figure 1.1a–d. Video stills from *Southwest of Salem: The Story of the San Antonio Four*: Anna Vasquez and Cassandra Rivera on the beach with Rivera's children, Michael (9) and Ashley (8), in 2000 (portions of this footage are played early on in the film and again at the end as the credits roll) and a family photograph, also from 2000, of Anna Vasquez and Cassandra Rivera with Rivera's children shown in the film. © Deborah Esquenazi Productions and Sam Tabet Pictures.

The film then cuts to footage of an interview with Vasquez's mother:

> VASQUEZ'S MOTHER: These two kids had two mothers. They took responsibility. Very responsible parents. I mean, if you could call them that, you know, I mean, they're not married or anything but they were totally devoted to each other, you know, just like a husband and wife. I did ask a priest about that once, I asked him, you know, what am I supposed to do, you know, she's my daughter, and she's involved with this other lady, what am I supposed to do, am I being faithful, um, in order to be faithful to the church, do I have to be, you know, apart from my daughter? Or separated from my daughter, you know? And he said, no. He said . . . the only thing that is required of you is to love her. That's all. He said, she's going to be receiving a lot of negatives in the world, you know, she's going to come against this prejudice. There should be one place where she can go where there is only love.

Here, the viewer witnesses Rivera and Vasquez's relationship as anything but radical or perverse. Instead, it is the very mundaneness of their story—

of meeting, coming together, and creating a family—that creates a relatable story. The images of the women and children in the home movie thus become authorized by Vasquez's Catholic mother, who compares the two to "husband and wife," and by the priest, who avoids judgement and imagines that structural violence ("negatives," "prejudice") might be countered by familial support. Thus, at the center of the documentary—and the affective response it works to create—is the understanding of the women as deeply enmeshed with family, friendship, and community. These representations lean in toward a politics of respectability, in which perversion can be imaginatively cast off from lesbian identity, a process that mobilizes particular racializing narratives.

Section III. "It's almost dreamlike": Violence, Illegality, and Testimony as Fantasy

The role of race remains complicated in the case of the San Antonio Four. As many scholars have observed, the racialization of Latinxs in the United States is a profoundly complicated matter, one that often confuses or displaces ethnicity for race, and that is riddled with inconsistent categories and representations. As Lee Bebout aptly notes, Latinxs are often positioned as either "people of color no different from African Americans or white ethnics like Italians, Irish, and other white ethnics before them," ignoring how "Mexican Americans are inheritors of at least two racial systems" and leaving "underexamined how Chicana/o inequalities and social nonwhiteness foster Anglo-American investment in whiteness."[45] While the wholesale process of Latinx racialization is beyond the scope of this chapter, it is nonetheless important to understand the impact of the women's racial identities on the proceedings of their cases.

To be sure, the early 1990s was a time of great national anxiety about Latinx immigration, as evidenced in the reformation of immigration and foreign-trade policies, as well as the expansion of militarization along the US-Mexico border. The decade began with the Immigration Act of 1990, a bipartisan, multilayered, and complex piece of legislation that reflected the country's vexed views on immigration. The act simultaneously increased overall legal immigration, though mostly for skilled workers; restricted some types of family visas while expanding others; offered Temporary Protected Status (TPS), which led the way toward allowing some migrants, including many Salvadorans, to come to the United States; and lifted the ban on gay immigrants, who were formerly classified under the medical category of "sexual deviant."[46] In 1993, Operation Hold the Line fast-tracked the use of military surveillance and force on the border as a means of policing and capturing undocumented immigrants. In 1994, the implementation of the North American Free Trade Agreement drastically contributed to economic devastation of the American working class, thereby adding to already existing narratives of anti-immigrant sentiment.[47]

While all of these events provide an important backdrop to the court's treatment of the San Antonio Four, it is also true that fear and tension regarding the border had already been linked to concerns over satanism only a few years earlier. In 1989, the murder of Mark Kilroy, a senior at the University of Texas at Austin, made headlines and was prominently featured on the reality television show *America's Most Wanted*.[48] While traveling with friends to Mexico for spring break, Kilroy was kidnapped by a cult described by the media as related to African diasporic religious traditions, including Santeria, Palo Mayombe, and Voudon.[49] Kilroy's body was found during a raid of a property owned by a local cult leader, in a building referred to as a "human slaughterhouse" that was covered in human and animal blood and remains.

When the leader of the cult killed himself after being surrounded by police, the cult's second-in-command, Sara Aldrete, became an object of fascination. Aldrete was a Mexican national who crossed the border on a daily basis to attend school in the United States, where she excelled academically, and was described as a "friendly, hard-working physical education major who had shown no signs of abnormal behavior or occult interests."[50] Yet, as one reporter explained, such deceptive behavior fit neatly within the parameters of a binational and bicultural existence:

> Aldrete was leading a double life of mind-boggling cultural contradiction. One life took place in the urban world of English, sports and academic achievement; the other in the rural terra incognita of Santa Elena, drugs and black magic. . . . In the bicultural society of Brownsville-Matamoros, Aldrete must have found it relatively easy to keep her two lives separate, switching back and forth as easily as she crossed the border, until events outside of her control forced her finally to choose between two incompatible realities.[51]

Here, Aldrete's portrayal is suggestive of long-standing American fears about the border as a lawless and permeable zone. Leo Chavez characterizes these ideations as representative of the "Latino Threat Narrative," which produces Latinx subjects as "unwilling or incapable of integrating, of becoming part of the national community. Rather, they are part of an invading force from south of the border that is bent on . . . destroying the American way of life."[52] These fears are then mobilized as a justification for anti-immigrant hostility and violence. In the midst of the reporting surrounding the Kilroy case, faculty at Cornell University published an editorial in the *New York Times* warning of "possible backlashes not only against santeros, botanicas and believers, but also against people of Hispanic and African descent in general" due to "inflammatory" reporting.[53]

While there is no way to know for certain if coverage of Kilroy's murder preconditioned attitudes toward the San Antonio Four, it is important to take seriously the overlap that existed between narratives of the Latino threat and the satanic panic ordeal. Certainly, racial difference must be understood to haunt any consideration of nonwhite, non-Judeo-Christian beliefs that employ religious rituals presumed unfamiliar to the "American" eye. That the women at the center of the trial had no affiliation with such religions, nor any history of such practices, was not made legible to the court. Instead, a hyperfocus on the details of the women's queer sexuality stood in for proof of satanism. Attorney Keith Hampton describes the testimony provided at trial as recalling the conventions of fairy-tale villainy:

> Fake stories, folktales, will look the same over time. It'll be like a certain motif, a pattern . . . you know, Hansel and Gretel or Sleeping Beauty. . . . The door opens, and it's her aunt Liz, "Come in, come in to my cottage, little girl." And then she starts yelling and screaming at her. So she becomes this ogre. On the floor were three nude women. They got on the bed and they started touching [the girls]. What did they say? They were silent. So it's imagery. It's too bizarre. It's almost dreamlike.[54]

Reflecting upon the case, Anna Vasquez lamented that she and her friends were "painted . . . as monsters."[55] Similarly, Cassandra Rivera explained the critical role that attitudes toward queer sexuality played in the verdict:

> At the beginning of our trial, during jury selection, the attorneys talked about us being gay as if it were a disease, or something to be frightened of— that we were not human. If people there had not thought about [our sexuality] as an issue, at the end of jury selection, I'm sure they felt differently. In closing arguments [the prosecutor] stated that we are gay and the victims are female. . . . Being gay does not make us perverts or sick people . . . DOES NOT mean that we are going to hurt small children. . . . [W]e are normal and humane people just like heterosexuals.[56]

While the introduction of the women's sexual orientation was indeed improper here, it is not particularly striking given the long history of homophobic attitudes present within the US juridical system at large, and in Texas in particular. Even as of 2019, "homosexual conduct" remains included within the Texas penal code as a Class C misdemeanor offense. That this law has not been removed from the code is striking given that sixteen years have passed since the landmark case of *Lawrence and Garner v. Texas*, when the US Supreme Court struck down the state's antisodomy law.[57]

As Nayan Shah has observed, while *Lawrence* is typically understood as an important event in the history of LGBTQ constitutional rights, it is also true that race played an important and often overlooked role given the racial identities of John Geddes Lawrence (white) and Tyron Garner (Black). Shah writes that "historically, concerns about interracial sodomy aggravated fears of sexual and social danger and catalyzed anxieties about the undermining of the social order."[58] While Shah emphasizes the way in which interracial sexual encounters have often occasioned policing and criminalization, he also demonstrates how the positionality of nonwhite subjects becomes the occasion for surveillance in the first place.

Describing how the verdict in *Lawrence* illegalized the sodomy law based on the presumption of a right to privacy, Shah asks, "Under what circumstances does a person have privacy, mobility, and freedom of intimate contact unfettered by government policing?"[59] When Lawrence and Garner were originally arrested in 1998, it was at the behest of a white neighbor, who called the police after witnessing "a man behaving erratically with a gun" (presumably Garner) in Lawrence's apartment complex. Responding to the call, police burst into Lawrence's apartment, caught the men engaged in consensual sex, and arrested them for "homosexual conduct." The two men were then convicted of "deviate sexual intercourse" in Harris County Criminal Court, a finding that would ultimately be overturned following the 2003 Supreme Court decision. As Shah observes, however, the men's racial identity is often omitted from narratives about the case, even though Garner's presence in Lawrence's apartment complex was the very issue that authorized the police's breach of Lawrence's private residence.[60]

Similarly, the legal theorist Kimberlé Crenshaw has argued that the absence of proper "frames" through which to understand intersectional identities and modes of oppression often means that social justice issues become legible only through one axis of difference. Moving from this observation to Shah's analysis of *Lawrence* and, finally, to the case of the Four, it is important to reflect upon the ways in which the publicity galvanized by *Southwest* has allowed the women's exoneration to become heralded as a victory for LGBTQ rights, even though at the time of the trial itself, LGBTQ rights groups were not interested in the case.[61] Yet since its release in 2016, eighteen years after the women were first arrested, *Southwest* has been nominated for and received numerous awards, including Outstanding Documentary at the GLAAD Media Awards (2017), Outstanding Documentary Feature at Outfest Los Angeles (2016), Best First Documentary at the Critics Choice Awards (2016), and Outstanding Documentary at the Frameline San Francisco International LGBTQ Film Festival (2016), among others. Recognized for its engagement with critical LGBTQ issues, the film is rarely cited in relation to questions of racial prejudice. Similarly, the film itself does not seek to question the women's ethnic or racial identities; instead, they appear simply as background facts in a story of legal miscarriage against four lesbian women. It is therefore clear which "frame" has allowed the case to become visible and mobilizable as a site of proper empathy.

Returning to Shah's assessment of *Lawrence*, it is worthwhile to think about the role that "privacy" and "mobility" played in the policing of the Four's "intimate contact." As young, Latina, working-class women inhabiting an area of the country that conjures the specter of migration and border crossing, in a state that has long had the highest rates of incarceration in the nation, the Four's right to privacy would have been uncertain under the best of circumstances. Their precarity was undoubtedly enhanced by their sexuality; three of the four had been kicked out of their family homes by disapproving parents, a fact that led directly to Mayhugh and Rivera's decision to rent an apartment together. In turn, it was not accidental that the crimes were alleged to have occurred at *this* apartment—a small domicile in a poor neighborhood, rented by two young, uncoupled lesbians whose use of the space was a continual source of speculation. It was *this* nonnormative space that became *the* scene of the crime, even as the actual physical evidence appeared to attest differently. While the girls testified that the women held them against their will, the space told a different story: the doors inside the house could not be locked and did not have knobs that were "too high" for the young girls to turn. In spite of these inconsistencies, the girls' testimony was treated as truer than the actual materiality of the space, suggesting, in some way, that the events that took place—which at the very least included a gathering of lesbian women—had the capacity to bend walls, whether through fantasy or "satanism." Observing this outcome does not imply a reification of scientific knowledge—that is, that the girls' testimonies should have been disregarded because they did not match the crime technicians' photographs and measurements—but rather, it asks what is at stake in the refusal to look at evidence that meets normative standards.

A similar question must be asked with regard to the expert testimony provided by Nancy Kellogg, the pediatrician who examined the girls after the alleged incident. Even at the time of the trial, existing medical knowledge did not support Kellogg's analysis. Later, during the investigation that led to the women's exoneration, it was noted that Kellogg identified "signs" of "sexual trauma" on the girls' genitalia that did not fall within existing diagnostic standards and that were in fact already known to represent simple forms of bodily variation.[62] Kellogg also emphasized her "concern that this could be Satanic-related," even though a number of the satanic ritual child abuse scandals had already received scrutiny and been discredited at the time of her examination. Describing the "fantastical" nature of the evidence presented at trial, Elvia Mendoza notes how the courtroom produced a "discursive dismemberment."

> With time, a Dalí-esque representation of the court trial emerged with hymens, breasts, menstrual blood, vaginas, ankles, wrists, buttocks, and fingers dispersed throughout the courtroom. . . . [T]he courtroom . . . came to produce what Foucault names a "world of perversion." Bodies, organs, excretions . . . all converged to ensure that by the end of the trials jurors felt morally obligated to convict . . . not for the crimes outlined in the Charge of the Court, but for the oversexed desires they came to associate with their lesbianism.[63]

Positioned against this disarticulation is the narrative offered by *Southwest of Salem*, which operates to challenge representations of the women and their sexuality as "fantastical," "monstrous," and "dreamlike." Using clips from the 1922 Swedish-Danish silent horror film *Häxan* (alternately translated as *The Witches* or *Witchcraft through the Ages*), directed by Benjamin Christensen, the documentary provides a counter to the imagery mobilized during the trial. The clips from *Häxan* feature images of immobilized waifs and dark monstrous hands; they are clearly outdated and fictional in nature, giving life to the claims of those who found the stories told by the alleged victims suspicious.[64]

At the same time, such imagery covers over and displaces the alleged victims' narratives, offering little resolution as to where their strange stories might have originated. At several points in the film, and in media reports covering the women's case, it is suggested that the accounts provided by the girls were based off of observations of their father's sexual activity with other women; Michelle Mondo, a reporter from the *San Antonio Express*, also implies that the accounts read like a description of pornography viewed by a confused child, wherein the girls represent themselves as surrogates in a perplexing and misconstrued sexual encounter. Yet whether the ideas were implanted fantasies constructed by the girls' father, grandmother, or agents of the criminal justice system who subjected them to extensive and repetitive questioning, it remains disconcerting that neither the film nor the publicity surrounding it addresses the potential issues of abuse that might have led to the girls' false testimony. Instead, because the women's transformation into "innocent victims" required the destabilization of the allegations against them, the girls' testimony could only be understood as fantastically false. With this denial came the erasure of troubling depictions that might have spoken to other forms of endangerment.

Section IV. "This could be you": Homonormativity and the Role of Public Sympathy

Southwest of Salem opens with a shot of Vasquez wiping tears from her eyes, explaining her initial shock and ongoing horror over the charges. Throughout the film, Vasquez is featured most heavily. In part this has to do with the material facts of the women's incarceration: while Ramirez, Rivera, and Mayhugh were not released until November 2013, Vasquez was released a year earlier, in November 2012, and was therefore able to be more fully involved in the film's production, including participating in screenwriting with Esquenazi.[65] Thus most of the scenes depicting life outside of prison follow Vasquez through her daily experiences at home, with her family, driving, grocery shopping, and so on. Substantially, however, Vasquez's centrality also allows the film to foreground a coherent narrative of familial unification and belonging. To this end, her mother plays a central role in the film. She is shown providing multiple interviews, speaking at public-awareness events, showing support and affection toward her daughter, and welcoming her upon release back into her childhood bedroom.

The film glosses over Rivera's and Mayhugh's families, though it is known that both did not approve of their daughters' sexualities, with Rivera's mother having kicked her out of the house during the year prior to her incarceration. Ramirez's family is of course the original source of the women's travails, given that the false allegations were testified to by her own sister's children. Present in the film are Javier Limon, her nieces' father, who main-

Figure 1.2.
Official poster for *Southwest of Salem: The Story of the San Antonio Four.* © Deborah Esquenazi Productions and Sam Tabet Pictures.

tains his own innocence in coercing his daughters' testimonies, and Stephanie Limon, the eldest of the two, then twenty-five years old. The film also depicts Ramirez's reunion with her children, now grown, upon her release from prison. Yet due to the centrality of Ramirez's role in the case itself, it is somewhat curious that Vasquez drives the primary narrative focus.

Publicity surrounding the film provides a similar orientation. The film's poster, for example, foregrounds Vasquez in sharp focus (fig. 1.2). Behind her, on either side and out of focus, are Rivera and Mayhugh, and Ramirez appears finally at the back. Some versions of the poster appear to have entirely removed Ramirez, while other publicity images cut out all of the other women's faces. Here, as in the interviews conducted in the documentary itself, the women's white prison uniforms are hard to read as anything but symbolic of their innocence; it is a color reflected in the background behind and above the women's heads and in the overexposed black-and-white mug shots lined up along the bottom of the poster. The contrast between the two depictions speaks to the question of representation, as the poster asks, "Do you trust the justice system to find the truth?"

A version of the poster image is also featured on the home page of the website dedicated to the documentary. There, a link to "press stills" reveals once more that Ramirez and Mayhugh are nowhere to be found. Instead, nine images are offered: one film poster, three images of Vasquez, one of Rivera, one of Vasquez and Rivera kissing, and three of individuals associated with the women's legal defense and the film production. A quick Google search of the film reveals similar images and proportionalities of representation. Finally, the film's two-minute trailer also features Vasquez; aside from the presentation of a brief mug shot from 1994, Ramirez only makes one brief appearance at the end. By contrast, the home video of Vasquez and Rivera kissing is played at three different points.[66]

Before considering what is at stake in foregrounding Vasquez's story (as well as the story of her relationship with Rivera) in a narrative produced to exonerate four women for a crime directly connected to only one them, it is first critical to understand the intentionality of this focus. In an interview following the release of the film in 2016, Esquenazi explains that after viewing the home videos depicting Vasquez and Rivera's relationship, she knew that it had to be central to the documentary's narrative:

> I did notice an absence of discussions of the fact that Anna and Cassie were in a relationship and were building a family together and were raising two kids together. And even that's like in the police report, like when they were giving their statements, they do mention it. But it doesn't really come up later. And I did want to ask myself, like *why is that? Why did they not say it?* It occurred to me, well, that's a real humanizing element. If you start to tell a jury about two women who are just living their lives and they're raising two kids, and you suddenly get to know the two kids and the kids are extraordinary and the kids are so well-adapted and there have never been any improprieties, no priors. And suddenly, you're like wait a second, the absence of this element of the story [is] incredibly homophobic because it's easy to demonize single women and keep to this idea that somehow they're sexual predators, that they are diabolical. And I feel like that was a really big turning point for the story perspective for me.[67]

In this statement, Esquenazi points to how the invisibility of Vasquez and Rivera's relationship might have damaged their case—not because of what the women meant to each other, but because of their representation of familial commitment and their ability to produce "well-adapted" children, in contrast to the ease with which "single women" can be "demonize[d]." It is an eerie moment that resonates with another of Esquenazi's statements about what drove her to create the film in the first place. After being sent some of the women's home videos by her mentor, the investigative journalist Debbie Nathan, Esquenazi describes her reaction: "I was like, oh my God, this is a story not just about injustice but about a family torn apart. It really hit home for me because at the time I was also in the process of coming out—I didn't come out until I was 33—and Debbie said to me, 'This could be you.'"[68] Read in concert with her other remarks, and in conjunction with Vasquez being featured in the film, it is fairly clear who Esquenazi thought "could be" her. Also significant is Esquenazi's description of Rivera's children as never having had "any improprieties, no priors," as if the relationship between the children's lack of criminality and their mothers' innocence would be self-evident. Such logic brings together ideas of criminality as inheritance, and the presence of normative familial ties as thwarting deviant behavior.

Throughout the film, the innocence of the women is constructed through a domestication of their identities. Interviews are intercut with extensive home-movie footage depicting family gatherings, tender embraces, and tears produced by the women's departure. Time and again, the women testify to the disturbing treatment of their sexual identity as necessarily tied to forms of deviance understood to be continuous with child molestation. Thus, their pleas for consideration require a disavowal of criminal culpability that continues to be associated with nonnormative sexualities and gender identities. That *Southwest* successfully does so through the subordination of Ramirez's story—a story harder to relate to, by virtue of the existence of intrafamilial abuse and betrayal—suggests the limits of social justice within a neoliberal frame. To become exonerated, to verify one's own lack of criminality, remains tied to the problem of casting out those who must be made criminal through the reification of binaristic paradigms of innocence and guilt.

This dichotomy has particular implications for both queer and Latinx subjects. As addressed earlier, the historic pathologization of queer sexuality has often led to attempts to divorce pathology from queerness rather than to interrogate the logic of pathologization itself. Similarly, because anti-immigrant sentiment continues to plague Latinx subjects, a desire to recast the immigrant as "not criminal" results in a fundamental misunderstanding of the role of law enforcement in the policing and production of citizenship. This in turn creates a dualistic narrative, one that emerges from the state and formally separates "desirable" immigrants from "undesirable immigrants"—as in the Obama administration's "felons not families" policy—and one that also comes from within many immigrant communities, who hope to prove themselves worthy of citizenship in contradistinction to those who are "illegal."

As the legal scholar Rebecca Sharpless writes, while "immigrants have been converted into criminals through the prosecution of behaviors associated with being undocumented . . . [t]he respectable immigrant narrative deepens the link between crime control and immigration enforcement, reifies our carceral state, and endorses extant societal inequalities that foster criminal activity."[69] Similarly, Lisa Marie Cacho uses the term "de facto status crime" to refer "to others' perception that a person of a certain status is certain to commit future crimes and may well have already committed crimes unwitnessed. A de facto status crime is not contingent on criminal conduct; it is premised upon bodies perceived to be criminal."[70] Of particular interest to the case of the Four is the way in which the "statuses" of queer and Latinx identities intersect. While *Southwest* succeeds in asking its audience to interrogate the women's criminalization, it remains unable to do so without mobilizing normative frames of kinship and affiliation. This shortcoming is reflective of the contradictions produced in a society that understands criminality as an "either-or" category, as well as an absence of analytical tools that account for the simultaneous pulls of rebellion and conformity. When pathways to visibility and belonging require empathetic engagement—"This could be you"—it becomes less and less possible to craft and sustain radical practices.

Section V. "Quality, objective science": Evidentiary Standards, Homonationalism, and the Prison-Industrial Complex

In June of 2019, Anna Vasquez was appointed by the Houston mayor's office to serve on the board of the Houston Forensic Science Center (HFSC), which reserves a seat for someone wrongfully committed. Prior to Vasquez, the position was held by Anthony Charles Graves, who had been wrongfully incarcerated at the age of twenty-six for eighteen years for murdering a family of six. Graves's arrest happened a year before Vasquez's, and like the Four, he was found guilty based on a very strange set of circumstances. Although he had no motive for the crime, he had no history of violence, and no physical evidence could be found linking him to the murders, he was convicted on the word of another man, who later admitted to having committed the crimes himself. During his tenure in prison, Graves was scheduled for execution by lethal injection on two separate occasions and spent sixteen years on death row, four of which occurred *following* the overturn of his conviction by a federal appeals court. In June 2011, he received $1.4 million as compensation for his wrongful imprisonment from the Texas governor's office. Four years later, in 2015, the prosecutor who handled the original case, Charles Sebesta, was disbarred after it was determined that he had withheld critical evidence in Graves's case.[71]

Like Vasquez, Graves has dedicated much of his postincarceration time to social justice projects that seek to overturn wrongful convictions. Since his release, Graves has testified before the US Senate "about the harms of solitary confinement"; joined the American Civil Liberties Union (ACLU) of Texas as the smart justice initiatives manager; served on the HFSC board; created the Anthony Graves Foundation, which "works to draw attention to problems within the American criminal justice system"; and published his autobiography, *Infinite Hope: How Wrongful Conviction, Solitary Confinement, and 12 Years on Death Row Failed to Kill My Soul*.[72] The ACLU has described him as a champion for criminal justice reform who "turned the tragedy of his wrongful conviction into a fight for a smarter criminal justice system."[73]

Yet what much of the publicity surrounding Graves's and Vasquez's exonerations and postincarceration activism fails to mention, however, is that their stories were far from unique. In fact, Texas continues to have one of the highest rates of wrongful incarceration in the United States. When the HFSC was founded in 2012, it was a direct consequence of a crisis that had unfolded in the forensic divisions of the Houston Police Department (HPD). In 2003, inspectors from the US Department of Justice found that HPD's crime lab suffered from "serious negligence" and breaches "of scientific standards."[74] As a result, the entire fingerprint and DNA analysis divisions were forced to close, and the city spent millions outsourcing their lab work. Meanwhile, at the federal level, the National Academy of Sciences released a statement in 2009 recommending that all "forensic laboratories be independent of law enforcement" due to ongoing difficulties with bias and improper conduct on the part of police departments. As the City of Houston was already working to rebrand its forensics department, the National Academy of Sciences report then became the occasion for the establishment of an independent forensic laboratory. Yet this lab was also under the control of the same local governmental offices that oversaw the HPD crime lab before it closed and that continue to oversee the HPD to the present day. Moreover, because the HFSC does not have a dedicated medical examiner's office, the center relies upon the resources and staff of the Harris County Institute of Forensic Sciences, which also previously provided services to the HPD crime lab. (Here, it bears recalling that Harris County was the location of the arrest and conviction of John Lawrence and Tyron Garner.) Finally, the HFSC remains located in the same building that houses the HPD, although its facilities are technically off-limits to law enforcement officials.

For all of these reasons and more, it is difficult to understand the HFSC as an entity that is entirely "independent" from the HPD. On the center's website FAQs, for instance, cost effectiveness and judicial efficiency are stressed. Under one of the questions—"Former Mayor [Annise] Parker said repeatedly HFSC must be 'truly independent.' Independent from what, exactly? And why is independence so important?"—the center provides the following answer:

> HFSC is independent from law enforcement agencies, prosecutors, elected officials and citizen groups, any of which could have an incentive to attempt to influence the scientific analysis of evidence. An important HFSC goal is to build public trust in the objectivity of evidence presented in criminal proceedings. *A juror who believes evidence has been externally influenced may be tempted to disregard scientific findings in favor of personal perceptions.*[75]

While the answer begins with an expected explanation regarding the potential influence or bias that could impact the processing of forensic data, it then moves the burden onto the public, emphasizing that if the crime lab is not well regarded (presumably referring to the HPD crime lab debacle), then jurors will not heed the information and will follow their "personal perceptions." In this way, the processing of forensic data is imagined as extractable from its social context. Justice is understood as achievable, augmented by a well-placed trust in scientific authority and the employment of proper experts.

This logic is echoed in Vasquez's own understanding of her place at the HFSC. In an interview with the Innocence Project of Texas—the organization that worked to exonerate the Four and that she now works for—Vasquez explains, "After spending almost 13 years in prison, I feel an obligation to ensure that my story prevents such things from occurring to other innocent people and helps improve the justice system. . . . Serving on HFSC's oversight board and helping to ensure it provides *quality, objective science* is one way to do that."[76] Here, Vasquez becomes instrumentalized as an agent of the state. Her presence at HFSC excuses her wrongful incarceration, suggesting that both she and law enforcement officials share the same end goal: the proper prosecution of crime. Certainly, given Vasquez's position as a person who has paid dearly for being wrongly accused of a crime, it is not hard to understand her desire to call attention to the importance of "accurate" police and evidentiary proceedings. At the same time, however, it is difficult to view her position at HFSC as anything other than a superficial placeholder. Unlike other members of the board, she is not a member of law enforcement, a legal professional, or a forensic scientist. She has no "expert" training to contribute that would safeguard against future violations. For these reasons, it would be easy to read Vasquez's inclusion at HFSC as a form of multiculturalist tokenism, but it also serves two more complex and specific functions.

First, it serves to reframe the narrative of the Four under the rubric of homonormativity and homonationalism. The span of years that passed during the women's incarceration was a particularly significant time period for debates over the civil rights of gays and lesbians, including both the passage and overturning of two key pieces of legislation: "Don't Ask, Don't Tell" (1994–2011), the policy that allowed gays and lesbians to serve in the military as long as they remained closeted, and the Defense of Marriage Act (1996–2015), which limited marriage to a union between "one man and one woman." As theorists reckoning with the arc of LGBTQ rights have observed, these seeming victories are in fact cause for trepidation. Writing about the rise of neoliberalism among wealthy, white gay elites, Lisa Duggan notes that support for gay marriage and military service represents a "New Homonormativity" in which

> there is no vision of a collective, democratic public culture or of an ongoing engagement with contentious, cantankerous queer politics. Instead we have been administered a kind of political sedative—we get marriage and the military then we go home and cook dinner, forever. . . . This New Homo-normativity comes equipped with a rhetorical recoding of key terms in the history of gay politics: "equality" becomes narrow, formal access to a few conservatizing institutions, "freedom" becomes impunity for bigotry and vast inequalities in commercial life and civil society, the "right to privacy" becomes domestic confinement, and democratic politics itself becomes something to be escaped. All of this adds up to a corporate culture managed by a minimal state, achieved by the neoliberal privatization of affective as well as economic and public life.[77]

Jasbir Puar has further proposed the concept of "homonationalism" to identify the ways in which the "imbrication of American exceptionalism is increasingly marked through or aided by certain homosexual bodies."[78] In this formulation, "good" homosexuals are contraposed to "bad" homosexuals (where the former category represents those who are normatively gendered, monogamous, white, and financially stable, and the latter represents everyone else), just as "good" homosexuals allow the United States to claim a progressive stance on sexual politics that aids in the demonization of nonwhite, non-Western, and non-Christian nations (as well as immigrants from these nations). Thus, the vision of a criminal justice system that allows for particular types of sexual and ethnoracial "diversity" in its personnel contributes to the logics of homonormativity and homonationalism.

Relatedly, Vasquez's role at the HFSC must be understood in relation to recent changes in the carceral militarization of the border. While the number of US Border Patrol agents hovered around nineteen thousand (with approximately eighteen thousand deployed at the southern border) in 2016, the Trump administration authorized \$297 million in 2017 for the hiring of an additional five thousand agents. Yet, importantly, these numbers were higher under the Obama administration (fig. 1.3). At the beginning of Trump's term, the ethnoracial makeup of the Border Patrol already comprised 50 percent Latinx persons, and the percentage has climbed since then. While this complicated positionality requires a far longer examination than can be provided here, it is important to note that Latinx Border Patrol agents are often quoted in the media as making a clear distinction between racial vitriol and racially nonspecific border regulations. For example, Salvador Zamora, a chief patrol agent in the El Centro sector, explains, "This is something I know burns inside a lot of the Hispanic candidates . . . what does this mean, to arrest somebody from my own, maybe my parents' hometown? . . . It's real simple: It's the law. It is right and wrong. It is not against any one race or any one ethnic group or any one particular group of people."[79] At the same time, because Texas has higher unemployment rates than most other states, and is a state where Latinx persons may rightly fear being read as "illegal," the incorporation of Latinx personnel into the Border Patrol is a complicated issue, where prospective employees may seek out employment on the border due to economic necessity or fear for their personal safety.[80]

Whatever the reason for the heightened application and employment of Latinx persons at the border, it is also striking to note that in spite of the funding allotted by Trump to expand patrol staff, the organization continues to suffer from a yearly rate of 6 percent attrition, producing a total number of employees that is actually lower than existed at the beginning of his administration.[81] Commentators have cited a wide array of factors that contribute to the difficulty in filling and sustaining Border Patrol positions, including poor working conditions with numerous physical and psychological burdens,

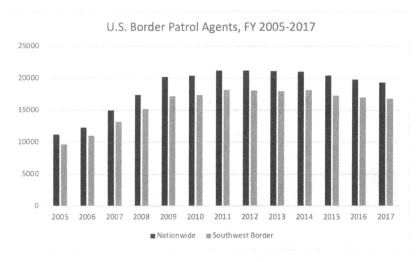

Figure 1.3. Number of US Border Patrol agents, 2005–2017. From Miriam Valverde, "Has the Number of Border Patrol Agents Quadrupled since 2005?," PolitiFact, February 1, 2019.

as well as the high rates of corruption and abuse that have characterized the agency for decades.[82] Further, as congressional appropriators noted, because border crossings were at an all-time low when Trump called for an increase in Border Patrol personnel, the proposal "'was not supported by any analysis of workload and capability gaps' that would allow them to assess whether the agents were even necessary."[83]

Bringing all of these issues together produces a troubling picture. On the one hand, the difficulty of maintaining employees in the Border Patrol, coupled with the high unemployment rate in a state that has the highest rate of Latinx residents, might serve to explain the heightened presence of Latinx personnel at the border. On the other hand, the fact that the Border Patrol is literally overstaffed but is perceived to be understaffed suggests that the overall effect and function (if not the intent) of overfunding the agency is the incorporation of Latinx persons into US law enforcement. What does this mean? In their study of Latinx Border Patrol agents, Jennifer G. Correa and James M. Thomas suggest that "the wielding of state power by brown-bodied agents to demarcate the US-Mexico border as a racialized space where brown bodies are constructed as 'threats' seems to cut against traditional understandings of race as 'familial.' In fact, it suggests that the contours of race are much more nuanced than previously understood, particularly within the context of the US-Mexico border."[84]

Figure 1.4.
Anna Vasquez
pictured with
Dr. Peter Stout.
From "IPTX's Anna
Vasquez appointed
to Houston Forensic
Science Center
Board," Innocence
Project of Texas,
June 18, 2019.

When thinking about this outcome in relation to Vasquez's inclusion within the HFSC, at a time in which Latinx people are experiencing heightened precarity under the global prison-military-industrial complex, it becomes clear that the instrumentalization of Latinx subjects as state agents also works to subsume and contain political dissent, while authorizing the law as a blind arbiter of justice. Overlaying these events with the trajectory of lesbian and gay rights–based claims for military participation and marriage equality—all of which are temporally synchronic—produces a narrative that allows for a reframing of the case of the Four in which the women's wrongful incarceration becomes imaginable only as the product of a particular set of now-outdated prejudices and misrepresentations.

The exoneration of the women and the placement of Vasquez at the HFSC further serve to quell remaining concerns about how the criminal justice system operates, how forensic science is often known to falter, and how queer people, gender-nonconforming people, and people of color disproportionately fill the prison walls. Thus, while the previous section of the chapter began with the ways in which media publicity for *Southwest* typically highlights Vasquez's face, it is perhaps fitting to close with a final image posted in 2019 on the website of the Texas Innocence Project—the organization that helped to exonerate the Four and that Vasquez also now works for—which portrays Vasquez with Dr. Peter Stout, CEO and president of HFSC (fig. 1.4). Both figures smiling into the camera, Stout sits while Vasquez stands in front of a backdrop with the HFSC logo repeated over and over on top of pale-gray molecule clusters. Bearing an official name tag, Vasquez quite literally appears as one of the official faces of the HFSC, even if neither her face nor that of her predecessor, Anthony Graves, can be found anywhere on the website of the HFSC board. Vasquez's presence within the HFSC is thus both hyperbolic and invisibilized, significant and unnecessary. She stands as a figure of wrongs righted, a symbol of justice served, and a marker of inclusionary politics.

Meanwhile, Nancy Kellogg, whose unfounded testimony became the lynchpin in the Four's indictment, continues to experience professional success. She has received numerous local and national awards, published over fifty peer-reviewed articles, spoken over two hundred times at conferences around the world, and held numerous leadership positions within the state of Texas and within the American Academy of Pediatrics. Currently, she serves as a division chief, a professor of pediatrics, and the program director of the Child Abuse Fellowship at the University of Texas Health Science Center at San Antonio.[85] Though she has long stood at the forefront of her field's clinical and research frontiers, she has never been held accountable for her inaccurate and outdated testimony in the case of the Four. Looking at her record of achievement, it becomes clear that her error was not that of an ill-informed, poorly trained, or out-of-touch physician. Rather, the only way to understand the fact that she has not been reproached for her work on this highly publicized case is because, on some level, regardless of their exoneration, it still seems believable within dominant cultural frames that a case involving *these* four women—by virtue of their ethnoracial, gender, sexual, and class identities—"could be Satanic-related."

CHAPTER 2

"A life is worth more than a penis": Lorena (Gallo) Bobbitt and the Domestication of Abuse

Men were supposed to be the ones with the soul; they were supposed to be spiritual, and women carnal. . . . So much is projected onto women: They want to "cut a man's balls," they're the "temptress," they keep a man from achieving.
GLORIA ANZALDÚA, "SPIRITUALITY, SEXUALITY, AND THE BODY"

American doctors pioneered penis reattachment surgery after Ecuadoran immigrant Lorena Gallo chopped off the one belonging to her husband. . . . [T]he only other instance of this . . . crime being committed against an American man occurred in 2011—by another immigrant . . . bride, Catherine Kieu.
ANN COULTER, ¡ADIOS, AMERICA!

On July 11, 2011, forty-eight-year-old Catherine Kieu Becker drugged the dinner she prepared for her husband with a sedative. She then tied him to the bed, cut off his penis with a kitchen knife, and sent it down the garbage disposal. She called 9-1-1 and reported the injury; responding officers stated that she said her husband "deserved it." During the trial that followed, the prosecution argued that Kieu Becker's actions were sparked by "vengeance, vanity and jealousy," due to her husband having recently filed for divorce, and his renewed interest in an ex-girlfriend.[1] An investigator with the local sheriff's department declared that "this case obviously is sexually motivated."[2] Kieu Becker's husband testified that "she murdered me that night. . . . I will never have a sex life again," and claimed that the assault was prompted by his wife's refusal to let him go.[3] By contrast, Kieu Becker's lawyer argued that her actions were guided by years of verbal and sexual abuse, including her husband's ongoing demand for "sex in ways that were physically painful."[4] Attempting to build toward a battered woman defense, Kieu Becker's attorney also explained that Kieu Becker "had mental health issues stemming from being molested as a child in Vietnam."[5] Ultimately, however, the defense was not successful. In 2013, Kieu Becker was found guilty of torture and aggravated mayhem and sentenced to life in prison, with the possibility of parole in seventeen years.[6]

Media coverage of the incident, while sparse, repeatedly highlighted Kieu Becker as an ethnic Other, existing at the margins of citizenship. Most reports removed her second surname, referring to her only by her Vietnamese surname, Kieu (she received the name Becker from her husband, a white American man ten years her senior). Some noted that she also went by the "alias Que Anh Tran." She was noted as being "Vietnam born," though she had been a US citizen for many years. Early reporting claimed that Kieu used a mysterious "unknown poison or drug" to taint the "tofu soup" she made, while the official toxicology reports revealed she simply used the prescription sleep medication Ambien.[7] Her courtroom presence was described as mysterious and strange, with references to "long dark hair [that] blocked portions of her face," her need to answer the judge's "questions through a Vietnamese-language interpreter," and the fact that she "did not speak, except to answer 'Yes.'"[8] No information was provided as to why the jury did not see Kieu Becker as a victim of spousal abuse, save for the frequent mention of her use of a likely ineffective public defender.

Several articles compared the Kieu Becker case to that of the 1993 Bobbitt case, when a twenty-three-year-old Ecuadorian immigrant named Lorena Bobbitt sliced off her (twenty-six-year-old, white, American) husband's penis and tossed it into a field, an act her attorneys framed as a response to years of abuse. Indeed, it was the only other known case like it in recent US history. But unlike what occurred in the case of Kieu Becker, Bobbitt was found not guilty by reason of temporary insanity and received only a forty-five-day commitment at a psychiatric facility. Media reports that compare the two incidents tend to leave Kieu Becker's story midstream and conclude with Bobbitt's successful defense strategy; no further explanation is offered as to Kieu Becker's claims of abuse, or of her inability to attain a similar verdict. While the Kieu Becker case did not succeed in garnering much attention, it was estimated that 60 percent of the American public followed the Bobbitt case; Lorena was also named one of *People* magazine's "25 most interesting people" in 1993, and *Vanity Fair* named her a "national folk heroine."[9]

In the mid-2010s, the story of the Bobbitts reemerged as a site of public interest in light of growing publicity surrounding sexual harassment and sexual violence, including the #MeToo and #TimesUp movements. In 2015, Lorena appeared as a guest on *Steve Harvey* and explained that she suffered from "battered woman syndrome."[10] In 2016, *Rolling Stone* ran a feature article about the couple, "25 Years Post-Castration."[11] In 2018, *Time* magazine published a retrospective on the case featuring the problem of domestic abuse.[12] In 2019, Amazon Studios and producer Jordan Peele (director of *Us* [2019] and *Get Out* [2017] and costar of Comedy Central's *Key and Peele* [2012–2015]) released a four-part miniseries entitled *Lorena* that "reframes Lorena Bobbitt's story around issues of sexism and domestic abuse," providing "a new view into how America got her story wrong."[13] Reviews of the series remark in similar terms that *Lorena* "finally puts Lorena Bobbitt at the center of her own story," changing her "place in the conversation about domestic violence."[14]

How can we account for the differences between the Kieu Becker and Bobbitt cases, from their enactment in the courtroom to their divergent portrayal by the media? Occurring nearly two decades apart, the events are connected by the women's claims of spousal abuse, by the specific nature of their violent acts, and—as attested to in conservative pundit Ann Coulter's jarring rhetoric provided at the opening of this chapter—by the fact that they both appear to feature "penis-chopping immigrants."[15] But this is where their similarities end. How did one woman end up with a life sentence, her story destined to obscurity, and the other become a "folk heroine" of domestic violence survivorship featured prominently in mainstream news accounts from the 1990s to the present? If the order of the cases were flipped—with Kieu Becker predating Bobbitt—a narrative of progress could be offered as an explanation, especially because at the time of Bobbitt's trial, the use of the battered woman defense was fairly unfamiliar to the court system. But the actual order of the cases, in which Bobbitt predates Kieu Becker, makes the story much stranger.

While much of the conversation that has taken place surrounding the Bobbitts—both in the 1990s and in the current moment—focuses on the court's lack of attention to Lorena's accusations of the abuse, the actual verdict in her original trial suggests otherwise. In fact, a 1991 study conducted by the National Institutes of Health—two years prior to her trial—showed that in cases of retaliation against alleged abuse, "even if a defendant can prevail on an insanity defense, she'll most likely be confined to a hospital for the severely mentally ill for a longer or equivalent period of time to her likely prison sentence."[16] Thus, given that Bobbitt was charged with malicious wounding, she should have faced a sentence of five to twenty years, even if it was served inside a psychiatric institution. Instead, she walked away after one and half months of hospitalization, while Kieu Becker will remain incarcerated for at least seventeen years, being eligible for parole at the age of sixty-seven.

Using this comparison as a springboard, this chapter focuses on the Bobbitt case, including an analysis of coverage of the trial at the time it occurred, as well as the public's renewed interest in it since around 2015. While I will return to the Kieu Becker case at the conclusion, the bulk of the chapter focuses on how Lorena Bobbitt's racial and ethnic identities impacted the outcome of her trial. I acknowledge, but then move away from, some of the more salacious details of the case in order to demonstrate its significance to broader debates about state intervention in violence against women that expanded throughout the 1990s. Indeed, at the conclusion of the trial, some feminist activists rejoiced at the verdict as a potential windfall for the uncertain fate of domestic violence legislation. Kim Gandy, executive vice president of the National Organization for Women, for example, explained that the verdict could lead to policy change, noting, "We're glad the jury rejected the twisted argument that a battered woman should be locked up in a prison cell. . . . [T]his whole saga drives home the need for swift passage of a comprehensive version of the Violence Against Women Act, which is stalled in the never-neverland of Congressional maneuvering."[17] At the same time, however, there was also tremendous concern that Lorena's actions and the court's verdict—often hailed as a form of radical grassroots feminism—would negatively impact the broader (white, mainstream) feminist movement, including the progress that had been made in the area of domestic violence policy. As the critic Katha Pollitt wrote in 1994, where disapproval for Lorena's actions existed, it stemmed from the "wish of educated female professionals" associated with the mainstream feminist movement "to distance themselves from stereotypes of women as passive, helpless, and irrational. From this point of view, women like Lorena, if not punished, taint all women."[18]

From the vantage point of the current moment—twenty-five years after the trial—this chapter argues that these "wishes" and fears were less about the specific details of the Bobbitt case and more about the implicit contradiction involved in domestic violence activism. Indeed, domestic violence activism existed in complicated relation to the feminist movement. On the one hand, the right to freedom from bodily harm and gender-based violence was a clear feminist tenet. On the other, the language of women-specific violence prevention and protection that emerged from the actual legislation was seen as concerningly paternalistic by many activists, even though it responded in direct proportion to the socio-juridical crisis of disproportionately high rates of domestic abuse involving male-identified perpetrators and female-identified victims.[19] Considerations of domestic violence thus emblematized what the historian Joan Scott has called "the paradox of feminism," which requires a simultaneous call to sex- or gender-based difference and human sameness.[20]

This chapter demonstrates how the Bobbitt case, rather than halting the slow progress of domestic violence activism that had been mounting since the 1960s and 1970s, worked to accelerate the materialization of relevant jurisdiction and public awareness in a very particular way—namely, through the mobilization of cultural and racial stereotypes surrounding Lorena as a Latina immigrant woman. In doing so, I illustrate how Lorena's narrative provided justification for the potentially disempowering rhetoric of domestic violence protectionism that had long troubled white feminism. Existing scholarship on the trial treats Lorena's gendering and racialization as an inevitable sign of 1990s anti-immigrant sentiment, through a reading of the media's use of adjectives such as "subservient," "oversexed," "hot-blooded," "stupid," and "small." By contrast, this chapter considers how Lorena's position at the intersection of a variety of unprivileged categories—Latina, immigrant, and noncitizen—was usefully mobilized for the broader white feminist project and, later, for the purposes of the state. I argue that race and cultural difference became critical fulcrums for addressing the issue of domestic violence in a way that sidestepped the problem of white women's potential disempowerment, and that even served to empower white women as the stewards of domestic violence protectionism. As Sara Ahmed has observed, "We need to understand how feminism was historically used, and is thus usable, as an imperial project, saving brown women from their culture and/or patriarchy. . . . If feminist agency is found in whiteness, then the passivity and helplessness of women of color becomes the occasion to demonstrate this agency."[21]

As this chapter demonstrates, while white feminist claims on behalf of Latina and immigrant women were presumably based in humanitarian interests, the actual chronology of US domestic violence policy tells another story. Rather than the United States' establishing itself as a beacon of hope for women experiencing domestic violence that could then be spread to "less evolved" societies (however problematically), the rise of official US domestic violence policy occurred simultaneously with advocacy for "special" provisions for Latina and immigrant women. As I demonstrate, such synchronicity was not only about the advancement of a type of imperial feminism for the purpose of "white women saving brown women." Rather, the project of "saving brown women" also provided a framework for "saving white women" through domestic violence awareness and policy advancements, while also avoiding the problem of white women's endangerment as a potential source of weakness, inferiority, or necessary social and political disempowerment. This bait and switch was accomplished through a process of queer racialization that positioned Lorena as a vector for the advancement of white feminism.

To these ends, after addressing the Bobbitt case and its representation by the media, I consider the evolution of US domestic violence policies both with respect to US citizens and in relation to immigrants with varying degrees of citizenship status, including the establishment of the "battered spouse waiver" in the Immigration Act of 1990 and the passage of the 1994 Violence Against Women Act. I address the rise of "battered woman syndrome" as a culturally meaningful and legally usable concept and consider social policy rhetoric surrounding the "special vulnerability" of Latina and immigrant women to spousal abuse. In examining the significance of the Bobbitt case to these issues, I unpack the relationship between the battered woman defense (deployed by Lorena's lawyers) and the insanity defense, as well as the potential application of both in cases pertaining to matters of racial and national difference. In doing so, I highlight how Lorena's positionality mediated the trial's verdict, her depiction by the media, and the lasting impact of both within the realm of US popular culture.

Section I. "A heinous act like none other": Lorena Bobbitt in the Popular and Scholarly Imaginations

Lorena Gallo was born in 1969 in Ecuador and was raised predominantly in Caracas, Venezuela, where her family relocated for economic opportunity. In 1987, she moved to the United States on a student visa, enrolling in Northern Virginia Community College. John Wayne Bobbitt was born in 1967 in Niagara Falls, New York. He grew up in a poor community, first raised by his mother and later by his aunt and uncle. John met Lorena at a Marine Corps officers' ball in 1988, when he was enlisted in the marines. The couple married nine months later in 1989, just as Lorena's student visa was expiring. Lorena described her attraction to John in the following way: "I thought John was very handsome. Blue eyes. A man in uniform, you know? He was almost like a symbol—a Marine, fighting for the country. I believed in this beautiful country. I was swept off my feet. I wanted my American dream."[22]

Unfortunately, Lorena's dream dissolved quickly. Her marriage was troubled from the beginning; John was increasingly physically, emotionally, and sexually abusive as time went on. He used "what she called 'Marine torture techniques' in which he would squeeze her face. . . . [H]e also would wrap his hands around her neck and choke her." "I couldn't breathe," she said. "There was no air."[23] By 1991, John was discharged from the marines and was unable to find steady employment, while Lorena worked as a manicurist at a local salon and supported them both on her salary. That year, she got an abortion, explaining that her husband forced her to undergo the procedure. Finding herself in a state of financial and emotional desperation, she embezzled $7,200 from her employer (who agreed not to press charges if Lorena paid her back) and got caught shoplifting from Nordstrom (for which she received community service time). The house Lorena and John had purchased then went into foreclosure, and the couple separated, then reconciled. By the time the notorious incident occurred on June 23, 1993, they were already in the midst of a second separation. Throughout their marriage, the couple had called the police to the house on several occasions—each claiming that the other was being physically abusive—though no charges were ever filed. The day before the incident, Lorena went to the police station and started to file charges of spousal abuse but allegedly did not want to wait the three hours for processing and thus left the station without completing the report.[24]

The night of the incident, Lorena was home alone. John was out drinking with a friend who had been staying with him at the time. When the two men arrived at the house, John's friend fell asleep on the couch in the living room, and John went into the couple's bedroom. Lorena claimed that he raped her at that time and that it was not an unusual occurrence, as he had done so on many occasions before. After John fell asleep, Lorena went to the kitchen for a glass of water; once there, she found an eight-inch carving knife, took it with her back to the bedroom, pulled back the bedcovers, and cut off John's penis. She then stole $100 and a Nintendo Game Boy from John's friend's possessions, while both men remained sleeping, and left the apartment, taking the penis with her. She started driving without a location in mind and threw the penis out the window into a field across from a 7-Eleven. She described her actions as a matter of self-defense rather than retribution: "I didn't want to teach him a lesson. . . . No, it was survival. Life and death. I was fearing for my life."[25]

In his own account of the night, John maintained that he did not rape her but also that because of intoxication he had no memory of what had happened. He believed that Lorena assaulted him because of jealousy over their separation: "If she couldn't have me, no one could."[26] After the fact, he stated that her actions were also motivated by her immigration status: "There was the green card, too. That didn't come to my mind at the time, but it's obvious. You have to be married to an American citizen for five years to get one, and we'd only been married for four."[27] When John eventually woke up and realized what had happened, he had his friend take him to the hospital. When the police found Lorena, she told them where she had left the penis, and they were able to retrieve it, put it on ice, and bring it to the hospital, where a team of surgeons successfully reattached it.[28]

Later that year, both John and Lorena stood trial: he for marital sexual assault and she for malicious wounding. John was found not guilty. Lorena was found not guilty by reason of temporary insanity and was committed to a psychiatric institution for forty-five days. Lorena's trial was broadcast in full on CNN and became an ongoing punch line in the popular-culture circuit, appearing as the subject of late-night talk shows, political cartoons, and comedy sketches. At the courthouse as the trial unfolded, "vendors hawked Slice sodas and hot dogs, penis-shaped chocolates, [and] T-shirts bearing the legend LOVE HURTS."[29]

From the beginning to the end, the US public was divided on Lorena's case. Some found her actions to be a sign of women's resistance to male oppression, "an ugly snapshot from the war between men and women."[30] Debra Haffner, executive director of the Sexuality Information and Education Council of the United States, noted that in the wake of the Bobbitt trial, "the avenging wife has become a new media model."[31] A feature-length article in *Vanity Fair* that interviewed Lorena called her a "national folk heroine," a term that quickly caught on in the associated press.[32] Support for Lorena was also notable among the local Latinx community. As Linda Pershing explains,

> A dozen Latino cabdrivers volunteered their services in transporting people to the site of her trial for free. In below-freezing weather, approximately two hundred people of Latin American descent, many of them men, kept a vigil outside the Manassas courtroom, cheering for Lorena when she entered or left the courtroom and carrying the Ecuadorian flags and signs with slogans like "Lorena, *estamos contingo*" (Lorena, we are with you).[33]

The press reported that the "crowd booed and whistled as John Bobbitt left" the courthouse, while Lorena waved and blew a kiss to her supporters.[34]

By contrast, others found the lenient verdict and sentencing in Lorena's case to be deeply problematic. *Newsweek* reported that Lorena's actions were "cringe-inducing, not empowering," a story comparable to other cases of violent and scandalous crime committed by female perpetrators, such as Amy Fisher (a seventeen-year-old who shot and wounded her married lover's wife in 1992) and Jean Harris (a fifty-seven-year-old who shot and killed her boyfriend in 1980 out of jealousy over his relationships with other women).[35] "These are women," the *Newsweek* article asserted, "who so strongly identify with their abusive, oppressive men that they find it untenable to simply walk away, but instead explode into violence."[36] Responding to debates over the Bobbitt trial, the cultural critic Barbara Ehrenreich argued that divisive attitudes toward Lorena represented a class schism in attitudes toward modern feminism:

> The really interesting thing about the Bobbitt affair is the huge divergence
> it reveals between high-powered feminist intellectualdom, on the one hand,
> and your average office wit or female cafeteria orator, on the other. While
> the gals in data entry are discussing fascinating new possibilities for cutlery
> commercials, the feminist pundits are tripping over one another to show
> that none of them is, goddess forbid, a "man hater." And while the pundits
> are making obvious but prissy-sounding statements like "The fact that one
> has been a victim doesn't give one carte blanche to victimize others," the
> woman on the street is making V signs by raising two fingers and bringing
> them together with a snipping motion. . . . They're tired of being victims.[37]

As Ehrenreich noted, while those at the front lines of the mainstream feminist movement (composed of upper-middle-class white women) despaired at Lorena's actions, working-class observers were "eager to see women fight back by whatever means necessary" against ongoing abuse.[38]

Of the limited scholarship that exists on the Bobbitt case, all of it was published in the decade or so immediately following the trial. Most of the literature focuses on one or more of the following three issues: first, the role of Lorena's and John's respective gender presentations in relation to the case; second, the psychoanalytic significance of the removal of the penis; and third, the meaning of the verdict for public attitudes toward domestic abuse. Jean S. Filetti notes that Lorena was able to successfully claim the effects of battered woman syndrome by fulfilling "society's expectations of the damsel in distress," which relies on the idea of "'incapacity and learned helplessness' . . . [and] emphasizes a woman's irrationality and passivity."[39] According to Filetti, the sheer brutality of Lorena's actions (i.e., her use of a large knife to sever a human body part) is so at odds with normative perceptions of femininity that it would be nearly impossible to reconcile Lorena's crime with her gender presentation, a disconnect that somehow served to "prove" the insanity of her actions.[40] Similarly, Robin Tolmach Lakoff suggests that the verdict in Lorena's case was the only one that could allow the jury to do one of its extralegal jobs: to function as a Greek chorus, a definer and reinforcer of community morals and values. An acquittal would have "sent the message" that Bobbitt's action was both legal and moral, which would have been clearly intolerable to the status quo. A guilty verdict would have implied, at least, that the act was rational, if not legal; that we the people . . . understand even if we don't quite condone. But the verdict of temporary insanity sent the most comforting (and conservative) message: such an act is crazy, without justification.[41]

In other words, the verdict enabled both the fact of domestic abuse and the necessity to defend oneself against it to be imagined as aberrations. As Patricia J. Priest, Cindy Jenefsky, and Jill D. Swenson argue, "American press coverage of John and Lorena Bobbitt emphasized the act of slicing off her husband's penis as 'unthinkable' and 'abhorrent' . . . 'a heinous act like no other' . . . 'primordial' . . . 'cruel and unusual.'" Through such use of "superlatives," these "structural press practices" served "to minimize rape and sexual/domestic violence" by "decontextualiz[ing] and individualiz[ing]" the issue.[42]

Scholarship addressing the case also notes the media's hyperattention to the injury John sustained, in a manner that excluded a more serious consideration of the long-term physical and psychological abuse that Lorena suffered at his hands.[43] As Melissa D. Deem writes, the "focus upon the body of John Wayne obfuscates the abuse suffered by Lorena Bobbitt. Masculine dismemberment monopolizes attention, turning it away from violence done daily to women's bodies."[44] Several scholars point out that even as the harm done to John was the central crisis of the Bobbitt case, the absence of "before-and-after photographs" speaks to the "highly censored" nature of images of the nude male body that serves to "efface" how "the materiality of the penis . . . reveals an instability at the center of phallic masculinity."[45]

Psychoanalytic approaches to the case debated the symbolic significance of forcible penis removal. Some works called Lorena's actions a form of "castration," while others noted the inaccuracy of the term in this case (i.e., castration is the removal of the testicles, not the penis). Daniel Dervin writes that John's body was "subjected to real castration" that "reduced [his phallus] to a penis."[46] Similarly, Diane Davis asserts that the most important part of the story was Lorena's choice to throw her husband's penis out the window of her car rather than destroying or keeping it: by "pitching it, she dis/covers a way out of the binary system all together, and so a way out of phallocentrism."[47] In these and other interpretations, critics note how the removal of the penis and/or the manipulation of the phallus functions as an incitement to discourse by the silenced, feminine body, exemplified by the focus on John's body and the nonattention paid to Lorena's.[48] As Marilyn Frye observes,

> John Bobbitt's penis signifies. But Lorena Bobbitt's vulva, clitoris, vagina, and womb are simply not in the story. News accounts reported that Lorena Bobbitt was "allegedly raped," but her genitals are not named. The word vagina was not oft repeated, not uttered at all, in fact, in any of the reportage I saw or heard. They did not say: he is accused of bludgeoning, bruising, and tearing her vulva and vagina. Her genitals do not signify; they are outside meaning, are not spoken, and do not speak. In the public and juridical realm, John Bobbitt's bodily sex distinction is significant: it is named, and it names. Entering that realm, Lorena Bobbitt's bodily sex distinction is outside meaning: it is utterly unuttered; it does not signify.[49]

Less attention has been paid to the racial dynamics at play between the couple. While a few articles mention the issue in passing, it is typically included as an example of the power imbalance between the couple, where it is noted that John is a two-hundred-pound, white, American, male marine, and Lorena is a one-hundred-pound Ecuadorian woman. Some note the frequency with which Lorena's actions were attributable to her ethnicity in media reports, where she was called a "hot-blooded Latina" and a "Latin firecracker."[50] Writing about the case as fodder for mid- to late-1990s comedy, Linda Pershing observes that "in some jokes Lorena, and by inference all Latinas, was portrayed as emotional, irrational, unpredictable, inept or stupid," or as a "castrating Fur[y]."[51]

Charla Ogaz and Suzana Sawyer both foreground issues of race and citizenship in their analyses of the case. Ogaz notes that media representations of the Bobbitt case demonstrate how Lorena was "raced/colored, sexualized, and classed (read: othered) in ways that make traditional paradigms of 'femininity' unavailable"—forms of "sexualization and exotification that result in different engendering than that of white women."[52] In particular, Ogaz points to the common mistake made in stories detailing the couple's travails, which alternately cite Lorena's nation of origin as Ecuador (her birthplace) and Venezuela (where she lived for part of her childhood): "Such inexactitude . . . suggests that it doesn't matter where she's from. Rather, the point seems to be to mark her as immigrant or alien/other."[53] Sawyer adds that from the perspective of Lorena's supporters in her home country of Ecuador, and perhaps also for some Latinxs in the United States, "this was a story about a First-World man exploiting a Third-World woman."[54] In the sections that follow, I consider Lorena's race and nationality as critical factors in the outcome of her trial, as well as the broader significance of the case to the trajectory of domestic violence policy.

Section II. "Cultural barriers": Domestic Violence Legislation and Immigrant Women

Several pieces of immigration legislation that occurred during the 1980s and early 1990s provide a critical context for understanding the significance of Lorena's positionality as a non–US citizen married to a US citizen. In response to a perceived increase in fraudulent immigrant marriages, Congress passed the Immigration Marriage Fraud Amendments (IMFA) in 1986, which lengthened the "timeline of immigration relief through marriage," requiring that the member of the couple who was a citizen or legal permanent resident "apply for a two-year conditional green card for their foreign national spouse," followed by a joint petition that must be filed by both spouses at the end of the trial period. The IMFA also required more extensive documentation demonstrating that the "marriage had been entered into in good faith."[55] These additional strictures placed a profound burden on victims of domestic violence in cases where an immigrant woman's abuser was also her sponsoring husband.

Concern voiced by domestic violence and immigration advocates during the late 1980s resulted in the inclusion of a "battered spouse waiver" in the new Immigration Act of 1990, which waived the required two-year waiting period for conditional permanent residents married to a lawful permanent resident or US citizen.[56] Nonetheless, as Susan Berger points out, the waiver required that applicants "maintained high levels of evidentiary proof of abuse and extreme cruelty," which had to be verified by "a mental health professional," a requirement that was difficult to attain and depended on an immigrant's financial status and linguistic abilities.[57] In requiring this burden of proof, the Immigration and Naturalization Service claimed that it "lacked the ability to evaluate the credibility of testimony from 'unlicensed or untrained individuals,'" which in turn necessitated that an evaluation be made by "a professional recognized by the Service as an expert in the field," restricted to "licensed clinical social workers, psychologists, and psychiatrists."[58] The shortcomings of this waiver in ameliorating the difficult situation experienced by many immigrant women led to the establishment of further provisions under the 1994 Violence Against Women Act (VAWA), which provided funding for the prosecution of violent crimes committed against immigrant women.

Emerging as the culmination of decades of activism, the passage of

VAWA legislation was a fraught issue for mainstream US feminism. While the right to bodily integrity was a clear feminist tenet, VAWA advanced the necessity of singling out "violence against women" and thus was perceived to be paternalistic by many feminist activists. Adding to the complexity of the issue was the fact that no matter how potentially conservative or mainstream second-wave feminist claims to bodily autonomy and safety were (insofar as they represented a very small segment of the population, i.e., white, upper-middle-class, and often heteronormative), they were still "left" of mainstream US politics. As one VAWA task force member described, the process of working on the act involved "passing feminist legislation without appearing too feminist."[59] The historian Irene Meisel argues that this was accomplished by "focus[ing] on VAWA's potential as anti-crime, anti-violence legislation and downplay[ing] its feminist credentials."[60] Framed as part of more conservative anticrime rhetoric, VAWA's passage cemented an alliance between feminism and criminal justice that Elizabeth Bernstein has termed "carceral feminism."[61]

VAWA also made special provisions for immigrant women, bringing them further under the scope of the law—first, by enabling those who experienced domestic violence to independently petition for lawful residency (in the event that the woman's potential sponsor was also her abuser), and, second, by providing an exception to deportation policy. In order to petition for residency or stalled deportation under VAWA provisions, women had to provide four justifications:

1. ABUSE—during the marriage the woman or her child was battered or subject to extreme cruelty by the woman's spouse.
2. VALID MARRIAGE WITH QUALIFYING SPOUSE—the woman entered the marriage with either a US citizen (USC) or Legal Permanent Resident (LPR) in "good faith" and has resided in the United States with the qualifying spouse.
3. GOOD MORAL CHARACTER—the woman has been a person of good moral character for the last three years.
4. EXTREME HARDSHIP—the woman's removal would be an "extreme hardship" to the woman or her child.[62]

Needless to say, the ability of a person who is already vulnerable as a noncitizen to demonstrate any of these points—through state-recognized forms of documentation, including "police reports, photos," community "affidavits," "or professional evaluations"—would be incredibly limited.[63] Similarly, the "moral character" clause is intentionally vague and defined by negation, requiring the exclusion of a lengthy list of individuals ranging from "habit-ual drunkard[s]" to illegal-gambling participants to those who have engaged in promoting "severe violations of religious freedom."[64] As the immigra-tion attorney Dree K. Collopy explains, "Even if an individual does not fall within one of these categories, [one] may still be found to lack good moral character."[65]

All of these factors work to produce a very narrow definition of an accept-able abuse victim and an acceptable VAWA claimant, requiring adherence to specific gendered and racialized stereotypes. In fact, much of the conver-sation surrounding VAWA's impact on immigrant women focused on the "special circumstances" that led to seemingly disproportionate rates of do-mestic violence in immigrant households. Interestingly, although the very premise of VAWA's self-petitioning clause for immigrant women illumi-nates how the required accumulation of citizenship through familial ties renders certain populations disproportionately vulnerable to invisibilized vi-olence,[66] literature surrounding the necessity of the law (and its later revi-sions) typically cited "cultural differences" as the primary reason for its es-tablishment in the first place. Academic studies, popular press reporting, and domestic violence activism all identified the prevalence and nonregula-tion of domestic violence in immigrant women's countries of birth, along-side regressive, culturally specific attitudes toward gender, as inducing inti-mate partner violence.

What is particularly concerning about this type of rhetoric—found, no less, in progressive forums—is that it so clearly aligns with conservative po-litical agendas. For example, the conservative pundit Ann Coulter asserts that the arrival of immigrants compromises US progress toward gender eq-uity and freedom from sexual violence:

> All peasant cultures exhibit non-progressive views on women and chil-dren; Latin America just happens to be the peasant culture closest to the United States. Mexicans alone constitute more than one-third of all le-gal immigrants and about 80 percent of illegal immigrants. . . . The media could have made this easy to see by reporting the truth about immigrant sex crimes. . . . What will America be like when it's majority Hispanic[?][67]

In Coulter's estimation—which clearly echoes then presidential candidate Donald Trump's 2015 remarks about Mexican immigrants being "rapists"[68]—gender and sexual regression in Latin America are simply matters of fact. As Lila Abu-Lughod, Kwok Pui-lan, Jasbir K. Puar, and other postcolonial the-orists have demonstrated, imagined constructions of "Other" cultures' standards of gender and sexuality have long been used as a justification for imperialism, military intervention, and nativism.[69]

Yet while Coulter's and Trump's rhetoric is particularly incendiary, it doesn't stand far apart from presumably more progressive attitudes toward immigrant women that have galvanized domestic abuse reform in the immigration law arena. In the context of discourse surrounding immigrant women's vulnerability to domestic violence, cultural differences are used to translate immigrant women's hesitancy to engage with law enforcement as a form of internalized repression stemming from culturally specific (read non-American, non-Anglo-European) gender roles that include an acceptance of domestic violence and a lack of individual willpower, rather than a matter of the state's failure to attend to basic human rights principles.[70]

Domestic violence services for immigrant women thus have often deployed the language of "cultural competency," a concept that emerged from early 2000s public health rhetoric regarding the necessity of instructing care providers in "cultural differences" in the interest of inducing patient compliance.[71] In the case of domestic abuse, which is both a matter of public health and a matter of law, the tasks of the state and of victims' rights organizations merge: police officers are "trained to recognize cultural barriers to investigating domestic violence and other crimes," while battered women's shelters work to employ multilingual staff, "rent Chinese and Vietnamese movies and . . . have plenty of tortillas in the house."[72] At the same time, these overtures toward difference are often limited. Because many shelters require victims to undertake counseling as a condition of residency, they will not accept women who are unable to communicate in English.[73]

Here, culture and ethnicity are understood to function as important individuating and collectivizing forces in ways that draw from developments in psychological research on domestic violence published during the 1980s and 1990s. During this time, researchers working on the problem of domestic abuse gradually moved away from "psychodynamic theories focused exclusively on the abused woman or on the man who battered," toward a more holistic, or "ecological," approach that considered other "environmental factors." In earlier conceptualizations, "abused women were seen as responsible for their plight because they were (a) masochistic, (b) suffering from learned helplessness, (c) mentally ill, or (d) experiencing severe intimacy-dependency conflicts." Those perpetrating the abuse, or "batterers," were understood to be "(a) alcoholics, (b) mentally ill, (c) generally violent, or (d) unable to tolerate intimacy."[74] By contrast, the new ecological approach focused on the broader context, including factors of socioeconomic hierarchy, gender norms, employment status, and, to a lesser extent, race and ethnicity.

As Kimberlé Crenshaw pointed out in her foundational 1989 essay on intersectionality, race—and its interaction with other conditions of identity and inequality—has often remained overlooked or misunderstood in discussions about the impact of violence on women of color.[75] In the context of domestic violence policy discussions—where the law was attempting to grapple with the precarity of domestic abuse victims, and the academic study of domestic abuse was moving toward ecological theorizations—"cultural differences" became a way of understanding domestic violence as an "environmental" problem, while simultaneously continuing to assign blame to individual women and their familial heritage. In these theorizations, domestic violence in "Other" cultures was typically described as a private family matter, a problem that was even without terminology in certain foreign languages.[76]

Ironically, and importantly for the purposes of this chapter, these critiques were concurrent with (rather than postdated) the emergence of US domestic violence law. Indeed, as the legal scholar Jenny Rivera wrote in 1994—the same year that VAWA was enacted—"local prosecutors and judges react differently to domestic violence cases than to other criminal cases. They often treat cases as inconsequential or private matters, ill-suited to state intervention."[77] Understanding the simultaneity of these phenomena reveals their coproduction—that is, that US domestic violence became a resolvable problem in the context of critiques about "foreign" immigrant, gender-based violence patterns. For example, in an article published in 1995, the legal scholar Linda Kelly explained the special difficulties facing "battered immigrants" in the following way:

> In some countries, domestic violence, while not only denied, may be found culturally acceptable. Other countries have only recently criminalized wife battering or violence against women. Only a few countries have programs or shelters to help abused women. . . . [W]ith limited acknowledgement of domestic violence in their own countries, battered immigrants may come to the United States unfamiliar with what legally available and socially acceptable recourse exists for victims.[78]

Such narratives worked to erase the long-standing dismissal of domestic violence victims in US jurisprudence. After all, battered women's shelters began appearing in significant numbers only during the 1980s and 1990s in the United States, and the issue of domestic abuse was still a fairly recent public priority.[79] As Natalie Nanasi points out, much of the domestic violence activism that took place during and prior to this period was a "direct response to law enforcement's unwillingness to intervene in 'family disputes' and sought to provide enhanced legal protections and assistance to survivors of domestic violence."[80]

What does it mean, then, that the battered spouse waiver, issued with the Immigration Act of 1990, actually preceded VAWA legislation? Certainly, VAWA included provisions relevant to immigrants with varying relationships to US citizenship, as I previously addressed. But it is also true that it stood as the first significant piece of legislation aimed at the general problem of domestic violence for the domestic population of US women. Understanding the chronological relation between these pieces of legislation requires understanding specific attitudes toward immigrant populations, particularly those from Latin America, which constituted the largest group entering the United States during the 1990s. To this end, it is important to consider how Latina women fit within social-scientific understandings of domestic violence.

In debates surrounding immigrant women and state intervention in domestic violence that took place during the late 1980s and the 1990s, Latina women emerged as the population at greatest "risk."[81] This endangerment was explained as being due to "certain basic cultural values that are held . . . and have a strong impact on [the] population," namely, "the centrality of family and the distinct gender roles."[82] Similarly, the 1996 *Statistical Handbook of Violence in America* cited "Hispanic women in intimate relationships" as the category most at risk for domestic violence.[83] Social-science research from this period, including work from legal theorists, psychologists, and sociologists, explained that "Latinas need support services—targeted to their specific needs—to a greater extent than other battered women."[84] "Cultural traditions," including "the strong patriarchal nature of Latino culture and the influence of Catholicism," were cited as "constraints" that made reporting domestic violence impossible without "challeng[ing] the core" of "Latina identity."[85] Scholars further noted that "male and female children" in "Latino culture" are "socialized differently from an early age," where "Latino boys are given more resources, priority, and freedom than those given to Latina girls."[86] As the psychologist Julia Perilla noted in 1999,

> Latino men (like men of many other cultures) learn from early on that their gender provides them rights and privileges that they perceive as the natural order of things. . . . [The Latino man] is accorded his rightful status: that of *jefe de la casa* (head of the household) who has absolute power and control over his family. Anything less than this is perceived as a serious threat to his sense of manhood.[87]

Perilla explained that by contrast, for Latinas, the concept of "marianismo" "defines the traditional roles expected of Latina women. The term is derived from [the Virgin Mary] whose attributes of self-sacrifice, abnegation, passivity, and sexual purity have been traditionally equated with the characteristics of *una mujer Buena* (a good woman). Traditionally, a Latina would derive her sense of identity and self-esteem from fulfilling specific cultural mandates."[88] Similarly, the legal theorist Berta Esperanza Hernández-Truyol wrote in 1997 that "Latinas are acculturated to be secondary, subordinate beings. The family always comes first. . . . Latinas are indoctrinated with the myth of *marianismo*," which requires "self-sacrifice, self-effacement and self-subordination."[89]

At the same time, however, Perilla, Hernández-Truyol, and others scholars writing during this period clearly state that there remained a lack of available data regarding domestic violence within Latino populations.[90] Hernández-Truyol attributed this absence to the fact that "Latinas as a group are so marginalized and invisible . . . [that] statistics are rarely available to allow commentators to bring them to visibility."[91] Perilla argued that the lack could be understood in relation to "both methodological issues and the heterogeneity of the Latino population."[92] The absence in available data noted here reflects a particular moment in which the question of cultural difference was increasingly becoming a broader public health concern. As touched upon in the previous section, the rise of cultural competency as a strategy for both research and clinical practice meant that cultural difference—whether ethnic, racial, religious, or some combination of all three—became a focal point at the same moment in which national policy debates occurred over the question of "violence against women." Much like the literature that identified the specificities of Latino or Hispanic culture as the source of Latina women's domestic violence victimization, studies on prevention also located cultural difference as a major factor in the process of ameliorating such violence. While these studies often proposed a correlation between general issues such as unemployment, alcoholism, and lack of education and the prevalence of domestic violence within the general population, they also singled out Latina women as most endangered by those issues.[93] For example, in a 2003 issue of the *Chicano-Latino Law Review*, Michelle DeCasas wrote that the women

> at greatest risk for injury from domestic violence include those with male partners who abuse alcohol, are unemployed, have less than a high-school education, and have a low socio-economic status. Hispanic women are more

exposed to these factors as a whole than are Black and White women. . . . [T]he poor economic and political position of Hispanics place them at a distinct advantage, thus causing Hispanics to experience and respond to domestic violence differently than White women.[94]

DeCasas's remarks are emblematic of research on "Hispanic women" and domestic violence that continually cites the population's special burden while not exactly explaining why its members are "more exposed" to risk factors than others. The question remains, then, why Latina women—US citizens and noncitizens alike, hailing from diverse ethnic, national, cultural, and religious backgrounds—were often framed as *the* group most impacted by domestic violence, and what consequences they experienced as a result. The implicit assumption seems to be that cultural difference shapes how women experience and react to trauma, and, for the reasons previously stated, that Latinas existed at a special disadvantage.[95]

Section III. "A pitiable woman of limited, child-like intelligence": Manufacturing Antipathy for John Bobbitt

The day after the verdict in the Bobbitt case, the *New York Times* described Lorena as "a pitiable woman of limited, child-like intelligence who endured years of abuse and finally struck back."[96] Throughout the trial, Lorena's intelligence was an object of ridicule. Recounting the testimony of Susan J. Fiester, medical director of the Psychiatric Institute of Washington and expert witness for the defense, the Associated Press reported that Lorena had tested at a "'borderline normal' IQ of 83."[97] Media reports that mentioned the test also conflated Lorena's alleged lack of intelligence with both her "severe mental illness" (alternately cited as "depression," "mania," and a "variety of mental illnesses") and her disfluency with English (represented as her general incoherency, a "thick accent," an inability to properly translate between languages, and so on).[98] As Lorena's attorney, Blair Howard, explained with respect to Lorena's statements in the aftermath of her arrest, "You have the problem of the second language, you have the problem of the woman who is hysterical at the time that the comments were made."[99] Nonetheless, all of Lorena's testimony, medical examinations, and press interviews were conducted in English, suggesting that she either was fluent enough for official purposes and therefore did not warrant a translator or, at the very least, was presumed to be reasonably fluent.

On the one hand, the overlap and misuse of language surrounding intelligence and mental illness reflects the culture of the time; after all, the Americans with Disabilities Act had only just passed in 1990, and the discourses used to address people with disabilities were less politically sensitive. On the other hand, the collapse of Lorena's ethnicity and foreign language skills, with the presumption of her mental illness or lack of intelligence speaks to centuries-old correlations between ethnicity, citizenship status, and mental fitness. As the historians Alexandra Minna Stern, Natalia Molina, and others have demonstrated, negative attitudes toward immigrants from non–Northern European nations have often been based in an assumed correlation between certain races, ethnicities, and "mental diseases or defects," wherein issues of intelligence and mental health have been used interchangeably.[100] Moreover, because the science of intelligence testing is itself rooted in the history of eugenic policy and has relied over time to greater or lesser degrees on fluency with English language and US culture, conclusions regarding Lorena's mental health and intellectual ability cannot be understood apart from her ethnicity and immigration status.[101]

At the same time, Lorena's mental state was not the only one that was disparaged throughout the trial. In fact, it is hard to find a mention of John without an accompanying critique of his intellectual abilities. Interviewers described him as "painfully literal," with "slow" speech, and jokes were commonly made that correlated his severed penis with his limited intelligence (e.g., "By his testimony [he] proves that his IQ is about as long as his equipment").[102] Physicians who spent considerable time with him working on his reconstructive surgery were quoted as stating that Bobbitt "is not a smart guy."[103] Even his attorney, Gregory Murphy, described having had an unspecified "psychological test done on John," which demonstrated that he was "not capable of really telling a lie, because he doesn't handle—he can't do the complexity that's required to make a—to see a lie, if you will."[104] Murphy also explained that "John suffered from a learning disability as a child" and "that even now John suffers from attention-deficit disorder. 'His attention tends to wander. . . . He'll be easily distracted in the course of conversation.'"[105]

Comments concerning John's lack of intelligence are typically presented alongside stories of his poor, single-parent upbringing. Describing the strange humor that continues to surround the Bobbitt case—which, after all, featured a horrific act of dismemberment following years of domestic abuse—a 2018 *Vanity Fair* article argued that John's background was the reason his story could never rise to the level of a real "tragedy" in the American imagination, as the genre "demands, if not nobility of birth, nobility of character. Sure, King Lear can descend from majesty to horror. But can John

Wayne Bobbitt, a man with the same name as a cowpoke movie star, a one-time employee of Red Lobster, who uses phrases like 'hurtin' for a squirtin" . . . ? No. Because . . . you can't fall from the bottom, can you?"[106]

In the 2019 Amazon docuseries *Lorena*, which claims to retell the case by centering Lorena's narrative "around issues of sexism and domestic abuse,"[107] John's intellectual abilities and impoverished background are presented as coproductive and are further tied to a narrative of racist violence. Interview segments are stitched together that explain how John's father abused and then left his mother, who was in turn "forced" to move with her sons to a predominantly African American neighborhood—a "ghetto"—in Niagara, New York. John claims that while living there, he and his family were the victims of several assaults: "At the time, there was a lot of hatred there. . . . [W]e were attacked by African Americans 'cause we were the only white family in a black community. And my mother was raped twice and they attacked me, knocked me down, busted my head open. . . . They burned down our house so my uncle had to come save us."[108] After his mother had a "mental breakdown," he went to live with other relatives. Recalling his childhood, John also describes abuse at the hands of a "pedophile uncle" from the ages of six to eight: "We were young and did alcohol and was involved and he, you know, molested some of us and, you know, we don't talk about it."[109]

John's description of his family's poverty and proximity to Blackness, as well as his lack of a nuclear family, combined with the aspersions cast on his mental abilities, work to inscribe him at the margins of normative whiteness. At the same time, his claims of intrafamilial sexual abuse—between his parents as well as between himself, other young boys in the family, and his uncle—work to destabilize his masculinity. (In a recent press interview, John describes how he "chose to be in the marines to work hard and be strong," particularly following his mother's decline in mental health.)[110] In *Lorena*, information about John's troubled childhood is presented in relation to his history in the pornography industry, highlighting the interrelationality among his lower-class status, marginal whiteness, and nonnormative masculinity. John's pornography career began in 1994, when he starred in the film *John Wayne Bobbitt: Uncut*, which still remains one of the highest-grossing films in the US pornography industry.[111] Loosely based on John's romance with Lorena, the film presents John fully nude, revealing the successful work of surgeons in reattaching his penis. During and after the trial, John intentionally pursued media attention—traveling on a forty-city speaking tour, appearing as a guest on radio stations across the country, autographing steak knives at public demonstrations, and, finally, appearing as a judge at Howard Stern's New Year's Eve pageant.[112] In 1996, Stern paid for

John to receive penis-enlargement surgery, which resulted in another starring role in a pornographic film, *Frankenpenis*.[113]

John's presence in the porn industry at once conforms to and flouts dominant narratives of normative masculinity upheld during the trial itself. On the one hand, his penis was at the center of the trial—it was the issue at stake in the crime and thus a matter of national debate. News reports called John's injury the "cruelest cut," "a fate worse than death," "worse than being killed," the removal of "a man's reason for living," and so on. On the other hand, images of John's body following the injury he sustained, as well as images of the unattached penis, were never shown to the public. (They are, however, both presented in the 2019 documentary *Lorena*, though the images are blurry and somewhat difficult to decipher.) At the same time, the frequent public discussion of John's penis, coupled with his presence in popular pornographic films, served to destabilize his masculinity.

As theorists of the gaze have long observed, the position of spectacularization is inherently feminized.[114] Placing gender into conversation with race, Richard Dyer has observed that the representation of nude white male bodies in popular culture is a rare occurrence, precisely because of traditional Enlightenment hierarchies that ascribe an inverse proportionality to intellectual ability and physical embodiment. Thus, individuals in positions of privilege by way of race, gender, class, and so on are typically understood to be the least attached to their bodily predispositions and thus to be rational, neutral subjects, not swayable by the passions of the body. In popular culture, it is therefore rare to find powerful subjects in states of undress that highlight their physicality. When they are presented in this way, they are typically muscle-bound, in order to connote the triumph of the mind's willpower over the body through ritualized acts of self-control and self-sacrifice.[115]

Similarly, Elizabeth Stephens notes that the absence of the penis from poplar cultural representations signifies "an instability at the center of phallic masculinity that its censorship has traditionally effaced."[116] Peter Brown, Elizabeth Grosz, and Leo Bersani, respectively, have also noted the difficulty of representing the materiality of the penis, particularly as it pertains to ejaculation.[117] "Men's refusal to acknowledge the effects of flows that move through various parts of the body from the inside out," Grosz writes, suggests an "attempt to distance themselves from the very kind of corporeality—uncontrollable, excessive, expansive, disruptive, irrational—they have attributed to women" throughout history.[118]

For all of these reasons, the presence of John's body in the media was a source of ambivalence. It was at once endlessly discussed and visually absent. It was fractured, successfully repaired, and ultimately deemed in need of a "franken" enhancement. And, finally, it was an emblem of identifiable normative masculinity that became a symbolically feminized form, through processes of both dismembering and spectacularization. These depictions, combined with narratives that invoked John's lower-class, unstable upbringing, produced John not only as a figure of marginal masculinity but also as a figure of marginal whiteness. The importance of his proximity to and distance from positions of power cannot be underestimated in terms of the public's reaction to the case, nor in the ultimate court verdict that leniently sentenced Lorena. For upper-class white feminists disconcerted by the sheer violence of Lorena's actions, her husband's marginal identity served to soften the blow: this was not the type of man *they* would have chosen; this was not the type of man *they* would find themselves in conflict with. Where sympathy for Lorena could be found, then, it was galvanized as much by public appreciation for her struggle as it was by a certain public distaste for John. Thus, when Lorena's lawyer, Lisa Kemler, urged jurors at the trial to remember (or perhaps to consider for the first time) that "it was his penis from which she could not escape. A life is worth more than a penis,"[119] it became possible to imagine the specificity of John and his body as sites of outrage that need not translate into a broader "man-hating" disposition.

Section IV. "An irresistible impulse": Battered Woman Syndrome, Temporary Insanity, and Gender Inequality

The Bobbitts' presence in tabloid journalism both during and after the trial was critical in shaping attitudes toward each of the parties. At the same time, the case took place at an important moment in the history of legal reform and was concurrent with three interrelated issues: the tightening of "insanity defense" standards in criminal law, the expansion of legal protections for victims of domestic violence, and the restructuring of US immigration law. While I address the latter two issues further on, this section addresses the first, which occurred following the passage of the 1984 Insanity Defense Reform Act (IDRA), and provides important context for understanding how and why Lorena was able to successfully deploy a version of the temporary insanity defense known as "irresistible impulse." Authorized as part of the Reagan administration's larger Comprehensive Crime Control Act, the IDRA followed and responded to the attempted assassination on the president's life three years earlier, when he was shot and wounded by John Hinckley Jr. in Washington, DC. When Hinckley was tried for his crime, he was found not guilty by reason of insanity and was committed to a psychiatric institution until 2016.[120] An ABC News poll revealed that 83 percent of Americans believed that "justice was not done" in the Hinckley trial. Significant outcry from the public and from prominent political figures led to the revision of the statute regarding the insanity defense, which primarily changed the burden of proof from the prosecution to the defense, thereby making the strategy more difficult to utilize, particularly with respect to a more ambiguous usage known as the "irresistible impulse" test.[121]

While all insanity defenses rely on claiming a lack of culpability due to mental illness, two criteria for the defense exist: the M'Naghten test and the irresistible impulse test. M'Naghten focuses on the defendant's cognitive capacities, or the defendant's ability to understand the consequences of their actions. By contrast, irresistible impulse focuses on the defendant's "volitional" capacities, or the ability to harness self-control.[122] Importantly, both the M'Naghten and the irresistible impulse tests use the term "insanity" as a legal concept rather than a clinical diagnosis, and both tests elide the distinction between intellectual impairment and mental illness.[123] Yet unlike the M'Naghten test, the irresistible impulse standard is harder to definitively prove, because it relies less on established criteria of mental acuity (however problematic) and more on variable psychiatric narratives.[124] Thus, the 1984 IDRA tightened the burden of proof necessary to claim an irresistible impulse defense, by requiring the use of "clear and convincing evidence" (i.e., more extensive expert testimony provided by the defense) that "at the time of the commission of the acts constituting the offense, the defendant" had experienced a "severe mental disease or defect."[125] During the Bobbitt trial, Lorena's lawyers used the irresistible impulse standard to argue that her actions were driven by years of abuse that led to an uncontrollable response. The success of this strategy, even in the face of new restrictions surrounding the court's tolerance for insanity defenses, was bolstered by increasing public awareness of the particular perils faced by those experiencing spousal abuse.

Originating with 1960s and 1970s feminist activism, official national interest in the problem of domestic violence began to rise during the 1980s. (Table 2.1 provides a chronological overview of the relevant national policy.) During the 1980s, congressional hearings were held and national coalitions were structured to address the issues of violence against women and children from the arenas of law (e.g., the 1983 Attorney General's Task Force on the Criminalization of Violence Against Women and Children) and public health (e.g., the 1985 Surgeon General's Report on Violence Against Women and Children).[126] By 1990, "violent and abusive behavior" became ranked as the number one health priority in the nation, and in 1992, the US surgeon general proclaimed "domestic violence as the nation's single greatest cause of injury to young women." This in turn led to the American Medical Association's decision to release standardized guidelines for doctors to screen all patients for domestic abuse. Then, from 1994 to 1996, the Centers for Disease Control and the National Institute of Justice executed the first National Violence Against Women Survey, providing "the first national data on the incidence and prevalence of intimate partner violence, sexual violence, and stalking."[127]

All of these developments took shape around the rhetoric of "battered woman syndrome" (BWS), a term coined by the psychologist Lenore Walker in 1979.[128] At the time of its original publication, Walker's work was part of a movement among social scientists to probe the origins and impacts of domestic abuse, in the interest of asserting the structural rather than individual nature of the problem. As "one of the first large scale empirical studies of violence against women" funded by the National Institute of Mental Health, Walker's study comprised over four hundred participants, analyzed "more than 5,000 variables," and was organized around "three specific theories": "learned helplessness, cycle of violence, and signs and symptoms of psychological distress."[129] In this and subsequent work, Walker describes BWS as a "subcategory" of post-traumatic stress disorder (PTSD) that incorporates three models—feminist, trauma, and biopsychosocial—which she explains as follows:

> The *feminist model* emphasizes that being a girl or woman places one in the highest risk category for becoming a victim of a man's violence, [and] victimization together with inequality in society can cause mental health distress. . . . The *trauma model* emphasizes that exposure to trauma can cause psychological problems in both healthy and clinical populations. . . . The *biopsychosocial model* emphasizes the response of the autonomic nervous system in dealing with traumatic stressors. . . . Continued dysregulation of these biochemical substances can negatively impact . . . [one's] ability to function and cause the anxiety, depression, avoidance, and other symptoms that are part of mental illness diagnoses.[130]

Taken together, these models provide for the means of recognizing domestic abuse as a multifaceted problem that in turn requires a multifaceted solution, including a combination of "social validation, support," "empowerment," and "verbal psychotherapy with or without medication."[131] While Walker's primary aim in developing the study was to work toward methods of treatment and prevention, she also realized from the beginning that it

Table 2.1. Protocols and events in international and US-based domestic violence prevention, 1979–2007

Year	Governing body or author	Protocol or Event
1979	United Nations	Convention on the Elimination of All Forms of Discrimination Against Women
1979	United States	Surgeon General identifies violence as "one of 15 priority areas"
1979	Lenore E. A. Walker	Coining of the term "battered woman syndrome"
1983	United States	Attorney General's Task Force on the Criminalization of Violence Against Women
1984	United States	Family Violence Prevention and Services Act
1984	United States	Insanity Defense Reform Act
1985	United States	Surgeon General's Report on Violence Against Women and Children
1986	United States	Immigration and Marriage Fraud Amendments
1990	United States	"Violent and abusive behavior" is ranked first out of twenty-two public health priority areas
1990	United States	Immigration Act authorizes the Battered Spouse Waiver
1992	US Surgeon General	Announces domestic violence as the "nation's single greatest cause of injury to young women"
1992	American Medical Association	Releases guidelines for doctors to screen for domestic abuse, including, but not limited to, "repeated battering and injury, psychological abuse, sexual assault, progressive social isolation, deprivation and intimidation"
1994	United States	Violence Against Women Act
1994–1996	Centers for Disease Control and National Institute of Justice	First National Violence Against Women Survey, which provides "the first national data on the incidence and prevalence of intimate partner violence, sexual violence, and stalking"[a]
1996	United States	Personal Responsibility and Work Opportunity Reconciliation Act; Illegal Immigration and Immigration Responsibility Act
2000	United States	Battered Immigrant Women Protection Act establishes U visas
2007	United States	U visa regulations issued

Note: This table is not intended to be all-inclusive, but rather notes relevant protocols and events addressed in the chapter. Information provided in the chart is culled from sources provided throughout the chapter unless otherwise noted.
[a] "Timeline of Violence as a Public Health Problem," Centers for Disease Control and Prevention, January 16, 2019, https://www.cdc.gov/violenceprevention/publichealthissue/timeline.html.

would likely be useful for the juridical arena, given that "it is rare that a battered woman does not have some contact with the legal system."[132]

Considering the use of BWS defenses in the courts from the late 1980s to the early 2000s, the legal theorist Susan Dimock notes that while the acceptance of BWS as a legal strategy is often thought of as a victory for survivors of domestic abuse, it has not come without a price. Dimock points to the fact that because the defense is considered an "excuse" rather than a "justification," it continues to establish separate standards for women's behavior as "irrational." While an "excuse defense" deems an action "wrongful" but excusable by way of the "individual characteristics of the defendant (such as mental disorder) or her circumstances (being faced with dire peril)," a "justification defense" deems an action "warranted and not wrongful" and rests "on the assumption that all persons should be subject to the same laws and held to the same standards of conduct."[133] The former is considered to be "individual or subjective," and the latter is understood to be "general or objective."[134] Dimock therefore argues that in being categorized as an excuse defense, the battered woman defense establishes a separate and unequal standard for legal reasonableness that foregrounds gender identity. As a result, "self-defensive actions of women" are considered to be "wrongful, but not blameworthy because we cannot hold battered women to the normal standards of reasonableness. Their actions must be seen as unreasonable, though excusable."[135]

Confronting domestic violence through the lens of BWS thus provided (and continues to provide) a critical paradox for (white, mainstream) feminist intervention. On the one hand, BWS offered the means to articulate the experience of gender- and family-based violence that had for so long been kept behind closed doors, and that had disproportionately impacted (and continues to impact) female persons. On the other hand, however, BWS constructs "women" as inherently different subjects whose cognitive capacities require alternative standards of reasonableness, which in effect means that they can never be understood as normatively reasonable subjects under the law.[136] The implications of BWS therefore extend beyond the parameters of its immediate usage and can even be understood as antifeminist, insofar as normative feminism stakes a claim for women's equality under the law. For this reason, the appearance of BWS as a clinical, legal, and cultural concept in the years following 1960s and 1970s feminist activism was jarring, because it recalled many of the issues that the movement sought to address surrounding sex bias, bodily autonomy, and women's equality under the law.

As the legal scholars Carole Pateman, Catharine MacKinnon, and Martha Nussbaum have made clear, women have long been understood as antithetical to conceptualizations of the "rational individual" that the law requires.[137] Much like the previous section's discussion of the white male body as a category that is constructed as universal and unmarked, US law is predicated on the construction of a universal, unmarked "rational subject." As a point of legal fact, this ideal subject is not gendered, raced, classed, or otherwise marked as differentially embodied. Yet as a matter of practice, this subject functions as male, white, upper middle class, straight, gender-normative, able-bodied, and in possession of a normative claim to citizenship. These particularities bias the law in favor of those who most closely adhere to these categories, and stem from earlier versions of US jurisprudence that were openly dependent upon one's identity.[138]

In cases dealing with criminal culpability, US courts have often treated women differently from men. As the criminologist Deborah Denno wrote in 1994, "Historically, commentators have explained women's lesser involvement in crime as an 'underachievement' attributable to their biology or sexuality. Moreover, they have often confused sex with gender, characterizing crime among females as masculine or malelike, a perspective that remains in current research on female crime."[139] Denno further explains that women typically have been associated with a "lower level of criminality because . . . they lacked the 'combination of intellectual functions' required of more demanding (i.e., masculine) crimes."[140] Researchers therefore sought out aberrational circumstances, including nonnormative sexual behaviors, drug use, mental illness, cognitive impairment, brain injury, and severe abuse, as an impetus for women to engage in criminal behavior.[141] (It should be noted, of course, that these attitudes are heavily raced and classed as well, a point to which this chapter will later return.) These attitudes have also led to greater leniency in verdicts and sentencing. For example, the use of BWS as a legal defense strategy uses pathology as an explanation for criminal activity but also provides the means to find a defendant not guilty or to apply different sentencing standards.

All of these issues were brought to the fore during the Bobbitt case. Many prominent feminists critiqued Lorena's actions. Naomi Wolf stated that the case only proved that "women are just as capable of mayhem and sadism and cruelty as men" and that "it's just not acceptable to support violence" under any circumstance.[142] Susan Estrich, a University of Southern California law professor and Democratic Party campaign manager, lamented that although Lorena was being treated as a "feminist heroine," she should be recognized as "a criminal" who did "a disservice not only to the cause of feminism, but . . . to the real victims of battered wives' syndrome—the millions of women who are beaten by their husbands and do not respond by assaults on their organs."[143] Rita J. Simon and Cathy Young, president and vice president of the Women's Freedom Network in Washington, DC, wrote similarly that "if feminism means equal rights and equal responsibilities, Mrs. Bobbitt's acquittal is not a victory for feminism. The decision trivializes female violence, infantilizes women and fuels hostility between the sexes."[144] These responses were representative of prevailing discourse that both recognized the problem of domestic abuse and eschewed it as a justification for retaliatory violence. Generally, these types of debates pivoted on questioning the broader consequences of BWS, both for victims of domestic violence and for the fundamental problem of women's inequality under the law.

Section V. "I will take you to my house": White Feminism and Lorena's Rescue

During the Bobbitt trial, Lorena's lawyers argued that she suffered from BWS and therefore could not be held responsible for her actions. The defense called Susan J. Fiester, a psychiatrist and medical director at the Psychiatric Institute of Washington, as a key witness to argue that Lorena was "a classic example of a battered wife, weakened by years of beatings, rapes, and threat." Dr. Fiester explained that Lorena "suffer[ed] from three major mental illnesses last June [at the time of the crime]: depression, post-traumatic stress disorder, and a panic disorder," and although she "may appear well put-together, she's a very fragile individual."[145] On the night of the event in question, Dr. Fiester asserted, John's rape of Lorena "unleashed a brief psychotic episode over which Lorena . . . had no control."[146]

In order to refute the prosecution's claims, the state called two forensic psychologists, Henry Gwaltney and Evan Nelson, and one forensic psychiatrist, Miller M. Ryans. At the beginning of the trial, all three of the state's experts disagreed with Dr. Fiester's testimony.[147] By contrast, they concurred with each other that Lorena could not be considered legally insane at the time of her actions. Dr. Gwaltney explained that although Lorena was "clinically depressed, frightened and emotionally overwrought when she maimed her husband . . . [her] act was a goal-directed, angry attempt at retaliation."[148] Similarly, Dr. Ryans testified that Lorena did not suffer from an "irresistible impulse, but an impulse that she did not resist":

When she stood at the foot of the bed, thinking about all these bad things her husband had done to her, at that moment she had a choice to make. . . .

She could either complete the act, or back off and leave. She chose to ampu-
tate the penis. . . . [T]here was no evidence she was out of touch with reality
or experiencing any delusions.[149]

Dr. Ryans and his colleagues arrived at this conclusion following extensive interviews with Lorena and consideration of the facts of the case. For
the prosecution's expert witnesses, the fact that Lorena had the presence of
mind to steal from John's sleeping friend before leaving the apartment, as
well as the fact that she had recalled the exact location in which she had left
John's penis, suggested that she was cognizant of her actions. Other details
of the night the crime took place further troubled them. For example, in
her immediate interactions with the police following the event, Lorena was
quoted as stating, "He always have orgasm and he doesn't wait for me to have
orgasm. . . . He's selfish. I don't think it's fair, so I pulled back the sheets then
and I did it."[150] Later testimony from an employee at the nail salon where
Lorena worked also revealed that in casual conversation, Lorena had threatened to cut off her husband's penis if she found him cheating on her.[151]

Surprisingly, however, by the end of the court proceedings, doubts about
Lorena's diagnosis were largely assuaged, and all of the experts agreed on
the diagnosis of BWS. This was made clear when midway through the trial,
Dr. Ryans requested to retake the stand to change his testimony, stating that
his opinion on the matter had been altered by evidence presented, particularly information provided by the defense witness Nancy Keegan, a customer
at the salon who had seen Lorena just days before the event took place.[152]
Keegan described Lorena as a victim of abuse, recounting that she had seen
"black and blue" marks covering her entire forearms:

I said, "How did you get those bruises on your arms?" And she looked at
me and said, "My husband hurt me." That's how he liked to grab her by her
wrists, and she said, "In our apartment he was going to drop me over the
railing and he said to me if I drop you I'm just going to tell everybody that
you jumped." I told her she needed to leave the situation that she was in. I
told her about places she could go, people that could help her. And as I said
that she became more and more frightened in appearance. She was trembling and shaking, um, to me she appeared terrified. And I said to her,
"You can't go home to this guy, I will take you to my house," and she said,
"No, my husband says if I leave him he will kill me, and he'll kill you. He'll
come after you." And I gave her a hug and it was like hugging my daughter, I mean, that's how small she was and I didn't want to leave her because
I was really afraid for her.[153]

When Keegan spoke further with Dr. Ryans in a separate interview, he became convinced that the symptoms Keegan described, including mood fluctuations—"shaking, crying, [and] trembling"—"were compatible with the diagnosis of post-traumatic stress disorder."[154] One of the jurors on the case explained that Dr. Ryans's second testimony became a turning point for deliberations, inspiring sympathy for Lorena and belief in her story.[155]

It is therefore important to ask how such a seemingly random witness—Nancy Keegan, a customer whom Lorena had only met once and who did not even notice the case proceedings until five months into the trial, when she happened to turn on the news that she had previously been "too busy" to follow—could have had such a strong impact on the state's attorney, the testimony of medical experts, and the jury's disposition toward the case. Certainly, even though there were some peculiarities in Lorena's accounting of the night of the crime, plenty of relevant evidence and testimony on the veracity of her claims had already been entered into the record. Photographs were shown of her bruised and beaten body. Several of John's acquaintances were called to the stand by the defense and explained how John "said he liked to make girls squirm and yell, and make 'em bleed and yell for help. . . . [H]e got excited by 'hitting [women] in the behind, making them scream, making them bleed and making them crawl.'"[156] The assistant manager at Bobbitt's apartment complex testified that Lorena "confided in her at least three times a week . . . [and] the tears would just run down her face."[157] All told, the defense called forty witnesses to support the severity of the abuse, and yet it was Keegan's testimony that was cited as making the strongest impression.

Looking at Keegan, who was everything that Lorena was not—a white, upper-class housewife, well spoken in English, a US citizen—it becomes clearer how and why her testimony was so effective. Indeed, Keegan's presence and tearful testimony fulfilled common narratives of white feminism as the proper savior of brown women.[158] As Sara Ahmed has observed, feminism continues to be used as an "imperial project," providing agency for white women through the marked "passivity and helplessness of women of color."[159] In keeping with this paradigm, Keegan offered Lorena "official" information regarding protection for abuse victims and clear instructions that she should "leave the situation she was in." Keegan also offered to take Lorena to her own home, suggesting that unlike Lorena's home, Keegan's residence was a site of safety and protection. Thus, Lorena—"as small as a child" in Keegan's sympathetic embrace—became a sign of the profoundly insufficient protections for certain women in certain situations. Keegan's testimony at once validated the appropriate course of action for domestic abuse victims *and* demonstrated how certain individuals could fall through the cracks. These cracks were important because they did not necessarily cast aspersions on the greater feminist project by infantilizing or pathologizing all women through the language of necessary assistance. They were instead directed toward a very particular type of woman, constructed through very specific intersections of race, class, and nationality.

Ultimately, sympathy for Lorena could and did exist precisely because of her positionality. She was normative enough to inspire concern (feminine in appearance, soft-spoken, light skinned) but also different enough to be separable from the average proponent of mainstream white feminist doctrine. As one reporter described her, she was a "small woman: five feet two inches tall, 95 pounds. In person she is far prettier than the tremulous girl with circles under her downcast eyes who appeared in court. . . . She never looked up . . . except for a few furtive glances. . . . She was too scared and nervous. It was obvious to those who fought for a look at her that *this was no trailer-park queen or hard-edged biker moll*."[160] She was at once a figure that was worthy of saving *and* a woman who had resorted to such a desperate act that she proved the necessity of alternative protocols surrounding domestic violence. In other words, she provided the means for justifying the BWS "excuse" (potentially for every victim of domestic abuse) in a way that avoided implicating all women's susceptibility to "irrational," "insane" behavior. Rather, Lorena's positionality as a noncitizen, non-American, nonwhite subject allowed for the co-optation of her story as one that could be equally influenced by the courts and by feminist activists who saw themselves on the side of the law, rather than on the side of victims and the disempowering circumstances that had created their violent predicaments in the first place. Lorena's case therefore allowed for a simultaneous disavowal of BWS and an instantiation of it in its proper time and place.

In order to better understand how this seeming contradiction took place, it is first necessary to understand how Lorena's position as a noncitizen and a Latina enabled her to function as the perfect center of a debate that seemingly did not incorporate issues of citizenship or race. The following section addresses how BWS became inflected with a discourse of "cultural difference" that provided the means to support the problem of domestic violence without conscripting white American women to a subservient position. In doing so, section VI considers the legal strategy known as the "culture defense" that was used disproportionately in spousal abuse and gender-based violence cases. By placing BWS (and the related battered woman defense) in conversation with the culture defense, I demonstrate how the particularities of Latina victimhood worked to permeate seemingly race-neutral discourses surrounding women's protection under the law.

Section VI. "A collision course": The "Culture Defense" and the Criminalization of Immigrant Men

Concurrent with debates over the use of BWS in the courtroom, another legal theory was also quietly gaining popularity: the "culture defense," sometimes also referred to as the "cultural defense." While Lorena's lawyers did not assert the culture defense on her behalf, it exists in close relation to the use of BWS in the case of immigrant women. Emerging as a phenomenon during the mid-1980s and becoming an object of debate among legal scholars by the mid-1990s, the culture defense relies on the notion of a "cultural compulsion, alternatively called cultural dictation," in order to identify "a state in which a person is fully under the irresistible sway of a cultural dictate."[161] In what follows, I explore the logic behind the culture defense, as well as debates that emerged in relation to it, from the perspective of prominent legal scholars writing in the 1990s, including Placido Gomez, Leti Volpp, William I. Torry, Holly Maguigan, Alice J. Gallin, and Kristen L. Holmquist.[162]

Writing in favor of the culture defense, Gomez explained that the courts were obligated to consider cultural difference when addressing legal culpability, as "punishment is only justified when (1) the action is morally condemnable, and (2) the actor is culpable."[163] For Gomez, culpability is necessarily mitigated by cultural "pressures that make it difficult . . . to comply with . . . societal norm[s]."[164] For Gomez and others, the culture defense could just as easily be applied for non-Anglo US citizens as it could for more recent immigrants. At the same time, many legal scholars pointed out that the culture defense was dangerously imprecise and often relied upon unquantifiable characteristics of degrees of assimilation to mainstream US culture.[165] As Volpp cautioned, "The concept of a 'culture defense' rests on the idea of a community not fully 'integrated' into the United States."[166] Torry further explained that the success of a culture defense relies upon understandings of "individuals' assimilative capabilities," thereby "entwin[ing] cultural identities with *individuals' responsibilities* rather than groups' rights."[167] Revealing the contradiction at the heart of the culture defense—in which "group" cultural standards are used to measure "individual" behaviors—Torry asserted that the culture defense cannot exist without a belief in "cultural determinism," which in turn must be understood as producing certain identifiable "compulsions."[168]

The strength of these imagined compulsions created further difficulties in the context of debates about domestic violence. Writing about the ethical challenges posed by attempting to attend simultaneously to issues of cultural difference and domestic violence, Maguigan observed that "feminist and multiculturalist reformers [were] on a collision course" in the arenas of legal and social policy. That is, by being willing to give victims of domestic abuse "cultural latitude" in order to legally consider acts of retaliatory violence as forms of self-defense under the battered woman syndrome theory, the courts also opened the door to leniency for the batterer as well. As Maguigan asked, "Can the courts permit defendants to introduce evidence of cultural background without condoning violence by men against women? In those trials in which cultural evidence is received, is the information entitled to such unquestioning deference that its receipt signals the recognition of a 'cultural defense' to male violence?"[169]

Similarly, Gallin argued that the culture defense worked to undermine "much of the policy lying behind the battered women's defense" and was "used primarily in cases of domestic violence against women and children" in order to justify a perpetrator's actions.[170] She warned that "successful use of the cultural defense often condones family violence that is generally condemned by American society," including actions such as marital rape and spousal murder as "retribution" for infidelity.[171] Gallin asserted that promoting the culture defense would only increase incidents of domestic violence in the United States, to rates comparable with other, presumably less evolved, nations.[172] This in turn would produce an understanding among "foreign" men that they need not "curtail their behavior" toward women and that US law would excuse forms of domestic violence within immigrant communities that it may not elsewhere. Gallin then juxtaposed the culture defense with the battered woman defense, arguing that while comparisons have been made between the two strategies, the former actually makes the latter necessary, as "the violence that the battered woman's defense recognizes is actually condoned and perpetuated by the cultural defense. . . . Thus promoting cultural diversity by using a cultural defense also promotes domestic violence."[173]

All of these conversations surrounding the culture defense speak to several assumptions implicit in claims that position cultural difference as inherently oppositional to the "progress" achieved by domestic violence advocates and policy changes. First, it suggests that conditions in the United States with respect to domestic violence are invariably better than those in other nations. Second, it suggests that many immigrants bring with them retrograde ideas of gender, kinship, and women's rights and, further, that "brown women" from these "foreign" countries and cultures require rescue from "brown men." Third, it represents culture as a concrete and quantifiable entity that is both measurable and usable by the courts, a context that relies on the law as a site of "perceived culturelessness."[174] As Holmquist explained, because the cultural defense requires a definition of the "defendant's 'culture,'" a "mini-trial . . . will take place (either actually at trial or within the decision-maker's mental processes) . . . regarding how well the actual defendant embodies this cultural dictate."[175] While on the surface this determination might have alleviated harsher sentencing in certain cases, it ultimately relied on oversimplified cultural stereotypes, establishing legal precedents that served to "bolster gender, race, and culture biases in public."[176]

Interestingly, much of the literature on the culture defense from this period points to its disproportionate usage in cases involving gender- or family-based violence. Yet what remained unspoken is the fact that this disproportionality must be understood as central to the defense's evolution in the first place. In other words, it was not an unfortunate "collision" that occurred between feminism and multiculturalism when it came to conversations about domestic violence and cultural diversity. Rather, debates about cultural difference had become critical forums for figuring out the problem of domestic violence—even when they only seemed to reference "American" women—and vice versa.

Here again, the Bobbitt case can be imagined as a litmus test for theorizations about gender, violence, and cultural difference. Firstly, Lorena's relationship to BWS cannot be understood outside of paradigms of cultural difference. Her identity and heritage were points of articulation during the trial and were also frequently portrayed by the media. As demonstrated in section I, stereotypes of the "hot-blooded" or "fiery" Latina—which included notions of uncontrollability, hypersexuality, and impulsivity—often accompanied popular press and comedic representations of the case. At the same time, however, mainstream sources also depicted Lorena on the other side of the virgin/whore dichotomy, remarking on her "white silk blouses" and "crucifix necklace." While some of the language used to describe her appearance read it as an affectation, it was more commonly referenced as central to her character as a "timid," "devout, unworldly, and deeply religious Roman Catholic woman," for whom divorce was an impossibility, "akin to 'humiliation' in her family, ruling out remarriage and children."[177]

In the only article featuring an interview with Lorena that appeared in the press prior to the end of the trial, she is portrayed as a tragic victim whose "American dream" brought her to the United States. She is quoted as comparing her immigration process to traveling to "another planet," where "everything is just pink and beautiful." The article also noted that Lorena accepted John's surprise marriage proposal early in their relationship because "her mother, who doesn't speak English, had no objections." Lorena then explains how at first she did not understand that anything was wrong with her "sex life": "I said, 'Well, maybe this is it. Maybe this is it when you're married.' I accepted that."[178] (Years later, she further stated that "I thought I was the only one suffering from domestic violence because I was younger and an immigrant from Venezuela.")[179]

Understandings of Lorena's vulnerability to spousal abuse were continually framed as a matter of cultural difference. Indeed, it is impossible to consider the outcome of the trial without thinking of the likely intersection between BWS and the available conceptual framework of the culture defense. Lorena's actions were seen as heated, strange, unfamiliar—the sign of mental instability and confusion. Importantly, because John was a white American, no similar concession could be made to justify his treatment of Lorena. Thus, the Bobbitt trial showcased the logic of BWS and the culture defense, without having to attend to a potential "collision" between the aims of feminism and multiculturalism that would have been raised by the specter of a "foreign," immigrant husband. Instead, Lorena's claim to BWS was only further enhanced by John's status as an American citizen who presumably "should" already adhere to progressive US standards. John's position as an uneducated, lower-class "brute" with a troubled past further enabled a critique of his abuse as a potential justification of Lorena's actions. At the same time, because John did not fully meet normative standards of white American masculinity, the public airing and condemnation of his abusive behavior could be separated from broader structural issues of sexism and gender hierarchy rooted in white mainstream culture.

Section VII. "The new Lorena Bobbitt": Uncertain Legacies

Returning to the case of Catherine Kieu Becker raised in the chapter's introduction, two questions remain after reviewing the Bobbitt case at length: (1) Why has there been so little coverage of the Kieu Becker case (even though it is only the second reported case of such a crime occurring in the United States)? And (2) why did Catherine Kieu Becker receive such a different sentence (incarceration for seventeen years) from Lorena Bobbitt (commitment to a psychiatric institution for forty-five days)? Ultimately, these questions and their potential answers are interrelated. First, it is important to understand the role of the internet and social media, which have exploded in the years since the Bobbitt trial. The sheer amount of information, "news" and otherwise, that is available to the average person has increased exponentially over the past three decades. Yet this increase in volume should not be mistaken for an increase in scope or actual content. Instead, it often makes it harder to decipher which stories are being silenced, giving the illusion that if something "important" is occurring, it will necessarily materialize in a popularly circulated and reproducible form.

A comparison of the coverage of the two cases reveals a striking disparity. A Google search of "Catherine Kieu Becker" reveals 5,950 hits, many of which are simply reposts of the same articles published by the Associated Press. Among these sources, very little information can be found about Catherine Kieu Becker, her life, her husband, her crime, or her trial. Only a few images of her exist online: a mug shot, an ID photograph, two images of her in court (one in prison blues, the other in a suit), and one from behind bars. By contrast, "Lorena Bobbitt" reveals 383,000 hits, populated by content that is widely varied and more deeply informative. Hundreds of images of Lorena circulate, many from the 1990s but others from the current moment as well as intervening years. In fact, the first image that appears when searching for Kieu Becker is a split screen that presents Lorena on the left, smiling in front of press microphones in 1993, and Catherine on the right, in a mug shot from 2012. The accompanying *LA Weekly* article states that Kieu Becker is "now unofficially known as the new Lorena Bobbitt." Though the author does not comment on the verdict in the Bobbitt trial, he does explain that the severity of Kieu Becker's sentencing comes as welcome relief: "While we sometimes wonder if the justice system treats the ladies with kid gloves (especially when it comes to their own domestic violence and claims for alimony), this here case of a pared-down pecker is being messaged with the utmost of due diligence. Men everywhere can exhale."[180]

To understand the relative absence of interest that surrounds the Kieu Becker case and the intense interest that followed and continues to follow the Bobbitt case, as well as their divergent verdicts, requires attending to the particular significance of each trial in its time and place. In a 2018 *Rolling Stone* article marking the twenty-fifth anniversary of the Bobbitt trial, the author asks what would happen to Lorena had the case occurred "now":

> Given the current anti-immigrant sentiment, particularly towards people who hail from countries south of the border, it's noteworthy that, back in the early 1990s, Gallo's story of coming to the U.S. in pursuit of the Amer-

ican Dream made her a more sympathetic victim. It's hard not to wonder if, in 2018, Bobbitt—an All-American, Trump-supporting ex-Marine with a fake Bob Ross painting hanging above his mantel—might have had the upper hand. Would Trump's America be more likely to rally behind Bobbitt's claim that Gallo was a liar and a gold-digger who maimed him because he was leaving her a year before she was eligible for a green card and . . . "If she couldn't have me, no one could"? Maybe.[181]

While it is of course impossible to know how Lorena would have fared today, the Kieu Becker case sheds some insight: no national debate and a harsher punishment.

That being said, it is also true that the 1990s are characterizable by their own anti-immigrant sentiments. The specific paranoia surrounding spousal (typically female) immigration led to legislative reforms throughout the prior decade, while domestic violence protocols for immigrant women were sold as part of a broader package of anticrime legislation that provided state protection according to very specific guidelines of merit, and necessarily at the cost of increased surveillance. The burst of popularity surrounding the Bobbitt trial and the relative silence surrounding the Kieu Becker trial also suggest that while the former was culturally meaningful, the latter was not. Ultimately, the idea that the Bobbitt trial set a precedent for domestic violence sufferers—for better or for worse—is belied by the Kieu Becker verdict. Instead, it suggests that the Bobbitt trial served its purpose, and that this purpose was not the protection of women from spousal abuse nor the exoneration of such women for acts of retaliatory violence. As the Bobbitt trial has become reappropriated for the late 2010s #MeToo media cycle, Lorena has once again become a figurehead for a movement she never claimed. Her story is repeated as one of triumph, featuring her exaltation (she is now a domestic abuse advocate, with a long-term partner and child) alongside John's deprecation (he remains a former porn star, who, since the trial, has racked up decades of domestic abuse allegations from other women and has served several prison stints). From the outcome of the Kieu Becker trial, however, it is unclear what the legacy of this triumphant narrative will hold for women who find themselves in similar situations, particularly for immigrant women whose ethnic, national, and racial differences place them at distinct structural disadvantages.

CHAPTER 3

"A troubled, battered mind": The Queer Lives and Deaths of Aaron Hernandez, 1989–2017

Football might be the most suitable metaphor to understand the role of Latinos in the United States today.

ILAN STAVANS, IN ALDAMA AND GONZÁLEZ, *LATINOS IN THE END ZONE*

You're never going to be totally safe from concussions in this game. . . . This is the only place where you can actually legally assault people.

STANFORD ROUTT, FORMER NFL PLAYER, QUOTED IN ASSOCIATED PRESS, "PLAYERS STILL WILLING TO HIDE HEAD INJURIES"

In April 2011, the New England Patriots' tight end Aaron Hernandez visited the Gardner Pilot Academy in Allston, Massachusetts, where he met with 120 third, fourth, and fifth graders to promote national Mental Health Awareness Month. Invited as a speaker for events focusing on "Latino mental health," Hernandez "interacted playfully" with the children and "stressed the importance of taking care of both mind and emotions because they are, in his words, as important as taking care of their bodies."[1] A "community hub school" that includes an "integrated focus on academics, youth development, family support, health and social services, and community development," Gardner Pilot is composed of 70 percent Latinx students, many of whom are first-generation or recent immigrants.[2] The academy also hosts a satellite clinic of the Lucero Latino Mental Health Program at William James College (formerly the Massachusetts School of Professional Psychology), one of the first graduate programs in psychology that expressly trains students in "Latino culture and language."[3]

Hernandez arrived at Gardner Pilot through his support for the Lucero Program, explaining, "I thought it was a perfect charity for me to get involved with. . . . It's geared toward training with mental health specialists with the Hispanic population." Media coverage of the event emphasized

Hernandez's "Puerto Rican roots," his desire to "give back to the community," and the importance of his "lending his name . . . to raise awareness about the need for culturally and linguistically appropriate mental health services to meet the unique needs of the growing Latino community."[4] After speaking with the students about football, Hernandez shared some of the struggles he faced growing up, which he described as a process of "making poor choices in trying to cope" with difficult circumstances, and continuing to "fight through those hard times."[5] But Hernandez's struggle was far from over. Only six years later, he was found dead by his own hand in a prison cell at the Souza-Baranowski Correctional Center in Lancaster, Massachusetts, where he had languished for two years after being found guilty of murder.

This chapter traces Hernandez's controversial short life and untimely passing at the age of twenty-seven (1989–2017). Born and raised in Bristol, Connecticut, Hernandez was a successful athlete from a young age and set several national records while in high school. He left home only a month after his seventeenth birthday, after graduating a semester early in order to join the University of Florida's football team in 2007. In 2010, he entered the National Football League (NFL) draft and joined the New England Patriots. By 2013, at the age of twenty-three, he was removed from the team because of multiple allegations of murder, culminating in his arrest for the shooting of a friend, Odin Lloyd. At the time of Hernandez's suicide, he was serving a life sentence for Lloyd's murder and was also a subject of interest in other ongoing homicide cases.

Following his death, public discourse swirled around the question of his mental health and the violent acts he had allegedly committed. Not only was it discovered that he suffered from an extremely advanced form of chronic traumatic encephalopathy (CTE), owing to a lifetime of repetitive head injuries both on and off the field, but information about his sexuality came to light as well in the days immediately preceding and following his suicide. Though Hernandez had lived publicly as a straight man with his girlfriend, Shayanna Jenkins, and their biological child, Aviel, rumors about his sexual relationships with other men surfaced in the wake of his incarceration. Two days before he died, he was outed by a radio-show host who made a joke about his queer sexuality.

This chapter considers the narratives that surrounded Hernandez's rise to fame in life and in death. It addresses how his racial, gender, and sexual identities operated intersectionally to shape the public's perception of his achievements, creating a path toward athletic and financial success that became coterminous with a descent into criminalization, debility, and, ultimately, death. In order to do so, the chapter draws upon the concept of "necropolitics," first articulated by Achille Mbembe and since deployed by critical race studies scholars as a marker of nonwhite subjects' paradoxical existence within symbolic and literal "death worlds."[6] This chapter considers how the exploitation of Black and Latinx men within the institution of professional football has served to reduce them to disposable bodies made to sustain and absorb endless corporeal damage. By thinking through how race has been used to mitigate definitions of "risk" surrounding CTE for football players alongside concurrent discourses that understand sexual identity as a corporeal "truth," this chapter locates Hernandez as a powerful figure through which to unpack the strictures of Latinx embodiment. Following Adrián Pérez-Melgosa's understanding of "low-intensity necropolitics," Lauren Berlant's concept of "slow death," and Jasbir Puar's theorization of debility, this chapter seeks to unpack the intersectional forms of oppression that constructed Hernandez as a disposable subject.[7]

But before going further, two caveats are necessary. First, like so many of the case studies in this book that revolve around phantasmic representations, while this chapter is interested in the narratives and forms of "evidence" marshaled in Hernandez's trials and in the related media coverage, it is not engaged in an empirical "fact-seeking" mission. That is to say, while there is a tremendous amount of contradictory information regarding Hernandez's own understanding of his sexuality, as well as the crimes he was arrested for, this chapter is not concerned with adjudicating the "truth" of his existence; these are only questions that Hernandez himself could answer. Here, I follow Lisa Marie Cacho's lead in questioning the role of "facts" in understanding "whose deaths are [understood to be] tragic and whose deaths are [understood to be] deserved."[8] Instead, she cautions, we must examine "how 'value' and its normative criteria are naturalized and universalized" in order to comprehend how nonnormative subjects are produced as "illegible."[9]

Although debates surrounding Hernandez's actions and identity continue to unfold, there is very little documentation of Hernandez's own perspective, and what does exist is filtered through media representations. For example, in an effort to gain insight into his psyche, a 2018 six-part series produced by the *Boston Globe* uses recordings of phone calls he made while incarcerated. The author quotes a conversation with Hernandez's cousin Tanya Cummings, in which he stated, "I'm just one empty person . . . it's been like that for so long."[10] While the media highlighted, decontextualized, and interpreted this statement and others like it as explanatory evidence of Hernandez's trajectory toward death, this chapter never loses sight of the context in which these types of comments were produced (e.g., within an involuntary setting, recorded without permission, and so on). Thus, I do not assume that any narratives that exist about Hernandez are empirically "true." Instead, I consider what these narratives suggest about the ways that race, sexuality, and nonwhite embodiment are representationally produced in the current moment.

The second caveat necessary to bear in mind at the outset of the chapter is that the arguments provided regarding race and sports often rely upon scholarship that directly pertains to African American, rather than Latinx, persons. Relatedly, it is also the case that the NFL is predominantly populated by Black athletes; as of 2018, the Institute for Diversity and Ethics in Sport reported that 70 percent of all NFL players are Black, 27 percent are white, 2 percent are Asian/Pacific Islander, and less than 1 percent are Latino.[11] Perhaps because of these disparities, existing scholarship on race and football in the United States focuses primarily on the experience of Black players. In highlighting Hernandez's case, this chapter does not seek to draw attention away from the disproportionate impact of the NFL on the lives of African American men, particularly with regard to emerging knowledge about the prevalence of CTE among professional football players. This chapter also does not seek to collapse Hernandez into the broader category of "men of color," which can sometimes serve to mystify important distinctions and inequalities. Rather, I argue that by considering Hernandez's "lives" and "deaths"—which I pluralize here to acknowledge the infinite number of rumors, stories, and reports that have come to circulate around him—we can better understand how rhetorics of anti-Blackness *need not always be attached to a Black body*. By understanding this distinction, we can better address how other nonwhite persons are marshaled in the service of racialized hierarchies that continue to value certain lives over others. Thus, this chapter pays attention to the mobilization of racial codes both in relation to Hernandez's Latinx identity *and* in relation to media representations that perpetually associated him with Blackness. These associations included pejorative stereotypes (e.g., the speculation surrounding his involvement with gangs and his alleged predisposition toward violence), his presence in a predominantly Black sport, and the fact that many of his highly publicized close personal relationships were with Black people. In doing so, I illustrate how Hernandez became conscripted within a process of queer racialization that enables the normalization and financial incentivization of corporeal trauma.

Section I. "A ticking time bomb": Acquired Trauma and Essentialized Violence

From the beginning of his football career, Aaron Hernandez was the subject of intense media attention. Initially, such scrutiny focused on his unusual talent, which put him on the fast track to college a year early and landed him a place on the New England Patriots' roster by the age of twenty. During his college career, his recruitment into the NFL, and his early years playing for the Patriots, Hernandez was lauded as a top-ranking tight end. At the same time, he was also heavily criticized for his off-field behavior, including his use of marijuana, his engagement in bar fights, and his association with purported criminal "gang" members. In spite of these concerns—or, one might argue, perhaps because of them, as I will address later—Hernandez remained professionally successful until his third year in the league, when he became associated with multiple shooting incidents that caused three deaths and one injury. Three of the cases made it to trial and resulted in indictments. The first case involved a shooting in 2007, when Hernandez was a freshman at the University of Florida, that resulted in the murder of Corey Smith, age twenty-eight, and the injury of Justin Glass, age nineteen; both Smith and Glass had reportedly been in an altercation with Hernandez and his friends at a bar during a previous night.[12] The second case involved a drive-by shooting in 2012, during Hernandez's second season in the NFL, that resulted in the death of Daniel Jorge Correia de Abreau, twenty-nine, and Safiro Teixeira Furtado, twenty-eight, an event that was linked to alleged gang activity. Finally, the third case involved the murder of Odin Lloyd, twenty-seven, the boyfriend of Hernandez's fiancée's sister, due to uncertain motives (a point I will return to shortly). While Hernandez was convicted only in the Lloyd case, the media was quick to portray this crime as linked to a broader history of violence and illegal activity. The discourse surrounding his trials and conviction was thus highly sensationalized but also worked to naturalize his path toward incarceration.

Following his passing by suicide, media attention turned toward another aspect of Hernandez's personal life: his potential sexual involvement with other men. Text messages and written correspondence between Hernandez and other men, coupled with the testimony of his former attorney, make clear that if he was not "gay," as the media framed it, he was, at the very least, not straight in the conventional sense.[13] Nonetheless, Shayanna Jenkins, Hernandez's longtime girlfriend and mother to his only child, has disputed any such desires or behavior on Hernandez's part, stating publicly that "there has been much speculation about Aaron's sexuality since his death. I can say this: he was very much a man to me. I saw no indication that he was gay or homosexual."[14]

While a few rumors had circulated earlier, widespread coverage of Hernandez's alleged sexual liaisons with other men began on April 17, 2017, just two days prior to his death, when Michele McPhee, an ABC News producer, made a series of crude comments about his sexual proclivities on a

Boston sports radio program, *Kirk and Callahan*, with hosts Kirk Minihane and Gerry Callahan.[15] McPhee had begun to investigate Hernandez's sexual past as a potential motive in the Odin Lloyd murder, speculating that Lloyd had threatened to out him. During the radio program, Minihane, Callahan, and McPhee mocked Hernandez's sexuality, joking that he was a "tight end on and off the field," "then he became a wide receiver," and he was "known to kick with both feet."[16] Other journalists have since criticized McPhee for her unethical public outing of Hernandez's sexuality based on unsubstantiated rumors. After Hernandez's suicide, McPhee attempted to rationalize these remarks as being "inelegant," and "not something [she] would have done if [she] wasn't on a sports-radio show," though she never admitted her potential role in his death, given its proximity to her comments.[17] She also subsequently published two articles in *Newsweek* that sensationalized his sexuality in relation to his suicide: "Aaron Hernandez's Sex Life Probed as Murder Motive, Police Source Says" and "'I Think I'm Going to Hang It Up, LOL': Aaron Hernandez Note to Prison Boyfriend."[18] Once Hernandez passed away, media interest only intensified on the subject of his sexuality, and three separate documentaries were produced by PBS, Lifetime, and Netflix, each of which examined the intricacies of his sexual history. Each tied his closeted sexuality to his untimely death.

Trailing behind coverage of Hernandez's sexuality as "the" cause of his death was strikingly sparse interest in the results of his postmortem brain scans, which revealed a severely advanced case of CTE previously unseen in such a young man. While CTE is diagnosable only in death, it is well known that it is a common occurrence among athletes in contact sports, especially football, and that it produces erratic and violent behavior. As Emily Harrison has pointed out, although the problem of sports-related head trauma is often thought to have been discovered in the late twentieth century through technological developments that enabled proof of brain damage, concern over the long-term effects of concussions dates to the founding years of football, during the 1880s and 1890s.[19] While CTE was not identified and named until 1949 by the British neurologist Macdonald Critchley, a similar syndrome was described in professional boxers in the 1920s. Labeled "punch-drunk syndrome" and "dementia pugilistica," this condition was thought to be caused by repeated blows to the head that produced ongoing "mental confusion." From the 1940s onward, researchers have also known that brain injury can occur even in cases where a concussion is not noticeable or diagnosed.[20]

Nonetheless, the issue received little attention until the early 2000s, when the US-based forensic neuropathologist Bennet Omalu "found changes consistent with CTE in the brain of ex–professional football player Mike Webster."[21] Following this finding in 2005, mainstream news outlets have increasingly reported on the ubiquity of postmortem CTE diagnoses in ex–football players.[22] In particular, the high-profile suicides of the former NFL players Junior Seau (1969–2012), Andre Waters (1962–2006), and Terry Long (1959–2005) have inspired significant public debate about the safety of a sport perceived to be "fundamentally dangerous."[23] Less often discussed is the fact that from 2005 to 2018, twenty former NFL players ranging in age from twenty-three to sixty-six took their own lives, sixteen of whom were since diagnosed with CTE.[24] As several critics have pointed out, these concerns have done little to reshape the game at the professional level. While the NFL has taken steps by adopting a concussion policy and settling a class action lawsuit that resulted in potential billion-dollar payouts to former athletes "who can prove they suffer from brain disorders related to their football careers," CTE remains diagnosable only in death through autopsy.[25] Moreover, as of 2018, the NFL had yet to make the appropriate payments to the families of players whose posthumous examinations revealed certain signs of the disease.[26]

In spite of these issues, preprofessional football programs continue to thrive. College-level programs have expanded in recent years to offer an even greater number of scholarships.[27] Since the 1980s, when the US Supreme Court ruled that colleges may "sell broadcast rights to the highest bidders," funding for college football has skyrocketed.[28] Long-standing racial disparities in the sport—which is 69.7 percent Black, 27.4 percent white, 1.9 percent Asian/Pacific Islander, 0.8 percent Latino, and 0.2 percent "other" at the professional level; and 54.3 percent Black, 39.8 percent white, 2.8 percent Asian/Pacific Islander, 2.3 percent Latino, and 0.9 percent "other" at the Division I college level—are further augmented by recent CTE findings, which have produced a "white flight" from football.[29] Yet for many poor young men of color, football remains one of the only ways to attend college.[30] As the journalist Albert Samaha writes, "Football reflects [the US] racial caste system: mostly black players sacrificing their bodies for the entertainment of a mostly white audience."[31] The historian Taylor Branch has noted the "unmistakable whiff of the plantation" in college football programming, a $4.2 billion per year sport that does not pay its players for any of their labor.[32] Recruited during high school, many of these players are expected to leave in the middle of their senior year and complete their high school degree through special classes in order to accelerate their participation on college teams.[33]

Certainly, educational and financial opportunities provided an incentive for Aaron Hernandez, who grew up as one of the only "mixed race, Puerto Rican" children in the working-class town of Bristol, Connecticut. Following in the footsteps of his older brother, DJ, who played football in high school and in college, Aaron's path seemed in a sense predetermined, and he began playing at the age of eight.[34] Both boys reportedly had a complicated relationship with their father, Dennis Hernandez, who trained them in the sport from an early age, kept strict household rules, and used extreme forms of corporal punishment. Recent interviews with those who knew Aaron and the Hernandez family have revealed that Dennis's violent behavior was not a secret; however, because Aaron was said to have a "wild streak," his father's abuse was often framed as keeping his son "in line." Similarly, coverage of Aaron's downfall often attributes his problems in college and the NFL to his father's unexpected passing in 2006, the same year he left home.[35] While reporters often linked Dennis's death to Aaron's decline, they did so by simplifying the narrative, portraying Dennis as a doting and supportive father whose presence was necessary for his sons' well-being. This story was part of a broader and commonly told narrative that describes Aaron Hernandez's childhood as a form of working-class idyllicism in which a "mixed-race kid (mom Italian; dad Puerto Rican) . . . had little trouble fitting into [predominantly white] suburban Bristol," presumably due to his skilled participation in local football.[36] Following Aaron's death, additional information came to light that he had also been a victim of ongoing childhood sexual abuse at the hands of an older family friend. Narratives that address this sexual abuse or his father's abuse (coupled with his father's reported homophobia) frame it as the "cause" of Aaron's secretive sexual involvement with men.[37]

In the wake of his death, media attention swirled around his troubled history and possible sexual partners, both inside and outside of prison. Less interest was directed toward the troubling facts surrounding his CTE diagnosis, which forensic pathologists called the "worst case" they had seen in a man so young. To be sure, there are many ways to understand the media's hyperfocus on revelations about Aaron's sexuality in the wake of important (and potentially exculpatory) forensic reports on his health status. Ongoing support for professional football—a multibillion-dollar industry—requires finding ways around growing scientific understandings of the prevalence and severity of CTE in former NFL players. Importantly, the focus on Aaron's sexuality helped to reorient the conversation about the meaning of his death, which quickly became linked to the murder of Odin Lloyd.

At the same time, understandings of Aaron's sexual appetites as polymorphous and perverse aligned well with existing and interlocking narratives about Latinx subjects, young men of color, and professional athletes.

In all of these identity categories, hypersexuality is often understood in relation to broader discourses of criminality, wherein "poor self-control" becomes a rationale for "bad behavior."[38] In Aaron's case, reports of failed drug tests, friendships with "shady characters," and a propensity for bar fights beginning at the age of seventeen were understood as a portent of tragedies to come.[39] In media representations of Hernandez's suicide, his alleged crime(s) were frequently interpreted backward with hindsight, and he became labeled a "ticking time bomb."[40] Commentators frequently noted how he had a "history of instability and volatility" and "later became criminally violent."[41] He was described as "a kid who was handed everything. Just a thug who got lucky," whose early success in athletics only served to sharpen a natural propensity for violence.[42] For example, a September 2017 article from the *Orlando Sentinel*, "Aaron Hernandez Had a Criminal Mind before CTE," voices a commonly held sentiment that CTE could not "turn" anyone into a "murderous thug." The author asks, "Of all the people who were posthumously diagnosed with CTE, why did only one start acting like a mob hitman? Maybe CTE aggravates a pre-existing condition. There is no doubt, however, that the condition existed long before Hernandez put on a Patriots helmet."[43]

When unpacking this article—and the dozens like it that describe Aaron as predestined for a criminal future—it is important to note the use of hyperbole that exculpates the sport at the expenses of the players. Authors speculated that Aaron's actions were due to a "pre-existing condition," but what exactly was this condition they referred to? Fatherlessness and its attendant forms of grief? The race- and class-based assumptions of how "thugs" and "mob" members are produced? Something else entirely? In their depictions of Aaron's life, professional success, and personal troubles—long before his suicide—reporters often suggested that his downfall was inevitable. At the same time, a relative absence of "blots" on his official record posed a problem. On the one hand, these missing blemishes signified the power of football to protect its players from criminal charges. On the other, the very absence of a full "record" of Aaron's alleged crimes made it impossible for anyone to say with certainty what he had been involved in. As a result, media sources often framed him as a con man, interpreting his friendly demeanor as a cover for a darker personality. People he worked with were quoted as saying that he was a skilled liar.[44] An American Football Conference scouting director explained that he was wary of Aaron because "people at the school [the University of Florida] would tell you, 'Every time there's an issue, he's around it,'" but that "they couldn't pin a lot of stuff on him." The scout said that Aaron was "very believable. Spoke well . . . but people that I talked to said that they didn't trust him, that he'd burn you."[45] Following his death, Aaron's agent, Brian Murphy, described him as "smart as hell . . . a survivor. A hustler."[46]

Throughout his media coverage, Hernandez was often represented as having a double personality, consisting of a "good Aaron" and a "bad Aaron."[47] As Dave Altimari, a journalist for the *Hartford Courant* who covered Hernandez's career and legal troubles, remarked, "Certainly in Bristol [Aaron] was considered like a favorite son. I think that people in general were shocked to find there was another side to [him] . . . rather than . . . the football player. . . . [A] lot of his friends were guys with drug records that no one really knew about."[48] Time and again, reporters questioned whether anyone ever really "knew" Aaron, suggesting that he had used his celebrity status to dupe the public. Aaron's attorney, Jose Baez, attempted to shake this anxiety by reframing his client's friendships as a form of simple loyalty to "guys from the neighborhood." Baez noted that "based on everything we investigated and saw, everyone who knew Aaron absolutely loved him. Aaron may have broken a lot rules but the fact is that he was so genuine, sincere, and likable that people didn't hesitate to go to bat for him."[49] Baez's favorable description appears to have been well founded, though such images were a far cry from Aaron's portrayal as a "thug." As his older brother, DJ, lamented in his 2018 biography, *The Truth about Aaron*, "To many, my younger brother, Aaron Josef Hernandez, was a monster."[50]

Section II. "There are no faggots in the Hernandez family": Homophobia, Gender Normativity, and Mental "Instability"

Beyond the double image of Aaron as "favorite son" and drug addict, family man and criminal threat, questions surrounding his gender and sexual identity produced a similarly ambiguous representation. In an interview with PBS, the investigative reporter Bob Hohler stated that Aaron lived a "double secret life even as a child," both because of the abuse he suffered silently at the hands of his father and because he "was exploring his sexuality and was involved with boys, which would have been an incredible offense to his father."[51] According to Aaron's older brother, DJ, their father was very critical of Aaron's gender presentation from a young age. Describing one particularly memorable incident, he writes,

> I heard my dad say, "Aaron, why do you stand like a faggot—with your
> hands clasped on your stomach and your elbows glued to your ribs? It's fem-

inine. Are you a faggot? Only faggots stand like that. There are no faggots in the Hernandez family." Aaron put his head down and he placed his
hands straight down by his sides. This wasn't the first time and wouldn't be
the last time our father grew angry over what he called Aaron's feminine
posture.[52]

DJ further described Aaron's earlier interest in being a cheerleader and how
his father "put an end to that really quick. . . . [I]t was not OK. My dad
made it clear that . . . he had his definition of a man."[53] DJ also recalled that
Aaron was troubled about his sexuality as an adult, noting that once, when
he "asked Aaron if he was gay," his brother threatened to "fucking kill" him
if he brought it up again.[54]

Importantly, in DJ's account—told primarily through the cowritten biography *The Truth about Aaron*—Aaron's experiences of abuse, attitudes toward
professional success, relationship with his ambiguous sexuality, and decline
into mental instability are portrayed as coterminous, even indistinguishable.
The deep connections among these facets of his personality, or, at the very
least, the *representation* of these facets of his personality, produce a complicated tangle of gender, sexuality, violence, and psychopathology. For example, descriptions of Aaron that sought to illustrate his mental instability often focused on nonnormative gendered behaviors, particularly the fact that
he was known to cry in public, a performance that many found jarring when
contrasted against the stereotypical masculinity expected of football players.[55] In an interview, the former Patriots receiver Brandon Lloyd observed
that "there would be swings where he'd be the most hypermasculine, aggres-
sive individual in the room, where he'd be ready to fight somebody in fits of
rage. Or he'd be the most sensitive person in the room talking about cud-
dling with his mother."[56] Lloyd also reported having been cautioned by another teammate, Wes Welker, who had previously played with Hernandez:

> He [Welker] is looking at me wide-eyed. And he says, "I just want to warn
> you that [Hernandez] is going to talk about being bathed by his mother. . . .
> He's going to have his genitalia out in front of you while you're sitting on
> your stool. He's going to talk about gay sex. Just do your best to ignore it.
> Even walk away." . . . It was like he went from this child-like, laughing, dis-
> ruptive behavior . . . and [then] he storms off in a fit of rage.[57]

Journalists also noted Hernandez's erratic behavior. One sports reporter for
the NFL Network who covered his career with the Patriots, explained,

In the locker room, [Aaron] was sweet and charming . . . sweet is a weird way to describe a man, but that's what he was—a sweet, endearing guy when he wanted to be. But the other part of it was that, emotionally, he was a wreck. It was not abnormal for him to burst into tears if he made a bad mistake. If he got humiliated in the meeting room, sometimes he would cry. That's not really normal behavior.[58]

Other evidence of his "abnormality" appeared in discussions surrounding the leaked results of his NFL scouting psychological assessment, in which he received the "lowest possible score" in social maturity.[59] In the preceding quotations, Aaron's "abnormal" emotionality is coded according to normatively gendered scripts. Even when he is described as "hypermasculine," the sheer excess of his mood swings renders him irrational and therefore deeply feminized. This feminization works to establish a connective thread between his purported mental instability and what is now "known" about his lifelong struggle with his sexual identity. Constructing an image of his mental incapacity as separate from, and perhaps prior to, the brain injuries that led to his CTE diagnosis, these portrayals also work to undermine the role of football in his decline, a point to which this chapter will later return.

In all of these accounts and more, Hernandez is described as a complicated figure whose internal contradictions were both at the forefront of his mind and beyond his control. As a young person reckoning with his sexuality in an impossibly homophobic culture, he was forced into a state of repression and hiding. Grappling with the cumulative effects of repetitive brain injuries, he turned inward, as he had been taught time and again by a sport that did not tolerate weakness. Indeed, it seems almost impossible to separate out Aaron's complicated relationship with his sexuality from his slow mental decline. Badly beaten by his father as a child for disciplinary reasons that extended across expectations regarding athletic success, gender presentation, and sexual identity, there is no way to pinpoint when his brain first became compromised, nor when he began to understand his sexuality in ways that did not meet a normative threshold. These connections are important to consider, because they produced a very specific nexus of vulnerability through repeated forms of victimization and practices of silencing. And yet making these connections is, in itself, incredibly problematic as well, gesturing toward the historical pathologization of queer sexuality, where abuse has often become understood as a "cause" of nonnormative sexuality, which in turn becomes understood as an undesirable "defect."

Much of the reporting that appeared following the release of rumors surrounding Aaron's sexual involvement with other men worked to conflate his sexual identity with his mental state. This conflation further naturalized his alleged participation in criminal activity and was even attempted as a prosecutorial strategy during his trial for the shooting of Abreau and Furtado. From the beginning of the trial, the case against Aaron was complicated by a lack of motive and the fact that the crime had occurred at a high point in his career. In the midst of this confusion, the prosecution alerted his defense attorneys (led by Jose Baez) that the state planned to provide testimony from an ex-girlfriend, Alyssa Anderson, who claimed that Aaron had admitted to her that he was gay years earlier. As Baez outlines, the district attorney intended to identify Aaron as a "closeted homosexual," whose "frustration and anger of being a closeted homosexual made him overcompensate as a man . . . and get angry enough to kill. In essence, being a closeted homosexual made Aaron a killer."[60] Importantly, then, the prosecution was seeking to offer Aaron's sexuality not in the interest of framing the murders as personally motivated (i.e., as a romantic relationship gone wrong) but rather to prove his propensity for violence and dishonesty.

Yet even without the use of this particular justification, the believability of Aaron *as* criminal was constituted by many factors, including his prior indictment in the Lloyd case. It is also true that rates of arrest and incarceration for professional athletes, particularly football players, are relatively high when compared to the general population. Thus, while there were certain aspects of Hernandez's predicament that were unusual (namely, the number of incidents he was linked to and the ongoing revelations made about his difficult childhood and sexual identity), it is not uncommon for professional athletes to find themselves in varying degrees of legal trouble. As James Patterson and Alex Abramovich point out, "accusations relating to armed robbery, kidnapping, forced imprisonment, and sexual assault . . . dogfighting . . . child abuse . . . domestic violence . . . drug trafficking . . . DUI manslaughter . . . conspiracy to commit murder . . . and murder-suicide" have been levied at NFL players on an ongoing basis.[61] Importantly, these charges and the publicity that surrounds them cannot be separated from the racial makeup of the NFL. Highlighting the role of race helps to explain the seemingly high arrest and incarceration rates for NFL members. In other words, if the arrest rates appear high for professional athletes, they are inflated only due to the predominance of African Americans in particular sports, who are disproportionately incarcerated within the general population.[62]

While a robust literature has emerged in recent years on issues of race, criminalization, and the prison industrial complex, little attention has been paid to the treatment of professional athletes, a group that might be best imagined as a racialized caste.[63] Much like conversations that collapse structural issues—for example, inequality, community surveillance, and racial profiling—into a logic that naturalizes the incarceration of certain populations, so too is the disproportionate criminalization of professional athletes often understood to be inevitable. As one *New Yorker* author wrote in reference to Hernandez, "When crime and sports interact, the lines separating the two are *naturally* blurry."[64] Of course, there is nothing "natural" about the blurriness of this interaction. Instead, it is guided by a logic of race-, class-, and gender-based stereotypes and represents a unique intersection between axes of difference that are especially salient in the contemporary "postracial" era. As the anthropologists Niko Besnier, Susan Brownell, and Thomas F. Carter contend,

> Some have argued that the dominance of traditionally oppressed groups in sport . . . is evidence that sport has become an even field in which meritocratic principles prevail, contributing to the gradual "de-racialization" of society. This argument quickly falls apart when one . . . considers sport as a hierarchical structure that continues to be regulated, owned, managed, and coached by (male) members of dominant racial groups and social classes. This situation . . . permeates sport at all levels.[65]

Thus, to the extent that sports recapitulate normative power dynamics, they also contribute to the logic of color blindness that obscures processes of racialization and racism.

In their assessment of the exploitation of African American athletes by college-level sports programs, the sociologists Lori Latrice Martin, Kenneth J. Fasching-Varner, and Nicholas D. Hartlep observe that "race and racism seldom enter the conversation . . . about whether college athletes should be paid . . . because many Americans believe sports are the only place where race does not matter."[66] Yet, as the authors note, the very fact that "young black males are overrepresented in high-revenue-generating college sports" should give us pause; that these young men are treated more "like commodities and less like students" necessarily conjures a complicated historical past in which Black bodies were sold and purchased for labor and entertainment purposes.[67]

This long-standing process of racialized commodification also has implications for the criminalization of Black student-athletes, whose behavior is heavily policed by coaches, campus security, and law enforcement.[68] As David J. Leonard points out, the criminalization of Black athletes in the realm of professional sports often revolves around media sensationalism focusing on fictitious gang ties and illegal gun ownership. "The discursive linking of black athletes to guns further invokes the sport/gang dyad," Leonard writes, while "urban/gun violence" is portrayed "as responsible for subverting sports . . . and for destroying athletes."[69] These associations are critical to bear in mind when reflecting upon Hernandez's treatment by the criminal justice system. As the following section documents, while Hernandez himself was not Black, he became a vector for anti-Blackness through his personal and professional associations. At the same time, his instrumentalization in this fashion becomes possible precisely because of perceptions surrounding his ethnoracial identity as ambiguous. In fact, the case alleging his involvement in the 2007 car shooting was only brought against him after his likeness was seen across the media in connection with the Odin Lloyd case. At that point, a witness in the 2007 shooting contacted the police to identify Hernandez, while in prior documentation, the shooter had been referred to solely as a "Hawaiian or Hispanic" male.[70]

Section III. "All-American thug": Criminalization, Bodily Confessions, and the CTE "Closet"

In a September 2013 feature article in *Rolling Stone*, "The Gangster in the Huddle," the authors call Aaron an "all-American thug," and a headline laments that he "might have been one of the NFL's all-time greats, but he could never escape drugs, guns, and a life of violence."[71] Here, contradictory imagery is offered: Aaron is at once "the" gangster in the huddle—a misfit in the realm of an "all-American" sport by way of his illicit activities—as well as a victim of circumstance, namely, the pull of his former ties to other "troublemakers." An image by Sean McCabe that accompanies the article tells a similar story (fig. 3.1). In the illustration, Aaron's neck and torso are covered with a red substance. He is posed against an abstract background that calls to mind graffiti spray paint or blood splatters, with giant golden bullets cascading diagonally from above his left shoulder. The shading in the image accentuates his shoulders, which are also placed against a white portion of the background. His head, arms, and lower torso appear darkened.[72] In this image, Hernandez appears larger than life. His direct gaze is disconcerting, and he seems confident, self-assured. The mixture of abstract and photo-realistic techniques used in the image speaks to the broader themes of the *Rolling Stone* article and others like it that construct Hernandez as an almost mythical figure whose "truth" is impossible to understand or, at the very least, is stranger than fiction.

Figure 3.1.
Artwork by Sean
McCabe, 2013. From
Ron Borges and
Paul Solotaroff,
"The Gangster in
the Huddle: Aaron
Hernandez; Inside
Dark, Tragic Life
of Former Patriots
Star," *Rolling Stone*,
September 12, 2013.

While McCabe's illustration of Hernandez is unique for its artistic rendering and use of collaged imagery, the representation of Hernandez as torso is part of a broader pattern that exists in media portrayals. Even in the years prior to Aaron's death, his body was a source of tremendous scrutiny. Beyond the usual commentary on athletes' large stature and "natural" athletic abilities, extensive commentary was held regarding the tattoos on his chest, back, and arms.[73] Descriptions of his suicide raised further questions about the meaning of the tattoos, with many speculating about a connection between the tattoos he had acquired over his lifetime and the inscription he carved on his forehead in blood immediately prior to taking his life. The scene of Aaron's discovery by prison officers became a sensationalized tableau:

John 3:16 was scribbled in blood on [his] forehead. . . . "For God so loved the world that He gave his only begotten son that whosoever believes in Him should not perish but have everlasting life." . . . Aaron Hernandez is naked, his tattoo-covered body dangling lifeless from a white bedsheet wrapped tightly around his neck. The bedsheet is attached to a bar in a back window, located a few feet higher than his six-foot-two, 240-pound frame.[74]

Figure 3.2.
Aaron Hernandez
with his lawyer, Jose
Baez. From Alex
French, "The Man
Who Knows Aaron
Hernandez's
Secrets," *Esquire*,
April 15, 2017.
© Chris Christo /
Boston Herald.

Rumors circulated surrounding his use of scripture. Was it an admission of guilt? A final plea of innocence? A message that had to be read in concert with the extensive tattoos that already covered most of his skin? This was also not the first time his tattoos had drawn media attention. Five years earlier, in the Abreau and Furtado trial, the judge ruled that prosecutors could use two of Aaron's tattoos as evidence of his crimes. The first tattoo the prosecution called attention to depicted "a six-shot revolver with five rounds of ammunition in the cylinder and one empty chamber, with 'God forgives' beneath," while the second portrayed a "semi-automatic pistol and a single spent shell casing with a wisp of smoke." According to the prosecution, these images should be understood as transparent in their representation of Aaron's guilt.[75]

Photographs that accompanied news reports of Aaron's trials and death also disproportionately featured his tattoos. In a frequently reproduced image of Aaron with Baez (fig. 3.2), Aaron's presence is strikingly large; his hand is posed by his mouth in a gesture that looks at once like a near fist and an attempt to make his words confidential. He smirks, suggesting an inappropriately casual attitude toward the trial (by contrast, Baez's grave face makes clear that the two men are not sharing a laugh). The prominence of the tattoos scrolling out of his sleeve augment his awkward presence; here, two men sit in formal suits, but there is no question as to who is attorney and who is client. Dozens of similar images of Aaron, photographed from the shoulders and chest up, continue to circulate on the internet, freezing him in a moment with a tattooed hand touching his face.[76]

Close-ups of Aaron's hands, both in and out of handcuffs, often accompanied the articles detailing his legal saga (figs. 3.3 and 3.4). Here, his hands appeared to exist independently of his body or perhaps to stand in for it. The use of his hands in lieu of other more familiar visual representations—namely, his face—simultaneously deny their owner's subjectivity and demonstrate how criminal identification continues to rely upon certain corporeal scripts. (Importantly, the tattoos that were said to be relevant to the case as "evidence" were on his forearms, not his hands.) Media coverage of his tattoos often debated their use value as evidence in relation to the historical usage of tattoos as a form of legal identification; at the same time, the sheer number of tattoos and their cryptic messaging was interpreted as a sign of perverse embodiment and mental illness.

As news of Aaron's indictment in the Odin Lloyd case became public and rumors about his sexuality began to swirl, images of his tattooed body also became fodder for internet memes. Figure 3.5 portrays an original image that social media users recirculated with textual edits to make light of his crim-

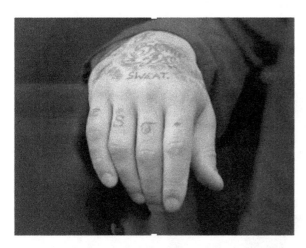

Figure 3.3.
An image of Aaron Hernandez's hand. From "Tattoos as Evidence: Aaron Hernandez's Far from the First," *Hartford Courant*, January 12, 2017. © David L. Ryan / Globe Staff / AP.

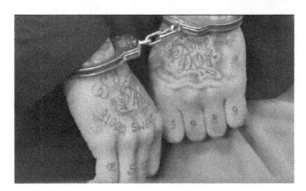

Figure 3.4.
An image of Aaron Hernandez's hands. From Beth Healy, "Part 5 of 6: Prison; A Room of His Own," *Boston Globe*, October 17, 2018. © John Tlumacki / Globe Staff.

inal charges (figs. 3.6–3.8). Using the peculiar positioning of his arms as a sign of surprise (rather than the simple effect of being unable to use one hand without raising the other when both are cuffed together), the memes suggest an ambivalence toward Aaron's agency. The symbolic weight of his covered mouth, the foregrounding of his arms, the positioning of his body, and the out-of-focus or cropped representation of his attorney all work to reframe a moment of fear and constriction into one of humor and entertainment. Ultimately, the image reveals a subject bound by the limits of his criminalized

Figure 3.5. An image of Aaron Hernandez that was recirculated as a meme. From Emily McFarlan Miller and Lauren Markoe, "Why Did Aaron Hernandez Write 'John 3:16' on His Forehead Before Killing Himself?," *Deseret News*, April 20, 2017. © Mike George / Pool / Reuters.

Figure 3.6. Meme, "AARON HERNANDEZ: HE JUST CAN'T STOP KILLING PEOPLE." From Randy Oliver, "Social Media Reacts to Aaron Hernandez Taking His Own Life in Prison," *Daily Snark*, April 19, 2017.

Figure 3.7. Meme, "WHAT THE F——K DO YOU MEAN 'THE PURGE' WAS JUST A MOVIE?" Twitter.

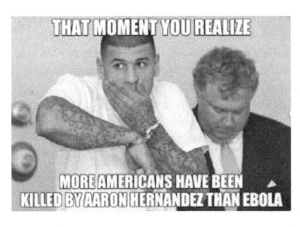

Figure 3.8. Meme, "THAT MOMENT YOU REALIZE MORE AMERICANS HAVE BEEN KILLED BY AARON HERNANDEZ THAN EBOLA." Me.me.

body, with his limp right arm pulled involuntarily to accommodate the intentional act of his left.

In all of these images and more, the use and manipulation of freeze-frame photography suggest the ways in which meme culture relies upon a halted temporality to gloss and reframe extreme forms of disenfranchisement. In her assessment of the 1992 Rodney King trial, Judith Butler explains how the immobilization of a video recording can be used to reverse intention, by invigorating familiar scripts of racial phantasmagoria. Describing how a bystander's video of police brutality became reinterpreted as an act of justifiable restraint, Butler writes,

The defense attorneys broke the video down into "stills," freezing the frame, so that the gesture, the raised hand, is torn from its temporal pace in the visual narrative. The video is not only violently decontextualized, but violently recontextualized. . . . In the place of reading the testimony alongside the video, the defense attorneys offered the frozen frame, the magnification of [King's] raised hand as the hyperbolic figure of racial threat, interpreted again and again as a gesture foreshadowing violence. . . . If the raised gesture can be read as evidence that supports the contention that Rodney King is "in control," "totally" of the entire scene, indeed, as evidence of his own threatening intentions, then a circuit is phantasmatically produced whereby King is the origin, the intention, and the object of the selfsame brutality. In other words, if it is *his* violence which impels the causal sequence, and it is his body which receives the blows, then, in effect, he beats himself: he is the beginning and the end of the violence, he brings it on himself.[77]

Writing in a moment prior to the explosion of internet meme culture, Butler nonetheless captures the ways in which the decontextualization of still images is critical to the (racial) schematization of the visual field. In the case of press coverage and media representation surrounding the Hernandez case, multiple modes of temporal interruption and spatial dislocation worked to render him "the beginning and the end of the violence."

Of course, Butler's argument takes on new meaning in the current era, which has become marked by a social media presence produced through a series of snapshot "moments when." More than a shorthand for a commonality of experience, the language of "that moment when" produces (and is produced by) the speculative tense of social media in ways that perpetually reframe past experiences and suggest the possibility of (predestined) future experiences as yet to come. This speculative tense has profound implications for populations who are bound by narratives and actualities of untimely demise. In these memes, the collapsing of temporal distinctions through the lens of (racialized) humor both immortalizes their subject and obfuscates his actual death.[78]

Representations of Hernandez as bound toward an inevitable life of crime and violence are further mirrored in conversations about the nature of CTE and its potential use as a legal defense. Although CTE has only recently become an issue of public debate, its prevalence and manifestation in professional football players raises important questions about the relationship between violence on and off the field. As Avi Brisman observes, research has begun to show that "CTE can promote changes in the brain that bring about many of the characteristics identified by some criminologists as criminogenic," or criminal behaviors produced through "biological factors of non-genetic origin."[79] Here, it is critical to unpack the uncomfortable coexistence of three issues: (1) the fact that CTE is disproportionately prevalent in football players; (2) the fact that professional football is disproportionately populated by nonwhite subjects, particularly in the most physically dangerous positions; and (3) the ongoing theorization of violent behavior as biologically determined, all of which harken back to earlier visions of biological racism that guided the original founding of the field of criminology.[80]

Yet disconcertingly, because CTE must be addressed, and must be acknowledged for its disproportionate effects, there is no real way to argue against the impact of biology on behavior without contributing to the type of logic that has been used historically to label certain "types" of people as inherently criminal. For example, in a 2016 ESPN article that speculates about whether the former NFL player O. J. Simpson may have CTE, quotations from Bennet Omalu (the neuropathologist who first discovered the prevalence of CTE in football players) and Dave Hojnowski (the equipment manager for the Buffalo Bills when Simpson played for the team) are used to discuss Simpson's head size as evidence of pathology:

> Another indicator for Omalu is the size of Simpson's head. Dave Hojnowski, who was a longtime Bills equipment manager, told NFL.com in 2011 that Simpson had "a big huge head" and had to wear a custom-sized 8¼ helmet as manufacturers during that time didn't make anything over 7¾. "If you have a bigger head that means your head is heavier," Omalu told People. "That means the momentum of your impact would be bigger. It's basic physics."[81]

More troubling still is the way that many news sources describe CTE and violent behavior as a chicken-and-egg scenario in which a player's potential predisposition toward violence is understood to have first attracted him to the sport. In this context, if CTE is acquired, it is understood to only augment a proclivity that already exists. The legal theorist Russell Spivak, for instance, even blames the acquisition of CTE on certain behavioral traits, "namely that more impulsive people are at a higher risk of acting in such a way to get a concussion."[82] For Spivak, if "concussive and sub-concussive blows alike make one more prone to CTE—implying those who play longer are more likely to develop the disease—then data on professional players' criminal behavior indeed suggests" a connection "between illegal actions and football," rooted in traumatic brain injury.[83]

While these "connections" seem fairly evident, it is also the case that analyses of them—from neurological, legal, and journalistic perspectives—never seem to question the legitimacy of allowing the sport to continue. Instead, debates veer toward whether CTE can be concretely diagnosed, formally tied to violent behavior, and subsequently used as a legitimate defense strategy. As a 2016 article in *Forbes* asks,

> How many people will use CTE as a legal defense for violent or criminal behavior, and how do you tell whether they really have CTE? CTE is not like obesity, where you can measure a person's body mass index . . . or malaria, where you can run a lab test. As can be the case with other medical conditions that have no definitive method of diagnosis, some will truly have the condition, and some will claim or believe they have the condition . . . without really having it.[84]

Here, the anxiety surrounding the use of CTE as behavioral justification is posed in familiar terms. While the author further speculates that CTE could become the "next" ADHD—by way of indeterminacy and overdiagnosis—the concern that the disease could be misused suggests that patients cannot be trusted to accurately or honestly claim its symptoms. Interestingly, this train of thought diverges from existing frameworks of legal "insanity," which do not require any actual verification of mental illness and often expand to encompass new medical findings (e.g., as in the case of Alzheimer's disease, which remains similarly ambiguous and idiosyncratic).[85] Instead, it presupposes the illegitimacy of CTE, or, at the very least, foregrounds patient opportunism as a hindrance to accurate understandings of the disease.

As the historian Keith Wailoo writes, medical conditions that present ambiguous symptoms often become points of political contention. In his work on the political history of pain, Wailoo argues that contemporary Americans' attitudes toward the management of disabling diseases have been shaped by broader negative dispositions toward dependence and state welfare; thus pain must be understood as "not just a clinical or scientific problem, but a legal puzzle, a heated cultural concern, and an enduring partisan issue."[86] In particular, he notes, "the problem of pain [is] in a sense a question of trust . . . the challenge of distinguishing people with true pain from 'chiselers' . . . [or] people seeking undeserved [assistance] through deceit and fraud. . . . What suffice[s] as evidence to validate a person's need?"[87] As Wailoo demonstrates, stereotypes of race, gender, and class have been used to categorize different patients and different diseases in relation to pain, producing an understanding of pain as "culturally specific" and, therefore, not objective in nature.[88] For this reason, Wailoo asserts that the racist and

sexist assumptions that produce figures like the "welfare queen" in US social mythology must also be understood to impact medicalized understandings of suffering, drawing a comparison to the government's undertreatment
of diseases that are disproportionately found in minoritized communities
(e.g., sickle cell disease, which predominantly impacts African Americans).[89]

In the case of CTE, similar rhetoric surrounding "deceit and fraud" is
used to discredit the disease's culpability in acts of violence and to dispute
the role of football in the production of the disease itself. Following Wailoo's
argument, this suspicion of deception must be understood in relation to the
population most affected by CTE—that is, predominantly athletes who are
African American men. When thinking about Aaron Hernandez, it is also
crucial to consider how other aspects of his identity—namely, the speculation that surrounded his ambiguous sexuality—already framed him as an
untrustworthy figure. That "rumors" of his "double life" surfaced around the
same moment in which information emerged about his diagnosis of CTE—
described by medical authorities as "the most severe case ever seen" in a person of his age—must be understood as significant to the ways in which the
disease continues to be approached with suspicion.

Perhaps more significant still is the way in which the disease itself has
been tied to practices of hiding and suppressing pain in a professional culture that does not tolerate weakness. In their research on the suppression
of concussion reporting and its relationship to neurodegenerative disease in
NFL players, Caroline E. Faure and Madeline P. Casanova describe the
constant pressure on players to ignore or downplay injuries for fear of being demoted or even removed from the team. Through a series of interviews
with former NFL players' wives, Faure and Casanova explain the prevalence of athletes' attempts to conceal their concussions from their coaches,
teams, and families. They describe how "concussion was thought to be the
most taboo of all injuries due to the injury's uncertainty" and how playing
in the NFL requires an understanding of what can and cannot be said out
loud, a fact that is at once imposed by the league and policed by the players
themselves. During the course of the interviews, Faure and Casanova document that many pending and adjudicated concussion-related lawsuits are
filed even without a player's knowledge and are levied by family members
who often remain silent on the subject in front of their affected loved ones.[90]

Strikingly, the "taboos" described by the players' wives, and by Faure
and Casanova's analysis, bear a critical similarity to the rhetorics of closeting that have shaped understandings and experiences of queer identity. Not
only does the need to veil one's physical or mental state align with the paradigm of the closet, but so too does life in a perpetual state of high-stakes

bodily hiding mimic the paranoia that accompanies repressed sexuality. At the same time, in both cases, this shrouding is linked to proper gendered comportment. Quoting from the sociologist Katie Rodgers, Faure and Casanova describe how in the "tough guy culture" of professional football, players' "understanding of their bodies 'leads to a disconnect between the emotional and physical self, including a repression of pain and other "weak" or feminized emotions such as fear or anxiety."[91] Thinking through these connections in relation to Aaron Hernandez, it is not a stretch to understand that the need to hide his pain (whether caused by childhood abuse or professional football), his sexuality, and his progressive neurodegeneration all functioned in concert. More significantly, these intersecting repressions operate at a larger institutional level to invisibilize the prevalence of traumatic brain injury among professional athletes in contact sports, industries that predominantly rely upon the labor and sacrifices of young Black men, whose masculinity is at once representationally hyperintensified and compulsorily interpolated.

That we, as a society, are inured to the violence displayed by football—and to the obvious pain that it causes its players—is an example of what Adrián Pérez-Melgosa calls "low intensity necropolitics." Drawing upon the work of Achille Mbembe (whose conceptual framework of "necropolitics" seeks to understand the role of state-instrumented death in the political management of populations), Pérez-Melgosa uses the terminology of "low intensity" to reference the effects of the omnipresence of certain dead and dying bodies. Focusing on the representation of Latin American migrants in film, he asks, "What effect does the reiterated representation of migrants as suffering bodies and corpses have on the social perception of real migrants and migration?"[92] To answer this question, Pérez-Melgosa points to a paradox of representation, or a "double semiotic bind," that occurs when films attempt to "portray the abused and dead bodies of migrants in an effort to dramatize the violence and hardships they endured." Yet in doing so, he writes, these films

> are simultaneously denouncing a human tragedy and reproducing a necropolitical logics of power. They identify the bodies of migrants as the natural sites where societies may deposit the negative affects generated by the shortcomings of the nation and capitalism. . . . The consistent focus on the dead bodies of migrants displayed in contemporary migration films reminds their main intended audiences . . . that the decision to migrate is an individual choice, and that once they are in transit between nations, they place themselves in a situation where death is the norm and life is a privilege.[93]

While this argument could certainly be applied more broadly to representations of dead and dying bodies of color in US media, it also has important connotations for the representations of sports that are predominated by nonwhite athletes and that naturalize injury, debility, and death.

Section IV. "A beautiful pathology": Monetizing Pain and Debility

In the case of CTE, the silence that surrounds these men's suffering is compounded by a lack of information and a lack of diagnostic technology. Because the determination of a CTE diagnosis can only be made postmortem through the examination of brain tissue, there is little incentive for those who suspect they suffer from the disease's symptoms to come forward. Even as researchers work toward new testing methods for patients prior to death, it is also understood as an irreversibly degenerative condition.[94] Harder still is the delayed symptomology, which does not appear within a concrete time frame and may take years to show its first signs.[95] Importantly, however, while these factors may contribute to the NFL's ability to deny an inevitable causal link between football and CTE, they do not completely account for the full range of attitudes toward this type of injury. Media depictions of the prevalence of head trauma in contact sports often portray it as an open secret whose concealment is supported both by professional organizations and by the participants themselves. As the San Francisco 49ers player Richard Sherman explains in a 2013 interview with *Sports Illustrated*,

> A NASCAR driver understands that anything can happen during a race; his car could flip at 200 miles per hour. A boxer knows when he goes in the ring what's happening to his body. Just like them, we understand [football] is a dangerous game with consequences not just in the short term, but for the rest of our lives. All of us . . . chose this profession. Concussions are going to happen. . . . Sometimes I can tell when a guy is concussed during a game—he can't remember things or he keeps asking the same questions over and over—but I'm not going to take his health into my hands and tell anybody, because playing with injuries is a risk that guys are willing to take. . . .
> . . . Do I think about the consequences 30 years down the line? No more than I think about the food I'm enjoying today, which could be revealed . . . to cause cancer or a heart murmur or something else unpredictable. Those are the things you can't plan for, and the kind of optimism I have right now is the only way to live. And the next time I get hit in the head

and I can't see straight, if I can, I'll get back up and pretend like nothing happened. . . .

If you don't like it, stop watching.[96]

Sherman's understanding of his career presents a classic problem in debates surrounding choice, coercion, and agency with respect to marginalized populations. Regardless of the structural forces that might help to land an individual in the NFL, political outrage at the health consequences of the sport can only serve to reinforce understandings of football players as intellectually ill-equipped to make their own decisions.

In interviews with the Associated Press, the former NFL players Maurice Jones-Drew, Justin Smith, and Mike Sellers reflected on their own attitudes toward concussions sustained during football:

> JONES-DREW: The bottom line is: You have to be able to put food on the table. No one's going to sign or want a guy who can't stay healthy. I know there will be a day when I'm going to have trouble walking. I realize that. . . . But this is what I signed up for. Injuries are part of the game. If you don't want to get hit, then you shouldn't be playing.

> SMITH: It doesn't take a rocket scientist to figure out if [you have] a concussion, you're probably damaging your brain a little bit. . . . Yeah I'd still play through it. It's part of it. It's part of the game. . . . And most guys—99 percent of guys in the NFL—are going to play through it.

> SELLERS: You want to continue to play. You're a competitor. *You're not going to tell on yourself.*

The Associated Press article noted that when it came to having a head injury, "other players would do the same: Hide it."[97] As the interviews reveal, the players' dedication to their sport is balanced with an acknowledgment of the potential consequences; or, perhaps more to the point, they describe an understanding that professional football and the experience of concussions are inseparable propositions. These men's narratives express awareness of and ambivalence toward the dangers of their sport, and their consciousness must not be read as reductively false. Further, as African Americans, their relationship to pain and pain reporting must also be understood as structured by the types of incredulity described by Wailoo. That is, the choice between reporting and not reporting injury in this context is not just a choice between playing with pain or not playing while receiving proper care. Instead, because there is no guarantee that a player's injury will be properly acknowledged (particularly in the case of undiagnosable head trauma), reporting may merely cause further harm.

In 2017 a federal lawsuit filed by former NFL players revealed that damaging and addictive pain medication is commonly used in "performance enhancing" capacities—namely, prior to, rather than after, a player sustains an injury. In particular, Toradol, a nonsteroidal anti-inflammatory drug, was cited as being offered "freely" to players "each Sunday to numb existing injuries" and "in anticipation of the inevitable aches and pains accrued" during games.[98] Former NFL player Eugene Monroe described the following experience:

> Before kickoff on game day, in NFL locker rooms all over the country, players wait in line to drop their pants. We call it the T Train . . . a bunch of really large guys waiting . . . to get shot in the butt with Toradol, a powerful painkiller that will help them make it through the game and its aftermath. . . . Some guys don't feel any pain for two days. Of course, that's the point of these drugs—they block out the pain and reduce inflammation. But they also temporarily mask injury. That's not a good thing if you get hurt during a game—you might need to address your injuries right away. But you feel nothing, so you do nothing.[99]

In the suit, the players linked Toradol to the danger of head injury, "claiming in part that Toradol had masked their concussion symptoms and increased their risk of suffering life-altering brain damage."[100]

Recordings of Hernandez's phone calls while in prison reveal the prevalent use of Toradol by the Patriots' medical staff, ostensibly under the direction of head coach Bill Belichick, even after new regulations were put into place. While on the phone with a former teammate who was suffering from broken ribs, Hernandez encouraged the player to ask Belichick for a Toradol shot, explaining, "It was illegal last year—the year we played—they made it illegal, but Bill still gave the shots. . . . If players want it . . . man they're getting that."[101] In other conversations, Hernandez also stated that he frequently used marijuana before games in order to block pain. While incarcerated, he tested positive for the pain medication Neurontin and was also suspected to have used the synthetic drug K2.[102] Years earlier, when police were attempting to uncover a motive in the Lloyd murder, speculation existed that the killing might have been drug related. In particular, investigations revealed that Hernandez was known to use phencyclidine—PCP or "angel dust"—a drug that was "first marketed in the fifties as a surgical anesthetic" but was later "banned for its psych-ward side effects: mania, delirium, violent hallucinations."[103] All of this information provides a picture of a person attempting to manage severe and long-term pain in a way that blurs the line between bodily and psychic injury. Many news sources also attempt to date Hernandez's drug use to early high school, which serves to further cloud the trajectory of football's role in his descent into CTE and its potential relationship to painkilling pharmaceuticals.

In her work on the obesity "crisis," Lauren Berlant offers a framework for rethinking the problems of sovereignty and individual autonomy under conditions of late-capitalist inequality. Berlant proposes that we need new ways to understand the "zone of ordinariness, where life building and the attrition of human life are indistinguishable," and where one may be compelled toward activities "that do not occupy time, decision, or consequentiality in anything like the registers of autonomous self-assertion."[104] To this end, she introduces the concept of "lateral agency," in which "agency can be an activity of maintenance, not making; fantasy, without grandiosity; sentience without full intentionality; inconsistency, without shattering; embodying, alongside embodiment."[105] Lateral agency is further a form of existence that plays out "in the scene of slow death" wherein "the structurally motivated attrition of persons notably because of their membership in certain populations, is neither a state of exception nor the opposite, mere banality, but a domain of revelation where an upsetting scene of living that has been muffled in ordinary consciousness is revealed to be interwoven with ordinary life after all."[106] Through the terms "lateral" and "slow," Berlant proposes an alternative construction of space and time that is particularly significant when thinking through the experiences and ontologies of health and disease. She calls attention to the simultaneous uses of the terms "chronic condition" and "crisis" in the rhetoric that surrounds obesity, noting in the first case how "disease[s] of time . . . can never be cured, only managed," and in the second how "the actuarial imaginary of biopolitics" transforms "cool facts of suffering . . . [into] hot weapons in arguments about agency and urgency that extend to imperiled bodies."[107]

Berlant's conceptual framework is instructive for considering the politics around CTE, concussion nonreporting, and professional football. Like obesity, CTE is at once a chronic condition and a "crisis"; it also exists without a cure, without a living diagnosis, and yet it is defined as degenerative. When the media refers to the current CTE "crisis"—which includes concerns surrounding youth contact sports, heightened rates of postmortem diagnosis in professional athletes, and researchers' race to find a solution—it shifts the focus away from the forms of slow violence that are coterminous with the disease's disproportionate reach across poor people of color. Nor does the discourse of crisis—which has ushered forth legal settlements and new league protocols but never the halting of the sport—account fully for the athletes themselves, whose choice to play hard must be rendered as something more than simple ignorance or an overt result of narrowed life choices. By moving away from a dichotomous framework that prioritizes "life building" over destructive activities, Berlant urges a reconsideration of life itself as a priori. To this end, she reflects on the common complaint that obesity is caused by modes of eating that serve "self-medicating" purposes, a turn of phrase often associated with inherently damaging or harmful behaviors.[108]

Building on Berlant's argument, Jasbir Puar observes that "slow death is not about an orientation toward the death drive, nor is it morbid; rather, it is about the maintenance of the living, the 'ordinary work of living on.'"[109] Writing about the politics of suicide and its cultural perception as the "ultimate loss of life," Puar suggests that we look to the "broader context of demands for bodily capacity as well as the profitability of debility, both functioning as central routes through which capital seeks to sustain itself."[110] While capacity and debility are often thought of in opposing terms, Puar suggests that they comprise the same neoliberal project that is geared toward the engineering of (un)healthy bodies. Moreover, while debility is presumably the undesirable position in this binary arrangement, Puar explains that this undesirability is only felt by the subject made to claim it, and is in fact ultimately a desirable—even necessary—position for the larger goals of what she calls the "liberal eugenics of lifestyle programming":

> Bioinformatics frames—in which bodies figure not as identities or subjects but as data—entail that there is *no such thing as non-productive excess but only forms of new identification.* This revaluing of excess/debility is potent because, simply put, debility—slow death—is profitable for capitalism. In neoliberal, biomedical, and technological terms, the body is always debilitated in relation to its ever-expanding potentiality.[111]

Applying this framework to the problem of CTE, it is immediately apparent that a careful consideration of the damaging effects of athletics on the bodies and minds of young men of color must move beyond a logic of disposability. In other words, the players' debilitation is not an unfortunate byproduct of the sport but, rather, is an inevitable outcome in an industry that continually monetizes participants' bodily differences.

One example of how this phenomenon operates can be found in the media coverage of Hernandez's late-stage CTE forensic diagnosis, which often describes his brain as a veritable gift to the scientific community, or a "perfect specimen."[112] Ann McKee, neurologist and director of Boston University's

Chronic Traumatic Encephalopathy Center, led Hernandez's diagnostic autopsy and is often cited on this issue. The following quotation appears on Boston University's website featuring faculty research, though various versions of it can also be found in numerous Associated Press sources. McKee notes that because of Aaron's "youth" and his body's "pristine condition,"

> *this* brain has been one of the most significant contributions to our work. . . . The integrity of the brain tissue is so well preserved that we're advancing our understanding of the disease at the submicroscopic level. We're able to do things in *this* particular brain that we aren't always able to do given the condition of a brain when we receive it.[113]

Explaining Dr. McKee's findings, the *New York Times* reports in even more macabre terms:

> *The* brain was sliced into sheaths, maybe a half an inch at a time, starting at the front. . . . What made *the* brain extraordinary, for the purpose of science, was not just the extent of the damage, but its singular cause. Most brains with that kind of damage have sustained a lifetime of other problems, too, from strokes to other diseases, like Alzheimer's. Their samples are muddled, and not everything found can be connected to one particular disease. *This* one looked as if it had been lifted from the pages of a textbook devoted to just one disease. "It's rare for us to get a brain of a person this young in such good shape . . . ," [McKee] said. "It's a classic case. And it tells us a lot about the disease. . . . He had a beautiful pathology, if you can call it beautiful."[114]

Profitable in life and death, capacity and debility, Hernandez and his brain have become a critical node on the trajectory toward an "ever-expanding potentiality" of neurological health and cognitive capacity. That Aaron's mind—referred to here as "this" brain and "the" brain rather than "his" brain—as well as those of other players, only became usable for this specific purpose after death suggests the ways in which the profitability of his short life was not an unanticipated "tragedy." Rather, it is a logical outcome of a profession that emphasizes hypercapacity through debilitating practices, of a bioinformatic culture that relies upon the ongoing consumption of vulnerable bodies. This practice is perhaps best summed up by Jose Baez's description of Hernandez's initial arrest and incarceration at the district attorney's behest: "They got themselves an NFL football player, they were gonna get a pound of flesh out of him."[115] Of course, they succeeded in appropriating much more than that.

CHAPTER 4

"Who's going to tell Sammy Sosa he is Afro-Latino?": Transraciality and Panethnic Latinx Authenticity

The hidden episteme in Rodríguez's pastoral is the rage at our embodied history, for while his wit may pass muster, his face does not.
NORMA ALARCÓN, "TROPOLOGY OF HUNGER: THE 'MISEDUCATION' OF RICHARD RODRÍGUEZ"

It's 2017 and just like a week ago somebody tweeted that Afro-Latina is a thing that Twitter made up a year ago, so you know, like people debate that we exist . . . like we're mythical or something. . . . So it's a never-ending battle—when you try to educate, they fight you back, like no, not really, you're not really here. So, are you talking to a hologram? It's actually a really advanced AI that's tweeting from my account, like I'm just a bot, I'm just a hologram.
ZAHIRA KELLY, "ZAHIRA KELLY DISCUSSES ACCOUNTABILITY & ASSERTING AFRO-LATINA EXISTENCE IN 2017" (YOUTUBE VIDEO)

In May 2017, the Colombian American musician Kali Uchis found herself in the middle of a controversy surrounding racial identity and her public aesthetic. Applauded for her "genre-bending" style that combines elements of pop, neo soul, rhythm and blues, and reggaeton, Uchis released her first independent mixtape, *Drunken Babble*, in 2012 at the age of eighteen. Her music has since enjoyed popularity on US and international charts, receiving multiple music award nominations, and has been featured in advertising campaigns and television programming. Yet as Uchis's success increased, so too did criticism over her self-presentation.

Critiques of Uchis often focus on her changeable racial appearance, referencing the differences between her portrayal on earlier works, such as *Por Vida* from 2015 (fig. 4.1), and more recent works, such as "Tyrant" from 2017 (fig. 4.2). In the former, the pastel color scheme, coupled with Uchis's skin tone, hair color, and makeup, recall a Marilyn Monroe aesthetic and appear dramatically different from the latter, which features a red and yellow design alongside a noticeably "darker" version of Uchis, with darker hair and skin tone and a very different makeup aesthetic. Reflecting on this shift, the cultural commentator Etienne Rodriguez notes that

> Kali Uchis very clearly presented herself as a *white Latina* in the past, and as such she benefitted from the privilege that comes with it. More recently, with the release of her newest single ["Tyrant"] and the announcement of an album, she has started to present herself as a brown Latina and appropriated the aesthetic of one. . . . Now I'm not saying that Kali Uchis intentionally made herself look like an urban Chicana so that she could sell records, but I am implying it.[1]

Rodriguez further explains that he was not the first to question the ethics of Uchis's stylization. Earlier in the year, a massive Twitter war occurred between Uchis and Esperanz Aguilera Fuentes (@SoyEsperanz), a Chicana/o studies student at the University of California, Davis. In her original tweet, Fuentes asked why Uchis was "suddenly brown," accusing her of capitalizing off of a racial identity that she could not rightfully claim.[2] In a later media interview, Fuentes explained, "Colorism is very real in the Chicanx/Latinx community. . . . [T]he amount of stigmatization, erasure and institutional oppression black and brown folks within the community face is why I had a problem seeing Kali Uchis take on a 'brown girl' narrative at her convenience."[3]

Uchis's response to Fuentes further enraged many fans. She first asked Fuentes to take down the tweets, explaining that she "has never considered herself white" and that she refused to identify as such: "I hate racism, I hate the criminalization of brown people, and all of that. Why would you try and make me seem like somebody that I hate?" She then explained that she had long been a supporter of Latinx, Afro-Latinx, and African American rights and had used social media to protest police brutality and police neglect. For example, following the 2016 murders of Alton Sterling and Philando Castile, Uchis highlighted community members' recollections that they had seen "the KKK passing out flyers" in the areas where they were killed, stating that the deaths should properly be called a "lynching." To call attention to the murders, Uchis posted an image on her Instagram account that read, "STOP TELLING PEOPLE OF COLOR THEIR EXPERIENCE IS AN ILLUSION."[4] While Fuentes agreed to take down the original tweets, she reported feeling "duped" and said she regretted her decision.

Figure 4.1. Kali Uchis, cover art for *Por Vida*, 2015. © Kali Uchis.

Figure 4.2. Kali Uchis, cover art for "Tyrant," 2017. © Virgin EMI Records, Universal Music Group.

Further responding to the conflict between Uchis and Fuentes was Zahira Kelly, an Afro-Latina artist and critic, who accused Uchis and her fans of using racial privilege to try to "censor" those who were skeptical of her image, adding that "Kali is also riding on neo-soul that Black women created, with no respect or homage given."[5] As the debate continued, Uchis remained firm that she had "always considered [herself] a person of color," but, she explained, "If you guys think I need to call myself a white Latina, then ok, I don't want to offend anyone and I definitely don't want to hurt anyone." Even still, Uchis claimed that this concession led to other detractors who complained that "she doesn't want to claim that she's a person of color because she hates herself . . . she doesn't want to be a person of color."[6]

In certain ways, there was nothing particularly new about the Kali Uchis debate. As scholars of US popular culture have noted, racial appropriation and exoticization have long formed the basis of mainstream "white" American entertainment and have taken a variety of forms, from the commodification of "other" cultures, to the outright theft of nonwhite art by white artists and white-owned industries, to the use and perpetuation of superficial racial stereotypes. As bell hooks has argued in her work on consumerism and racial representation, "Within commodity culture, ethnicity becomes spice, seasoning that can liven up the dull dish that is mainstream white culture. . . . Otherness . . . is offered as a new delight, more intense, more satisfying, than the normal way of doing and feeling."[7]

At the same time, the (mis)appropriation of race, and the quest for racial

authenticity, can move in multiple directions. In particular, nonwhite artists are often criticized for not being authentic "enough," whether authenticity is read in relation to skin color or sociocultural upbringing. Popular
Black female-identifying artists such as Nicki Minaj, for example, experience multidirectional criticism; Minaj's aesthetic has been decried as both
exploitative of Black women's bodies and potentially white seeking, given
that she often wears light-colored contact lenses and straight hair exten-
sions. To be sure, Black women have long been required to adhere to particular white beauty standards in order to be treated with respect and humanity; this requirement has also shaped the trajectory of the American music
industry and has determined its anointment of particular artists and its neglect of others.

What makes the Uchis controversy more complicated, however, is that
unlike the category of "Blackness"—a racial identification that an artist like
Minaj is unequivocally identified with—the categories of "whiteness," "non-
whiteness," and "person of color" are all potentially applicable and meaningful when thinking about Uchis's positionality. In other words, while
it is inarguable that Minaj is "Black" according to US standards of racial
identification—this is not a category she can escape from or change even
if she desired to—Uchis's identity is less clear. (Indeed, the first suggested
question provided by Google when searching Uchis's name is, "What race
is Kali Uchis?") As Zahira Kelly notes, this lack of clarity can only exist for
someone like Uchis who is potentially legible as "white"; by contrast, "those
of us who are visibly and permanently brown and black don't have the op-
tion of just tanning or staying out in the sun and changing hair color to play
to whatever preferences arise, we must simply deal with being excluded and
dehumanized."[8] Kelly's remarks point to the difficulty in thinking through
Uchis's identity from the standpoint of both US and Latin American racial frameworks. For Kelly, the same colorism that enables Uchis's success in
the US music industry also produces the exclusion of darker-skinned people
throughout Latin American media.

At the same time, however, the racial status of persons of Latin American
descent in the United States is hardly resolved. This fact can be seen in the
collection of data for "official" purposes (e.g., the census, school enrollment,
medical care, and so on), where, depending on time and place, the identification choices for Latinx persons change. Sometimes, one's race is requested
in a separate category; at other times, "Latino" and/or "Hispanic" are given
as choices within categories of race or ethnicity; and at other times still, one
may be asked to identify as "non-Hispanic white," "Hispanic white," "non-
Hispanic Black," or "Hispanic Black." As Cristina Mora has argued, while

"Hispanic" and "Latino" are technically ethnic designations, they have been produced and imagined as racial designations through comparative frames (as I discussed in this book's introduction).

In this chapter, I consider how the ambiguity surrounding the category of Latinx itself—how it intersects with, eclipses, and/or stands in for categories of race and ethnicity—relates to a source of consternation within contemporary US racial politics: transracialism. Historically, the term "transracial" has been used in reference to children who have been adopted into families of a different racial background than their own. Since the 2010s, however, various forms of US media have seen the rise of the term in relation to the idea of race as a voluntary or changeable entity, drawing upon definitions of transgender identity.[9] Mainstream awareness of the new use of the term occurred following the 2015 Rachel Dolezal controversy, in which a white woman who "passed" for Black was publicly outed.

While many scholars and commentators have explained the ways that transraciality problematically appropriates the rhetoric of transgender identity and rights, this chapter argues that transraciality also harnesses the conceptual framework of racial and ethnic ambiguity produced by state-sanctioned definitions of Latinx identity as a pluralistic and ill-defined category. I argue that the fundamental ambiguity surrounding Latinidad has had increasingly profound implications for the ways that racial difference and classification become played out in the early twenty-first century. In other words, I suggest that the demographic categories of Hispanic white, Hispanic Black, non-Hispanic white, and non-Hispanic Black (and beyond) have served to produce confusion over the saliency of ethnicity and race as meaningful categories, as well as over the primacy of ethnicity over race (and vice versa). In doing so, I address how ongoing uncertainty surrounding Latinx identity has provided an imaginative space for rethinking race as a mutable category (i.e., as constantly changing, coterminous and/or divergent with ethnic identification, and so on). Ultimately, not only has this mutability created a springboard for transracial thought, but, as the examples provided in this chapter demonstrate, it has functioned simultaneously to authorize a devaluation of Blackness *and* to exteriorize anti-Black sentiment as a problem of "Other" nations' colorist attitudes.

Unlike the previous chapters that focused around singular case studies in order to explicate broader cultural phenomena, this chapter pulls together several incidents to examine and contextualize the relationship between Latinidad and transraciality. To this end, the chapter begins with an analysis of academic and popular comparisons made between Dolezal and Caitlyn Jenner (the former US Olympian who publicly announced her gender transition the same year as the Dolezal controversy). The chapter then thinks through the commonness of cross-racial performativity within popular US cultural forms, addressing narratives of racial "passing" as evidence of the predominance of the Black/white binary in the US racial imaginary. Following from this, the chapter considers how Latinx theorizations of *mestizaje* have produced a fluid understanding of ethnoracial identification.

Finally, the chapter addresses two popular media controversies surrounding Latinx identity and processes of racialization. First, I consider an instance from 2010 in which African American professional baseball player Torii Hunter called out his former teammate Vladimir Guerrero (who was born in the Dominican Republic) as "not Black" and stated that Guerrero and other Major League Baseball athletes hailing from Latin America were "imposters." Second, I consider the significance of ongoing debates surrounding the use of skin lighteners by former professional baseball player Sammy Sosa (also from the Dominican Republic). By evaluating the conversations surrounding Guerrero's and Sosa's relationship to US-based notions of Blackness and Afro-Latinx identity, these sections explore how ongoing confusion over Latinx ethnic and racial identity is produced through a process of queer racialization that simultaneously enables transraciality and invisibilizes Afro-Latinx subjects.

Section I. "Trans": Intellectual and Ethical Caveats Critical to the Transgender-Transracial Comparison

Before delving into the first part of the chapter, I must offer a quick series of caveats. First, it is important to note that critics and activists have argued that the use of "transracial" (in the sense employed by Dolezal) is damaging to transgender identities, persons, and rights. I therefore acknowledge that any analysis of the cross traffic between forms of bodily alienation based in a "trans" framework enters into potentially treacherous territory. While this chapter probes the contours of identity, embodiment, and dysphoria with respect to gender and race, I firmly reject the sort of thinking that denigrates transgender people, whether through discourses of psychological aberrance, social incredulity, or political infidelity. This rejection includes the types of semantic debates or forms of discursive "logic" that, if pushed to extremes, would trespass upon the legal rights, civic protections, and healthcare access necessary for the survival of transgender persons. Further, while the central purpose of this chapter is not to ethically evaluate other individuals' or groups' use of transgender rhetoric for alternative purposes, it is critical to acknowledge that such uses are appropriative and serve to diminish transgender activists' painstaking efforts to carve out consideration for basic rights, respect, and humanity. With these basic principles in mind, the chapter nonetheless demonstrates that an analysis of transraciality—as an identity and as a social phenomenon—is necessary not only because it exists but also because of its broader political stakes in relation to other marginalized identities and peoples.

To be sure, one issue raised by the use of "trans" in a racial rather than a gender framework is the way in which the juxtaposition of these contexts produces transgender subjectivity as inherently white. This problem is continuous with what trans of color and queer of color scholars have observed with respect to the fight for transgender rights: namely, that although trans people of color and queer people of color often experience the greatest level of personal and community endangerment, the public face of the transgender identity and rights movement is typically white. Similarly, when "transgender" and "transracial" are thought through as parallel forms of "trans," gender and race are produced as comparable rather than intersecting categories, and thus those with multiply marginalized identities become invisibilized. Instead, by taking an intersectional approach to the question of transgender politics, we must learn how the process of gender transformation impacts racial identity, which is, in itself, always already gendered. As C. Riley Snorton has argued, the "category of transness is a racial narrative."[10] With these statements clearly in mind, this chapter offers a juxtaposition of politico-cultural phenomena—transraciality and Latinx panethnicity—in order to think through how each produce a model of fluid, ambiguous, and appropriative racial identity.

Section II. "Unsettled identities": Scholarly Debates over Transraciality

In May 2017, the same month of the Uchis controversy, another debate over a question of racial identity emerged in a very different context: an academic journal. This argument began when the philosopher Rebecca Tuvel published an article in *Hypatia: A Journal of Feminist Philosophy* that resulted in a virtual firestorm of condemnation and outrage from within the academic community. The essay, "In Defense of Transracialism," assumes the form of a standard scholarly essay but came under scrutiny due to its central premise: that the support for transgender rights should entail the subsequent and parallel support of "transracial" rights. Tuvel argues, "Since we should accept transgender individuals' decisions to change sexes, we should also accept transracial individuals' decisions to change races."[11] In order to establish this equivalence, Tuvel compares two figures who became fodder for public debate in the early months of 2015: Rachel Dolezal and Caitlyn Jenner.

Because of both the timing and the titillating nature of the Dolezal and Jenner stories, their comparison was perhaps inevitable and indeed inspired a veritable frenzy, as everyone from reporters to talk show hosts offered opinions. Dolezal also underscored the comparison in an interview on *Good Morning America*, during which she described herself as "transracial." Here, she spoke of her experiences as a dysphoric child, explaining that her discomfort with a white racial identity began at the age of five, when she recalls "drawing self-portraits with the brown crayon instead of the peach crayon" and "black, curly hair" in lieu of her naturally straight blond hair. In subsequent interviews, Dolezal reiterated her claim to a Black identification and repeatedly self-identified as Black. Although she knew she had no African heritage, she had spent years serving as a representative of the African American community in the state of Washington, where she was the head of a local NAACP chapter and an instructor of Africana studies at Eastern Washington University. When pressed to elaborate on her identification with Blackness, she explained,

> From a very young age I felt a spiritual, visceral, very instinctual connection with "Black is beautiful" and, you know, just the Black experience and wanting to celebrate that. I didn't know how to articulate that as a young child. You know, in kindergarten or whatever, you don't really have the words to say what's going on. But certainly that was shut down. I was socially conditioned to not own that and to be limited to whatever biological identity was thrust upon me and narrated to me, so I felt pretty awkward.[12]

While Dolezal describes her appropriation as an attempt to circumvent the limits of social conditioning, the actual performance of her racial identity relies heavily on the blunt technologies of racial appropriation. A self-professed "Black hairstylist" and a diligent tanner, Dolezal's postures of Blackness require a superficial mimicking of phenotypic Blackness and Black style. In this way, Dolezal joins a longer tradition of white American appropriation of Black culture that vacillates between claims of authenticity and intentional performance, igniting anger from across the political spectrum.

Critics of Tuvel's comparative treatment of Dolezal and Jenner asserted that the juxtaposition was disrespectful toward transgender people and rights. The philosopher Nora Berenstain, for example, wrote that Tuvel was guilty of "egregious levels of liberal white ignorance and discursive transmisogynistic violence."[13] Similar remarks could also be seen across social media. Mere days after the appearance of Tuvel's article, an open letter to the editors of the journal circulated online, garnering hundreds of signatures from scholars. The letter requested that the journal retract Tuvel's article because of "a failure in the review process" (even though the normal peer review protocol was followed), which they cited as causing "harm to the communities who might expect better from *Hypatia*."[14] In an even more unusual move, one of the journal's associate editors, Cressida Heyes, posted a note on *Hypatia*'s Facebook page criticizing Tuvel's work and apologizing for its publication.[15]

As further debates ensued in the following weeks, disagreements over Tuvel's argument cracked open (at least) two bigger questions. First, why did this particular essay inspire such vitriol when similar arguments had been made by other scholars in the recent past? Certainly, regardless of one's political or philosophical position on this type of comparison, there is no doubt that it already exists in the realms of popular culture and academic scholarship. Second, how can we make sense of the ways in which the narrative of gender transition has increasingly been appropriated by individuals who claim other forms of identitarian alienation, such as race in the Dolezal case? To be sure, an important and fair critique of Tuvel's essay was a common objection to her lack of scholarly background in the fields of transgender studies and critical race studies, documented in the article's failure to fully engage with relevant scholars in these areas.

At the same time, other recent publications from nonspecialists with related theses have received no such complaints. The sociologist Rogers Brubaker, for instance, published a book-length essay in 2016 with Princeton University Press entitled *Trans: Gender and Race in an Age of Unsettled Identities*, which directly compares transgender and transracial identities, bodily transitions, psychological narratives, and discursive representations. At the outset of *Trans*, Brubaker, who specializes in European political thought, states explicitly that he is not an expert in the materials at hand, explaining that he is "an outsider not only to the fields of gender and transgender studies but also to the experience of crossing racial or gender boundaries" and that his "analysis is no doubt shaped and limited by my own identity as a cisgender white male."[16] While Brubaker's book did inspire some critical reviews, they were largely of the standard polite scholarly ilk; there were no campaigns launched against him, no calls to retract his work, nor any sort of responses in keeping with the scandal that emerged over Tuvel's essay.[17]

Tuvel is also not the first nor the most provocative scholar to compare the issues surrounding Dolezal and Jenner. In a 2015 article entitled "Rachel Dolezal Is Really Queer: Transracial Politics and Queer Futurity," the sociologist Angela Jones asserts that transracialism might be best understood within a framework of queer political and intellectual life, positing that transracial transition

> seems like testimony to the potentiality of queer world making . . . that people can and do craft subjectivities that bring them joy, and that disrupt hegemonic discourses in the process. . . . If [Dolezal] identifies as black because it fills her soul with joy, and helps her achieve self-actualization, and has also used her position as a black political figure to fight racial injustice, why the backlash? The backlash is because people *are* afraid of a queer planet. Subjectivities are ours to craft, and while it is arduous to escape the hegemonic discursive power regimes that imprison our bodies, it is an exercise of agency, empowerment, and queerness to challenge such discursive power regimes.[18]

Comparing Jones's argument to Tuvel's, it is hard to understand why the two did not elicit similar responses; in fact, Jones's statements have yet to be criticized.

One theme present throughout assessments of Tuvel's work has been a concern over the forum in which it was published, namely, a feminist journal. Yet surely such unease is a bit dubious, given that there has never been a singular "feminist" perspective on trans identification. In fact, it is often the case that certain strains of feminist and transgender political, cultural, and intellectual perspectives clash. Feminist arguments with gender transition, and, consequently, with transgender people, extend back to Janice Raymond's 1979 tome *The Transsexual Empire: The Making of the She-Male*. Emerging from the intellectual and social tumult of second-wave feminism, Raymond made a name for herself by denouncing "transsexuals" and "transsexuality" as manifestations of a patriarchal society. She vilified male-to-female (MTF) trans people as interlopers who co-opted women's space and experiences and female-to-male (FTM) trans people as cowardly self-haters who betrayed women by actively identifying with male oppressors. In her view, trans people's commitment to traditional gender roles meant that they were, in the end, always antifeminist.[19]

Over time, as transgender identities and individuals became more visible in popular cultural spaces and within scholarly circles, Raymond's antitransgender feminist positionality became known as trans-exclusionary radical feminism. A fairly recent example of this line of thinking can be found in the feminist scholar Sheila Jeffreys's 2014 book *Gender Hurts: A Feminist Analysis of the Politics of Transgenderism*, which argues that "transgender theory and practice contradict the very basis of feminism, since feminism is a political movement based upon the experience of persons who are women, born female, and raised in the female sex caste." Jefferies even extends her critique to the use of "queer" theory and the deployment of "queer" activism, noting that because such projects separate sex (as a biological concept) from gender (as a sociological/cultural concept), they have produced "a queer assault on feminism" that has operated to erase lesbian feminist peoples, politics, and goals.[20]

In contestation of these positions, trans activists and scholars have critiqued cisgender feminists as bigots who exclude trans women from calls for women's rights and sociopolitical justice and who portray trans people, particularly trans women, as predatory and threatening to cis women. Transgender writers such as Julia Serano, Emi Koyama, and Bobby Noble explain that the exclusion of trans women from feminism only serves to undermine its liberatory goals, in a manner similar to the earlier failures of mainstream feminism to include and represent lesbians and women of color. Building upon the "lavender menace" debate that fractured early second-wave feminism (in which many heterosexual feminists sought to ban lesbians from the broader movement), Serano contends that the exclusion of trans women from the category of "woman" engages in the same sort of divisive politics. Serano asks readers to consider how the same arguments being used against trans women today have been used by heterosexual feminists against lesbians in the past (e.g., both have been imagined as a threat to "real" women's safety, both have been dismissed as peripheral to the mainstream feminist movement, and so on).[21] Similarly, Koyama compares the exclusion of trans women from feminism to the racial animus that has divided feminist communities from the 1970s to the present moment.[22] Noble further asserts that the critique of transgender feminists and feminism by cisgender feminists serves a project of "feminist fundamentalism" that produces a violent and forcible normalization of the category of "woman" at the expense of all trans people.[23]

Thus, from Raymond and Jeffreys to Serano, Koyama, Noble, and beyond, it is clear that tensions continue to exist between and among certain cisgender feminists and trans communities. The appearance of Tuvel's article in the context of a self-defined feminist journal is therefore not improper, but instead builds upon a longer contestation over the boundaries of feminism and the place of those who defy positions of normative existence. To imagine Tuvel's argument as blatantly antifeminist seems to require the following logic: first, that transracialism, in and of itself, constitutes a derogation of transgender identity and personhood; and second, that feminism proper desires no affiliation with such ideations. Yet if we know that some feminists have quite literally argued against the ethical viability of transgender existence, and that some transgender activists have directly lamented their marginalization and depreciation at the hands of such feminists, it would seem that the "feminist" rebuke of Tuvel is curiously counterfactual. It is therefore worth considering that the anger extended toward Tuvel's position is less about a deep concern for transgender identity and personhood and more about a larger discomfort with the politics of nonnormative embodiment and corporeal transformation.

Section III. "It's not something you can choose": Racial Authenticity and Transracial Identity

The term "transracial"—and its corollary, often used interchangeably, "transethnic"—has recently made its way into common usage on a number of internet sites, particularly the social media and blogging platform Tumblr. According to these sites, the designation "transracial" (or "transethnic") seeks to represent a type of identification in which a person rejects their assigned racial identity. This rejection typically takes place in the following fashion: a transracial person is born into a particular body, family, and culture that assigns them a racial identity they find alienating, and they instead feel that they belong to a different racial group. Thus, a transracial person might feel highly dysphoric—meaning they might experience the feeling that they are in the "wrong body" and may express the feeling that they should have different phenotypical features. Drawing on more familiar narratives of transgender dysphoria, individuals who identify as transracial describe a sense of improper embodiment that is both painful and disorienting.

Very little information exists on the transracial experience from a firstperson perspective, but what is available can be found largely in online forums. In particular, Tumblr has served as a site for anonymous postings by individuals who identify as transracial, as well as their detractors. While these postings are informal and unattributable, they nonetheless raise many of the same issues debated in academic settings. Tumblr conversations surrounding transracialism address three concerns: (1) the unprovenness of transracial identity according to scientific standards; (2) the fear that transraciality, as an identity and a concept, poses a threat to transgender persons;

and (3) consternation over the (in)ability of certain individuals to claim certain identity positions.[24] Each of these concerns deals with the question of transraciality as an authentic, or "real," identity, as can be seen in the following excerpted posts from Tumblr conversations:

> People who say others should just stop being transethnic completely miss the point that it's a real thing real people feel. It'd be like someone telling you not to be anything else you can't help—it's not something you can choose. And people are just gonna go ahead and assume you're lying or trying to get attention or something. How the fuck do you know what's going on in my head? Have brain scans conclusively proved transethnicity to be fake or some shit? The stuff I feel over that is real, even if no one believes me or tells me I'm faking or trying to appropriate stuff. It's there and it's not gonna go away by anyone telling me or any other transethnic person to "stop."[25]

> There isn't one single thing I gain by coming out as transracial. Not one thing. But I couldn't keep lying to myself about who I was on the inside. It was like a nightmare, having to live like someone I wasn't. Seeing a white face in the mirror, but knowing I was African American on the inside. It was incredibly debilitating to live like this. . . . Transracial people are here, we're real, so you'd better get used to it.[26]

> Unlike gender dysphoria, there is no biological basis for "feeling" like you are a race other than white. Unlike transsexualism, transethnicity is a phenomenon that has only been observed in young white pseudo-activists who have nothing better to do than play at being disenfranchised. Science says you're ridiculous so kindly shut the fuck up and get back to your regularly scheduled boring privileged lives.[27]

While scholarship does exist on the question of how race becomes mediated through virtual forms, the issue of transraciality *as itself a virtual phenomenon* has yet to be addressed. By this I mean to call attention to the fact that in spite of the possible existence of transracial sentiments throughout various time periods and representative media, growing public awareness of, interest in, and claims to a transracial identity are all products of a virtual era in which "anonymous" spaces allow for debates that might otherwise not find a forum. Likewise, the transformations of the self that have become enabled by the internet—that is, self-fashioning projects that exist in everything from social media sites, to dating apps, to video games—

have provided a unique site for contestations over race that cannot exist in the "real" world. As the media studies scholar Lisa Nakamura has written, while the internet might have had the potential to be a "race-free" space—insofar as it is anonymous—in practice, it became a locus for the reinstantiation of race. As Nakamura explains, the place of race in virtual practice cannot be separated from the historical moment in which the internet emerged as a mass technology, namely, its simultaneity with the "neoliberal discourse of colorblindness." Nakamura argues that the "emphasis on privacy, competition, lack of regulation, and 'nondiscrimination'" (nondiscriminatory access) touted by proponents of the internet "not only opened the door" to understanding it "as a utopian space for identity play, community building, and gift economies," but also served to "echo the language of color blindness or 'genteel racism'" that characterized 1990s political discourse.[28]

Yet even if transraciality has been facilitated by the types of anonymity and virtual realities afforded by the internet age, the possibility of racial transformation has long been the subject of other popular cultural forms. Indeed, countless stories of racial passing, alienation, and misrecognition can be found in US texts dating back to the nineteenth century, particularly in stories surrounding the "tragic mulatta" figure, including Lydia Maria Child's "The Quadroons" (1842) and "Slavery's Pleasant Homes" (1843), William Wells Brown's *Clotel* (1853), Charles W. Chesnutt's *The House behind the Cedars* (1900), Nella Larsen's *Passing* (1929), Jessie Redmon Fauset's *Plum Bun: A Novel without a Moral* (1929), Vera Caspary's *The White Girl* (1929), Fannie Hurst's *Imitation of Life* (1933), Elia Kazan's *Pinky* (1949), and Danzy Senna's *Caucasia* (1998). Narratives of passing—which typically involve a person of color passing as white—are a staple of American fiction, including works such as James Weldon Johnson's *The Autobiography of an Ex-colored Man* (1912), Colson Whitehead's *The Intuitionist* (1998), Philip Roth's *The Human Stain* (2000), Gene Luen Yang's *American Born Chinese* (2008), and Helen Oyemi's *Boy, Snow, Bird* (2015). In each of these examples, characters voice a desire to become "white"—to take on, in other words, the racial identity of those with social, political, and economic power. Thus, it may be tempting to read them as the unfortunate but logical by-product of a racist society—the result of a systemic institutional racism so invasive that it not only oppresses people socially and politically but also invades the psyche, eliciting the longing to transform from a degraded minority into a powerful majority figure.

Carrying this line of thought through becomes more difficult, however, when we consider the fact that the desire for racial transformation does not move in just one direction. And perhaps more to the point, most documented instances of transracial identity involve a white person who desires to transform into another race. This type of transformation is also a long-held theme in US popular culture, from literature, to music, to cinema. As scholars have documented, forms of white racial nostalgia, fetishization, and appropriation that long for nonwhite cultures, identities, and bodies structure the backbone of American cultural production.[29] Such narratives also describe the basis of white privilege, which proceeds through channels of invisibility, universality, and malleability. Reflecting upon the question of transraciality, the philosopher Kris Sealey explains,

> The range of agency made available to someone like Rachel Dolezal, to transition from a white to a black person, supposedly without unintended consequences, is just not the same as the range available to a black person. . . . [A] comportment that claims to be able to fully opt out of racially-constituted privilege seems bound to the privilege upon which this comportment rests.[30]

Similarly, in the *New York Times* Charles Blow describes the Dolezal controversy as

> white privilege at a spectacular level. This could not happen the other way around. . . . And because it doesn't flow both ways, there is a privilege in the ability to even perform blackness in this way. . . . A person like Rachel has the privilege to present and perform blackness because we are conditioned in America to accept those presentations [as a part of white hegemony].[31]

The critical race theorists Marquis Bey and Theodora Sakellarides further explain that "Blackness—despite its undeniable constructedness—carries a very real and lived visceral history that cannot be overlooked. . . . [T]his visceral history is sidestepped, bypassed, and cheapened when a person of racial privilege such as Dolezal attempts to disavow their privilege and thus their complicity/responsibility in that violent history."[32] Here, Bey and Sakellarides raise an issue that many note as problematic with respect to transracial identification: namely, the meaning of race as a historical category, as tied to particular social circumstances, forms of state administration, and ancestral cultures. While this argument can sometimes be understood in terms of heritage or even biological gatekeeping, Sealey explains otherwise:

> There does seem to be some core that is misrepresented (if not outright violated), in a case like Dolezal's. This "core" . . . while not genetic in the

strict sense, does unavoidably inform what it means to be (and to not be) black. . . . Said otherwise, the biology of race is really about a relationship—namely, a relationship between actual genetic ancestry (on the one hand), and the cultural and social signification of that ancestry (on the other), which then allows ancestry to mean certain things, in certain contexts, for certain groups of people. Hence, the role and predicative force of ancestry, in my racial identity, is not biological at all, but rather, social (or cultural).[33]

Nine years before the Dolezal scandal, the philosopher Cressida Heyes proposed a similar logic to explain why gender transitions must be distinguished from the possibility of racial transitions: while "sex-gender . . . is essentialized as a property of the individual's body . . . race is essentialized with reference to both the body and ancestry."[34] Rather than interpreting racial identity as reflective of phenotype, Heyes cites the legal history of the "one drop rule" for African American identification in the United States as proof of the fact that "race is taken to be *inherited* in a way that sex is not."[35] In other words, the "realness" of race—albeit as a social construct—is produced through discourses of inheritance. Gender, by contrast, is a more individualistic form of identification.

Following the Tuvel controversy in 2017, Heyes extended her argument regarding the distinctions between gender and race in relation to transgender and transracial identity, arguing that any comparison between the two was unethical:

> To compare ethically the lived experience of trans people (from a distinctly external perspective) primarily to a single example of a white person claiming to have adopted a black identity creates an equivalency that fails to recognize the history of racial appropriation, while also associating trans people with racial appropriation. We recognize and mourn that these harms will disproportionately fall upon those members of our community who continue to experience marginalization and discrimination due to racism and cisnormativity.[36]

Thus while Heyes disavows transraciality as a "real" phenomenon, she also points to an anxiety about the negative impact transracial rhetoric can have on the lives of transgender people. This concern is realized in critiques of transracialism that use transphobic rhetoric to devalue both groups. In this configuration, both forms of identification are seen as fantastical, where race (just like gender) is understood to be merely a collection of physical traits that is irreducible to a feeling or essence. This perspective builds upon the thinking of the aforementioned feminist scholar and antitransgender thinker Janice Raymond, who suggests that while it may seem easy to make a comparison between an individual who might have "always felt like a 'white trapped in a Black body,' [just] as the transsexual commonly says that he is a 'woman trapped in a male body,'" it would in fact be incorrect to do so; she notes that "there is no demand for transracial medical intervention precisely because most Blacks recognize that it is their society, not their skin, that needs changing."[37]

Thus, the comparison between gender and race in the case of trans identity falters in many ways; perhaps most importantly, it makes it difficult to see how categories function intersectionally. As Raka Ray has written with respect to the common comparisons made between Caitlyn Jenner and Rachel Dolezal,

> By allowing Jenner and Dolezal to stand in for transgender and transracial, treating Jenner as if she has only a gender and Dolezal as if she has only a race . . . [the] logics of race and gender [are kept] apart. . . . Yet, the social violence visited upon some transwomen and not others, the privilege that accrues to some transwomen and not others, have everything to do with ancestry.[38]

Likewise, C. Riley Snorton has argued that we need only to look at the precarity of Black trans lives to understand that the "category of transness is a racial narrative."[39] Snorton dates this narrative to the history of slavery, observing that "chattel persons gave rise to an understanding of gender as mutable and as an amendable form of being," while the "narrative of fugitivity" frequently "included cross-gendered modes of escape."[40] At the same time, the "color line was produced and policed by black women's reproductive capacity . . . [which] necessitates an encounter with the figure of the black maternal as a character and as the ground of nonbeing that engenders black manhood."[41] Examining the historical evolution of transgender identity and the conditional forms of societal acceptance that have accompanied transgender "celebrities" such as Christine Jorgensen (the former US Army private from New York who underwent gender-altering surgery in 1952 and became a media sensation), Snorton argues that anti-Blackness has always been a "critical paradigm" in the production of white trans identity.[42]

Similarly, Tey Meadow observes that "the social forces at work in trans 'recognition' politics may underwrite some of the most pernicious forms of racialized violence in the contemporary United States, lending themselves to projects to ossify racial categories, rather than to disrupt them."[43] This "ossification" ironically is produced through and by discourses of gender and sexual liberation. As C. Riley Snorton and Jin Haritaworn have noted, the "universalized trajectory of coming out/transition, visibility, recognition, protection, and self-actualization largely remains uninterrogated in its complicities and convergences with biomedical, racist, neoliberal, and imperialist projects."[44] Here, transness becomes subsumed within the types of ideologies and practices that are harnessed under homonationalist sentiment (as I addressed in chapter 1). In the sections that follow, I consider how the development of Latinx identity, as well as current debates surrounding its parameters, may help to unpack the meaning of transracial identity.

Section IV. "To condemn our origins and deny our hybridism": Mestizaje, Latinx Panethnicity, and Afro-Latinx Invisibility

"Latinx" is a complicated signifier. It is at once the product of a history of activism among groups of people who have genealogical ties to Latin America and, in its various incarnations—Latina/o, Latin@, Hispanic, and so on—a concept that has emerged from governmental schemes of classification. In her work on the history of "Hispanic" as a popular term (which originated in the 1960s, was concretized by the 1990s, and became used somewhat interchangeably with "Latino/a/@/x" by the 2000s), Mora asserts that ambiguity has always been central to its definition. A critical component of this ambiguity, as she points out, is the way that Latinx is technically an ethnicity but ultimately functions *as* a race. This functionality can be seen in the rhetoric of government studies that compare Latinx persons to other racial populations, and in the platforms of civil-rights-era activists, who compared the plight of Latinxs to that of African Americans in a bid for equality. Arguably, the ambiguity surrounding Latinidad has only increased with the recent appendage of the *x* to "Latin" in lieu of the *o* and *a*. Richard T. Rodríguez writes,

> In ways that I'm weary of just anyone embracing Latinx—like queer—at the expense of non-normative people and communities whose lives are constantly . . . at risk, I am vigilant in not smothering people in blanket terms for gains that have more relevance for those with the privilege to name. . . . [W]e cannot simply use Latinx without acknowledgment of its discrepant gender politics, nor can we map it on to people's lives, histories, and bodies uncritically. For if the X is to simply become something to which anyone can easily lay claim, we will need to aggressively pose the question: Why

adopt it at all if the ultimate goal is to cross out any traces of queer assertion and affirmation?[45]

Invoking a comparison to the appropriation of "queer" as a catchall for diverse sexual orientations and political positions, Rodríguez suggests a more careful attention to the ways in which universalizing categories impose upon different individuals in variable ways. But if the *x* is a fairly recent application—one that has grown out of and alongside queer discursive strategies—the idea behind Latinidad as a space and an identity position of multiplicity (whether with respect to gender, sexuality, ethnicity, or race) is not new.

Indeed, any consideration of ethnoracial identity and fluidity with respect to Latinx subjects must begin with the concept of mestizaje. In Latinx studies, and almost always in Chicanx studies, the term often represents the "racial mixture" of European and Native American peoples; sometimes, it is also applied to include intermixture between these groups and African peoples. While a full exploration of the concept is beyond the scope of this work, it is important to understand its basic principles, as well as the major debates that continue to swirl around it. In Latin American letters, mestizaje has long been considered a generative concept, providing a rich and malleable conceptual framework for thinking about the construction of ethnic, racial, and national identity. Marilyn Grace Miller describes the term as inspiring an almost cultish allegiance, even as it "has been employed in radically distinct ways," producing a "range of meanings . . . [that] is surprisingly extensive and often frustrates attempts at providing coherent contexts for its examination."[46]

While the term existed in prior eras, it was not until the turn of the century that Latin American writers began to celebrate its potentially positive connotation. Written in New York in 1891, the Cuban exile José Martí's famous essay "Nuestra América" begins this tradition by arguing that decolonization would produce an end to racism: "[There] can be no racial hatred, because there are no races. . . . The soul, equal and eternal, emanates from bodies that are diverse in form and color. Anyone who promotes and disseminates opposition or hatred among races is committing a sin against humanity."[47] Drawing upon this vision, the Mexican thinker and politician José Vasconcelos wrote *La raza cósmica* (1925), which argued that Latin America would come to produce a "cosmic race" of citizens who would usher in a utopic age:

We have four stages and the four racial trunks: the Black, the Indian, the Mongol, and the White. The latter, after organizing itself in Europe, has become the invader of the world and has considered itself destined to rule, as did each of the previous races during their time of power. It is clear that domination by the whites will also be temporary, but their mission is to serve as a bridge. The white race has brought the world to a state in which all human types and cultures will be able to fuse with each other. The civilization developed and organized in our times by the whites has set the moral and material basis for the union of all men into a fifth universal race, the fruit of all the previous ones and amelioration of everything past.[48]

Thus, for Vasconcelos, conquest and colonization are events not to be lamented but rather to be understood as an opportunity for the human races to evolve into a greater spiritual whole.

Vasconcelos also envisioned the future of Latin America in contradistinction to the United States, where racial hierarchy and segregation appeared inseparable from any future vision of the nation:

The ethnic barricading of those to the north in contrast to the much more open sympathy of those in the south is the most important factor . . . because it will be seen immediately that we belong to tomorrow, while the Anglo-Saxons are gradually becoming more a part of yesterday. The Yankees will end up building the last great empire of a single race, the final empire of White supremacy. Meanwhile, we will continue to suffer the vast chaos of an ethnic stock in formation, contaminated by the fermentation of all types, but secure the avatar into a better race. . . . What is going to emerge out there is the definitive race, the synthetical race, the integral race, made up of the genius and the blood of all peoples and, for that reason, more capable of true brotherhood and of a truly universal vision.[49]

In Vasconcelos's estimation, the concept of mestizaje was inseparable from a progressive view of the future, in which a people made strong by mixture and transcultural exchange would come to supersede those who clung to antiquated visions of white supremacy. Yet even within this optimistic vision, Vasconcelos demonstrated that the ideology of mestizaje need not preclude the reality of racism. Instead, *La raza cósmica* clearly engages with racial prejudice, including rhetoric surrounding the purportedly displeasing aspects of Black people's appearances and the "savagery" of pre-Christian Indigenous peoples. (Later on, he would recant the entirety of the text's premise as a youthful folly drawn from his "adolescence in the tropics.")[50]

Scholars such as Rafael Pérez-Torres and María Josefina Saldaña-Portillo have demonstrated how the figuration of mestizaje can also be used as a means of racialized denial, a way of disavowing some forms of racial identity by subsuming them under an unstable narrative category. As Pérez-Torres writes, within Mexican contexts, mestizaje has produced an ideological "flight from the Indian," whereas in Chicanx contexts, it has operated as a "race *toward* the Indian."[51] In the former circumstance, the desire to escape racist rhetoric that characterizes Indigenous peoples as archaic and primitive is recast within romanticized terms, producing a historical trajectory that imagines Indigeneity as part of a national, imperial past and obscures its present existence. In the latter circumstance, mestizaje has been reshaped to fit the boundaries of ideological necessity in which a romanticized rendering of a heroic Indigenous past is reinvigorated—not only to justify land claims but also to condense the messy mix of political disenfranchisement, cultural alienation, and economic oppression surrounding Chicanx communities into a simplified narrative of "Indigenous resistance" to imperialist policy.[52]

Gender and sexuality have also been central to the construction of mestizaje, largely as expressed through Mexican mythology surrounding the parentage of mestizo people, which conjures the rape of an Indigenous woman named Malintzin Tenepal (known as "La Malinche") by the Spanish conqueror Hernán Cortés. Within Latin American letters, the story of La Malinche and Cortés is best known through the narrative provided in Octavio Paz's essay *The Labyrinth of Solitude* (1950), which delineates Mexican national identity through the narratives of geopolitical and sexual conquest. In this essay, Paz writes that Mexican identity is animated by a narrative of reproduction through imperially sanctioned sexual violation, in which an Indigenous woman is raped by a white colonist and thereby produces a mestizo child. This in turn produces a fundamental discomfort with the colonial "father"—who is white, remote, brutal, and so on—as well as the Indigenous "mother," who becomes known as *la chingada*, or she who is raped, violated, and contaminated. As inheritors of these traumatic origins, Paz characterizes Mexicans as

> desir[ing] to live closed off from the outside world and, above all, from the past . . . to condemn our origins and deny our hybridism. . . . The Mexican does not want to be either an Indian or a Spaniard. Nor does he want to be descended from them. He denies them. And he does not affirm himself as a mixture, but rather as an abstraction: he is a man. He becomes the son of Nothingness. His beginnings are in his own self.[53]

As Miller observes, because of these fraught origins, the mestizo often comes to stand as the "embodiment of betrayal, deception, craftiness, opportunism, and moral degradation."[54] These negative attributes are often correlated with the maternal figure of La Malinche, whose sexual violation is imagined as a form of treachery: "She does not resist violence, but is an inert heap of bones, blood, and dust."[55]

Even still, the concept of mestizaje has also been taken up by later scholars and activists in more radical ways. As Sandra K. Soto observes, Chicana authors have often produced "writing that recuperates Malinche ('the native woman') from a feminist and sex-positive vantage point." In doing so, "Chicana feminists have refashioned the meaning of *mestizaje*; while it still connotes racial hybridity, it now privileges a deeply indigenous and feminine ethos and always manifests itself in the female embodied form."[56] Gloria Anzaldúa's *Borderlands / La Frontera* (1987) stands as the epitome of this reformulation. In this text, Anzaldúa proposes the notion of *new mestiza* consciousness, which foregrounds plurality, contradiction, and ambiguity, in order to move away from static binaries and rigid norms. For Anzaldúa, the new mestiza is a product of existing in literal and symbolic borderlands, "*una herida abierta* where the Third World grates against the First and bleeds":

> As a *mestiza* I have no country, my homeland cast me out; yet all countries
> are mine because I am every woman's sister or potential lover. (As a les-
> bian I have no race, my own people disclaim me; but I am all races because
> there is the queer of me in all races.) I am cultureless because, as a feminist,
> I challenge the collective cultural/religious male-derived benefits of Indo-
> Hispanics and Anglos; yet I am cultured because I am participating in the
> creation of yet another culture, a new story to explain the world and our
> participation in it, a new value system with images and symbols that con-
> nect us to each other and to the planet. *Soy un amasamiento*, I am an act of
> kneading, of uniting and joining that not only has produced both a creature
> of darkness and a creature of light, but also a creature that questions the
> definitions of light and dark and gives them new meanings.[57]

As Soto explains, the flexibility and ambiguity at the heart of Anzaldúa's theorization has "appeal[ed] to poststructuralist feminist thinkers" for its radical potentiality, while simultaneously and unintentionally serving to collapse Indigenous and Chicana positionalities. In doing so, Anzaldúa produces a "racial category" that is "paradoxically both hybrid and fundamentally indigenous."[58]

Other scholars have pointed to additional difficulties surrounding the positive use of "mestizaje" by Latinx writers. Hiram Pérez notes that the term often eclipses the presence of African peoples and heritage. Addressing Martí's "Nuestra América," Pérez calls attention to Martí's use of "mestizo" even when "the word 'mulatto' would much more accurately describe the history of race mixture in Cuba and the racial demographics of the island."[59] In other words, even though colloquially "mestizaje" may be used to signal racial mixtures that include persons of African descent and histories of African slavery across the Americas, it is striking that "mulatez" is not used in a similar capacity. Writing about the distinctions and connections between the terms, Alicia Arrizón asserts that both "mestizaje" and "mulatez" are best

> understood as figures of cultural hybridization, countering the normative, reductive representations of "authentic" racial and cultural identities. . . . In contrast to the subjectivity reflected in the term *mestizaje*, which refers to the blending of indigenous and the Hispanic worlds (or other European cultures), in the Latin American cultural context, *mulatez* is the marker of the black-hybrid body.[60]

While Arrizón sometimes opts to use the terms interchangeably, she also draws out a critical specificity present in "mulatez" through the history of African slavery. As she explains, the term "mulatto" is "derived from the Latin *mulus*, meaning mule," and has been used across the Americas since the inception of the transatlantic slave trade. Applied in this way, the term conjures a very particular tactic of dehumanization and commodification used against persons of African descent. (Nonetheless, Arrizón is careful to explain that the slave trade and the production of mulatez cannot be understood in isolation from the forces of colonization that also generated the concept of mestizaje.)[61]

At the same time, the relative celebration of the term "mestizaje" when compared to "mulatez" across the field of Latinx writing mirrors a deeper problem involving the marginalization of Blackness and Afro-Latinx subjects. Caught between the invisibilizing pressures of mainstream white US culture on the one hand and normative Latinx culture on the other, Afro-Latinx histories and identities are often erased, mishandled, or deemed inauthentic. As Tanya Kateri Hernández has observed,

> Many Latino Studies scholars have thus far been content to focus on the mestizaje pride without thoroughly interrogating the subtext of White supremacy. . . . [I]f the mestizaje race relations mindset were indeed such an

enlightened space one would expect race relations with Afro-Latino/as and Anglo-Blacks in the United States to embody the fantasy of racial democracy so often touted in Latin American countries.[62]

Hernández further asserts that mestizaje, "upon being transported to the United States by Latino/as . . . becomes a pathway to assimilation" that moves away from Blackness toward whiteness.[63] Isabel Molina-Guzmán writes that this conceptualization of Latinidad is also enforced by the mainstream media, in which Latinxs are racialized "as brown in relation to whiteness and blackness. . . . [They are] not quite white but rarely black, instead occupying a panethnic identity space of racially ambiguous . . . brownness."[64] For these reasons, Keara Goin has proposed the term "marginal Latinidad" to refer to "the positioning of Afro-Latino subjectivity as geographically marginal to the 'heartland' of America," where Blackness is perceived to "taint" "normalized or generic Latino subjectivity."[65]

Similarly, in her short graphic work *Baina Colonial* (2016), Zahira Kelly addresses the paradoxical ties of identifying as Afro-Latina. Reflecting upon how quickly identity politics can shift, she documents how claiming African ancestry does not necessarily promote recognition of Afro-Latinx subjects, as can be seen in figures 4.3a–d. Here, Kelly demonstrates how discourses of color blindness continually serve to erase the presence of Afro-Latinx subjects, who remain politically and culturally underrepresented and disproportionately disenfranchised in both Latin American and US contexts. As Kelly explains elsewhere, "A lot of people use the terms 'yo soy Afro Latino, yo soy Afro Latina,' but they negate their Blackness. . . . [People] claim the terms but don't want to accept the fact that they're Black."[66] Thus, Kelly states, "Afro-Latinx has now been co-opted by Latin Americans who do not get read as Black in daily life. To where they're telling visibly Black Latinas they are too Black to be Afro-Latina. Somehow a term for Black pride became colorist and anti-Black."[67] At the same time, Kelly notes, some people refuse to acknowledge the very existence of Afro-Latinx people:

> It's 2017 and just like a week ago somebody tweeted that Afro-Latina is a thing that Twitter made up a year ago, so you know, like people debate that we exist . . . like we're mythical or something. . . . So it's a never-ending battle—when you try to educate, they fight you back, like no, not really, you're not really here. So, are you talking to a hologram? It's actually a really advanced AI that's tweeting from my account, like I'm just a bot, I'm just a hologram.[68]

Figure 4.3a–d. Zahira Kelly, *Baina Colonial*, vol. 1, 2016. © Zahira Kelly.

As the Afro-Dominican author Ana M. Lara explains, Afro-Latinxs are "so invisibilized as citizens that we don't even appear as a sector in statistical data, because the data is not segregated by ethnic composition, which creates the assumption of the inexistence of race."[69] Suzanne Oboler and Anani Dzidzienyo similarly observe,

> Whether in official documents or academic studies, the racial/color dimension is consistently neglected, such that many . . . do not take seriously . . . that Latina/os "can be of any race." . . . This has deprived us of an opportunity to further unravel the changing meanings of Blackness in US politics and sociocultural relations. . . . In the heavily race-conscious US context, the Afro-Latina/o category (even though it usually goes unofficially recog-

nized) points to the existence of often-overlooked discrepancies not only of national origin, social status, and language, but also of race and color, which can deeply differentiate . . . daily experiences and life chances.[70]

Frances Negrón-Muntaner has also called attention to the invisibility of Afro-Latinx identity through her analysis of multicultural Barbie dolls. Describing the controversy that ensued over the introduction of a Puerto Rican Barbie in 1997, Negrón-Muntaner explains how the doll immediately frustrated consumers. First, it was seen as too "white" because of its skin tone and its origin story printed on the back of the box, which stated "that the island was discovered by Columbus . . . connot[ing] that all Puerto Ricans are fundamentally Europeans."[71] The doll's hair was also a source of contention: those residing on the island commended the doll's straight, black hair, while Puerto Ricans residing on the mainland found the texture inauthentic, even though they simultaneously decried the possibility of the doll having "bad hair." Ironically, as Negrón-Muntaner writes, changes to the doll's skin color and hair to move away from a white aesthetic would result in a Barbie that would "not have looked much different from Black (African American) Barbie, thus undermining the notion of essential differences between both groups, and any modest racial capital that light-skinned Puerto Ricans may wish to claim in the colonial metropolis."[72] For those debating the doll's authenticity, then, a Black Puerto Rican Barbie was an impossibility for two reasons: because it could not stand as representative of all Puerto Ricans, owing to colorist prejudice and deeply held attitudes surrounding racial authenticity, and because there was no obvious way to visually signal an Afro-Latina identity without having the doll appear *as* African American, thereby erasing the possibility of Afro-Latina identity and personhood.

Taken together, these perspectives—Kelly's description of herself as a "hologram," Lara's assessment of Afro-Latinxs as an "inexistent" demographic category, and Negrón-Muntaner's explanation of the impossibility of an Afro-Latina Barbie doll—produce a troubling picture that suggests a profound marginalization of Afro-Latinx identities and peoples. In the sections that follow, I consider how the marginalization of Afro-Latinx people intersects with broader issues of anti-Black racism and colorism in two public controversies surrounding Latinx identity and Blackness. In doing so, I consider how the category of Latinx—whether viewed through the lens of panethnicity (as constructed through state-sponsored regimens and activist-based forms of strategic essentialism) or the lens of Latinx-based cultural production (as conceived of through theorizations of mestizaje)—has produced an ambiguous conceptual space critical to, but unacknowledged by, those who claim a transracial identity. More importantly, I identify how the insufficiency of Latinx as a category for representing all Latinx persons is produced by the very same logics of fungibility and universality that allow for the appropriation of transgender transformation for transracial purposes.

Section V. "They're imposters": Major League Baseball and the Displacement of African American Players

In March 2010, the professional baseball player Torii Hunter found himself at the center of controversy after he said the following in a press interview:

> Fans look down from their seats onto the baseball field, see dark-colored skin and might assume they are African-American players. But increasingly, the players instead hail from the Dominican Republic, Puerto Rico, or Venezuela. People see dark faces out there, and the perception is that they're African-American. . . . They're not us. They're imposters. Even people I know come up and say, "Hey, what color is Vladimir Guerrero? Is he a black player?" I say, "Come on, he's Dominican. He's not black." As African-American players, we have a theory that baseball can go get an imitator and pass them off as us. . . . It's like they had to get some kind of dark faces, so they go to the Dominican [Republic] or Venezuela because you can get them cheaper. It's like, "Why should I get this kid from the South Side of Chicago and have Scott Boras represent him and pay him $5 million when you can get a Dominican guy for a bag of chips?" I'm telling you, it's sad.[73]

Immediately condemned as racist, Hunter expressed shock and dismay. In a follow-up interview, he explained, "What I meant was they're not black players; they're Latin American players. There is a difference culturally. But on the field, we're all brothers, no matter where we come from, and that's something I've always taken pride in: treating everybody the same. . . . Where [a person] was born and raised makes no difference."[74] Hunter felt that his remarks had been mischaracterized, though he admitted to regretting his "choice" of the word "imposter." "I'm not going to apologize," he stated. "I told the truth. . . . It ["imposter"] wasn't a racist word. I can't believe that people take that as racism. Maybe it was the wrong word, but I do too much in the community to make this one word ruin anything."[75]

Those who voiced support for Hunter noted that he had long been supportive of fellow players of all backgrounds and was known for his philanthropy in underprivileged communities. For example, in 2009, Hunter received the Branch Rickey Award for his work with children at his Torii Hunter Project, a program that aims "to increase the opportunities for America's youth to enjoy the game of baseball in inner cities and beyond, and to provide an equal playing field for everyone, regardless of race, ethnicity, and skill level."[76] Former Major League Baseball (MLB) star Reggie Jackson, identified in the press as "an African American who is also of Latino heritage," suggested that Hunter's comments were taken too harshly, even if they were misguided. "If you say minority, I don't separate it as African-American, Latin American or Asian," he explained. "There are a lot of minorities here, man. There's an opportunity for all of us."[77]

By contrast, Hunter's detractors fell into two camps: those who found his comments prejudiced and injurious to foreign-born players, and those who found his comments unintelligent and incorrect. Those in the latter camp criticized Hunter's "misunderstanding" of baseball's economics. White Sox manager Ozzie Guillén, who originally hails from Venezuela, was widely quoted as "laughing" at Hunter's comments. Guillén said that Hunter could not be more incorrect in his estimation of the league's misuse of Latin American players. Guillén recalled, "I remember in my time, one scout goes [to Venezuela and] 30 players show up. Now 30 scouts go there and one player shows up."[78] Citing a number of multimillion-dollar contracts held by new Latin American recruits, he explained,

> In our country, we play baseball. That's no choice. Here [in the US] you can play basketball, you can be another athlete, you can do so many things when you have the opportunity. And that's why there's not many [African American] players out there. . . . I keep saying a lot of times, in ten more years American people are going to need a visa to play this game because we're going to take over. We're going to.[79]

While the Associated Press presumably sought Guillén's opinion as an MLB coach and a person of Latin American descent, many sports commentators came to similar conclusions. One explained that Hunter's remarks were "evidence that the culture of baseball is still hopelessly backward on matters of race" and that they served as "proof that ballplayers aren't entirely clear on the business of the game":

> Not to say that baseball hasn't richly earned Torii Hunter's paranoia, but the man gets so lost inside his own crackpottery that he fails to see which way the exploitation actually runs. . . . Real Black Person Torii Hunter

made $200,000 in his first full season in the majors. Meanwhile, [Cuban-born] Aroldis Chapman is in the first year of a six-year, $30.25 million contract (with a $16.25 million signing bonus)—money that adds up to many, many, many bags of chips, all for an imitation black person.[80]

Likewise, another sports reporter explained that while

U.S.-born blacks are subject to the draft and can be paid peanuts for years[,] Dominican or Venezuelan players get big signing bonuses. . . . Hunter's comments speak to our nation's profound immaturity when it comes to race. A mindset that makes rigid and often artificial census categories like "black" and "Hispanic" take on much more significance than is warranted and causes us to lose sight of what's really important. . . . The big picture: baseball is a truly international, multi-ethnic game in ways that, say, American football will never be, and that if there's a meritocracy anywhere in this country, it's in professional sports.[81]

In a similar vein, former MLB player Tony Menéndez lamented,

We are in the 2010s, and, for the good sake of baseball, stop the differentiation of whites, African-American, and Latinos. Major league baseball must . . . understand more than ever it is an international game and there should not be any differentiation of colors. If you know the Latino Angels players . . . there are some from the lightest . . . to the darkest . . . skins. Latinos are brothers no matter their color.[82]

In these estimations, Hunter's remarks are understood as outdated, "hopelessly backward," "crackpot," "immature," and missing "the big picture"— or, as one blog put it, "Torii Hunter's stupidity is not news" (comments that come with their own racial charge). The commentators gloss over the potentially racist content of Hunter's interview as a matter of misunderstanding that is symptomatic of broader racial misunderstandings held by specific people (Hunter) and within specific industries (baseball and professional sports). The solution posed to Hunter's remarks is thus a familiar multicultural paradigm: to rise above it, to progress beyond it, or to just get over it.

By contrast, criticism of Hunter that focused on the racial content of his remarks, namely his use of the term "imposters," expressed outrage at Hunter's prejudicial language and queried why some of the league's players weren't "Black enough" for him. Many articles featured a side-by-side photograph of Hunter and Guerrero in the same uniform, presumably to illustrate the fallacy of Hunter's claims (fig. 4.4). In these images, Hunter's and Guerrero's skin tones are shown to be similar, with many observing that in an earlier era, both men would have been required to play for the so-called Negro leagues and would have been ineligible to join the MLB.[83] Similarly, Menéndez railed against the double standard that seemed to motivate Hunter's apologists:

> I really would like to know if, during a similar interview, a Latino player in a similar context would have said the word "Negro" before calling such people "imposters" in the majors. I bet the whole media would have exploded on it. If it would have been a Dominican Republic or Venezuelan player, no matter his skin color, people would have asked immediately for his deportation. . . . Puerto Rican players cannot be deported as the island is a United States territory, but they would have felt the wrath all season long. . . . There would have been no pardon no matter what they would have said later, like they were misquoted because of their poor English. . . . Hunter should . . . start apologizing.[84]

While Menéndez made an important point about the way that immigrants, as well as Latinx US citizens, are held to higher standards of patriotism than "average" Americans, he also raised the stakes of Hunter's remarks. Nowhere in the original interview does Hunter use an outdated racial pejorative to refer to persons of Latin American descent; indeed, there was no corollary in Hunter's remarks to the word "Negro" invoked by Menéndez. Arguably, my highlighting his use of this term moves contrary to the spirit of his remarks. But there is also something interesting and significant in the introduction of this term in this context; there is a sense that for Menéndez, too, all persons of darker "skin color" do not comprise the same racial categorization.

Further, while many critics suggested that Hunter "owed an apology to Latinos," there was surprisingly little outcry from Latin American/Latinx MLB players and Latin American/Latinx commentators. While this absence may speak to an issue of internal racism (the unwillingness of many Latin Americans and Latinxs to be associated with Blackness, a matter addressed later in the chapter), it also signals a broader ambiguity surrounding the overlap or discontinuity between Latin American–based and US-based racial categorizations. This ambiguity is ultimately cultivated by the industry of baseball, which claims a very particular racial origins story that follows a path of segregation and integration. Yet as the historian Adrian Burgos Jr. has written, "One of baseball's long-held myths [is] that the zenith of African American participation in baseball was 28 percent in 1975," following the

Figure 4.4.
Los Angeles Angels
teammates Torii
Hunter and Vladimir
Guerrero, ca. 2010.

decline of the Negro leagues and the desegregation of MLB. Instead, however, this number always included players who would by most standards be considered Black *and* Latinx, "hid[ing] from plain sight the active participation of Latinos both in the years of pioneering integration and in the decades that followed." In prior years, "the overwhelming majority of [Latin American immigrants] who ventured North to play professionally in the United States did so by performing in the black baseball circuit where over 240 Latinos [US and foreign-born] participated. Conversely . . . 53 Latinos appeared in the majors," all of whom were considered to be white passing.[85] (In the earliest years of MLB, the first Latino players, Armando Marsans and Rafael Almeida from Cuba, were introduced in 1911 as "descendants of a noble Spanish race, both of no ignoble African blood . . . two of the purest bars of Castillian soap that ever floated these shores.")[86] For Burgos, "[in] discounting the status as fellow blacks of those from Latin America, the history of how profoundly the color line affected Latinos, especially black Latinos, is minimized," while also covering over "the choices the MLB has made in pursuing Latin American talent after it had dismantled the black baseball infrastructure that had been established and sustained by the Negro Leagues."[87] Jennifer Domino Rudolph explains similarly that baseball "casts Afro-Caribbean players via narratives of immigration, and less often blackness."[88]

Other critics writing about the Hunter controversy noted that while he may have been incorrect in his estimation of the financial inequities in the game, and while his use of the term "imposter" was clearly inappropriate, he was not incorrect in observing the trend in MLB recruiting abroad. Those who wrote about the incident in relation to the history of baseball often naturalized the outsourcing of US baseball as part of a broader narrative of deindustrialization. Some suggested that unlike other sports, baseball's "ethnic mix tends to reflect the underclass at any given moment," which in the present moment "isn't necessarily domestic but can reside beyond borders. . . . The game's makeup reflects as much those who need to play baseball as those who want to play."[89] Others observed that inarguably, "both black and white players are being replaced by Latinos. Now, some of these Latinos are Americans, but many of them are immigrants who were groomed in training camps in their home countries." It was pointed out that even if notable superstars from Latin America were given multimillion-dollar signing packages, many others were signed early on as a "cheap substitute" for US-born players in the MLB amateur draft.[90]

Statistics charting MLB demographics beginning in the early 1990s—the period generally associated with the lamentable "decline" in numbers of Black baseball players—reveal that both Black and white participation has steadily decreased (fig. 4.5a–b). (Importantly, however, this has meant a decline from 18 percent to 10 percent for Black players, and from 68 percent to 60 percent for white players, who still form a clear majority of the league; more recent statistics suggest that 8 percent of the league's players are US-born African Americans and 27 percent are foreign-born players, largely from Latin American nations.)[91] Bearing out Burgos's claim that Afro-Latinos have consistently participated in the league, the statistics for players identifying as "African American and Latino" have stayed relatively steady. This in turn provides an important context for reading the dramatic increase in participants identified as Latinos: namely, that these players must be white identified. In other words, while Hunter's comments identify Afro-Latinos as "imposter" replacements that the league all too readily—and increasingly—uses to fill spots that might otherwise have gone to US-born Black players, the category of players that has risen in direct proportionality to US-born Black player decline is *white* Latinos. What this means on some level is that Hunter is in fact correct: when the MLB advertises itself as an organization committed to the advancement of African American players, it is in fact padding these numbers with a supplemental group—"African American and Latino players"—who might not be US born and who might racially identify as white. Meanwhile, Afro-Latinx players are blamed for the league's increase in outsourced recruiting efforts, when numerically, these efforts have pulled in a greater number and percentage of white Latinx players.

This bait and switch is significant beyond the parameters of league publicity. Indeed, when considering the decline of Black participation in MLB, it is also important to understand the factors that produce such a decline as

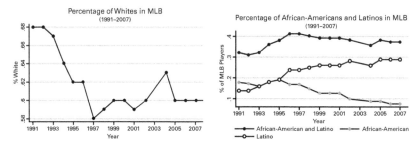

Figure 4.5a-b. (a) Percentage of "white" players in Major League Baseball, 1991–2007; (b) percentage of "African American" and Latino players in Major League Baseball, 1991–2007. Institute for Diversity and Ethics in Sport, 2008.

well as its effect on sporting culture, including its impact on preprofessional baseball leagues, ranging from grade school to college programming. As the journalist Deron Snyder explains, "Black kids have fallen away from baseball at an accelerated rate during the past 30 years. Basketball offered a quicker path to success—no spending several years in the minor leagues—and football grew to become the nation's most popular sport. Besides, baseball is expensive, hard to organize and requires more extensive groundskeeping."[92] In his own narrative of finding baseball, Hunter describes similar issues:

> I was a football player as a kid. Football was my life where I grew up. But people like Scipio Spinks, who pitched in the major leagues and saw me play, and my grandfather were able to convince me that I could have a long career in baseball and not tear up my body. I am grateful I listened to them and followed this path. Now I'm dedicated to spreading the word to other young kids.[93]

In this blog post, written in the midst of the controversy surrounding his "imposters" interview, Hunter explains why baseball is so important for African American youths in particular. As I addressed in the previous chapter, Hunter is correct in his estimations that baseball is a "better" sport for athletes than football—providing longer careers, more stable economic prospects, and the benefit of not "tearing up" one's body.[94]

Thus, while I have no interest in justifying Hunter's word choice or its potentially negative impact on Afro-Latinxs, it is nonetheless important to think through the relationship between the prospects available to young US-born Black athletes and the intentional recruitment of foreign-born athletes who read as "Black" in the US context but whose identity is far more complicated in an international context. Further, it is striking that although Hunter was quoted as including other players in his remarks ("As African American players, we have a theory that . . ."), reporters did not follow up on who these other "African American players" were who might or might not have agreed with him, nor was it even a topic of discussion that Hunter implied his sentiments were widely held. It is also important to note that his use of the terms "imposter" and "imitator" were treated transparently: no one even suggested the possibility that he was attempting to signal a racialized and racist strategy mobilized by the MLB's recruitment pattern. Instead, the conversation circled around Hunter as the single source of racist remarks. Taking Hunter seriously would thus require a greater structural critique of the MLB and of race in US sports more broadly.[95]

At the same time, even as many have attributed the decline in African American participation in baseball to the celebrity cultures of basketball and football, it is also true that these other sports have seen no real change in their racial composition during the period purportedly marked by a Black "exodus" from baseball.[96] What does this mean? On the one hand, it confirms Burgos's understanding of the incorrect mythology surrounding African American participation in the MLB, which has always reflected an inflated estimate of African American participation. During the post-segregation era, the use value of this inflation was clear: to reflect well on the MLB's integration efforts. During the current era, this inflation serves a similar purpose, while also serving to mystify the steady decline of African American participation.

On the other hand, it also suggests that the opportunities for young African American athletes are not as great as they are often imagined to be, framed in the popular narrative of American sports as a site of true meritocracy. Hunter's reading of Afro-Latino players as "imposters" is therefore significant not because of what it may mean about his own personal racial politics (or those of his fellow players, whom he claims share his opinions, if not linguistic choices) but rather because of what it means for the political use value of Afro-Latinx players for the MLB and, more broadly, for the political use value of Afro-Latinxs for US racial politics.

Section VI: "Things are rarely black or white": The Trouble with Sammy Sosa's Skin

In one commentary about the Torii Hunter debacle, Daniel Cubias connected Hunter's misstep to rumors only a year earlier, in 2009, that the veteran MLB player Sammy Sosa had been whitening his skin:

I may owe Sammy Sosa an apology. In a recent post, I wrote about Sosa's apparent use of a skin product designed to make him appear whiter. I wondered if the baseball great's light skin was a capitulation to the colonizer mentality. . . . As we know, Hispanics can be of any race or skin color. I myself am a light brown. Sosa, a Dominican, is obviously a dark-skinned Latino. Many people have wondered if he is trying to renounce his Hispanic and/or black status. As it turns out, maybe Sosa isn't to blame if he wants to be white. Apparently, some of the man's fellow players think that he is not really black in the first place.[97]

Reflecting on Hunter's description of Guerrero as "Dominican . . . not black" and on the photographs that accompanied the media stories (see fig. 4.4), Cubias further writes, "I have no idea if Guerrero considers himself black. Perhaps he answers, 'Hispanic' or 'Dominican' or 'human' or 'right-handed slugger' when asked about his status. But he's certainly within his rights to say, 'black' or 'black Latino.' In the picture below, Hunter is on the left. Guerrero is on the right. *One of them is positively not black.*"[98] Cubias's sarcastic commentary raises several important points. He illustrates how the categories of "Black" and "Latino" are understood at times to converge and at others to be mutually exclusive. His words also demonstrate that even if Hunter's questioning of Guerrero's Blackness was politically incorrect, certainly the query would be impossible to clearly answer.

And then there is Sammy Sosa, whose appearance has changed dramatically over the past ten years. To this point, progressive typologies of his face can be found across the internet (fig. 4.6). As the journalist Yesha Callahan observes, "Currently there are 2,217 photos of Sosa in Getty Images. And if you look at the photos from the last couple of years, you can watch Sosa turn into a 'white' man with a couple of page clicks."[99] Another media outlet noted that he "could [now] easily be mistaken for a white man. . . . Sosa is almost unrecognizable."[100] Speculation surrounding Sosa's skin color began after he appeared at the Latin Grammys in 2009 wearing green contact lenses.[101] Shortly thereafter, he gave an interview on the news program *Primer Impacto*, which airs on the US-based Spanish-language network Univision (available in the US and Mexico), explaining,

It's a bleaching cream that I apply before going to bed and [it] whitens my skin tone. . . . It's a cream I have, that I use to soften [my skin], but [it] has bleached me some. I'm not a racist, I live my life happily. . . . What happened was that I had been using the cream for a long time and that, combined with the bright TV lights, made my face look whiter than it really is.[102]

Figure 4.6. Progression of images of Sammy Sosa circulated on Reddit.

Sosa's description was confusing. He seemed to admit to using a skin-lightening product while also saying that his skin tone might have been a side effect of a moisturizer and bright television lighting. Nonetheless, the 2009 interview remains the only time Sosa has ever publicly addressed this issue and has therefore been quoted ad nauseam across media outlets.

Since that time, scathing critiques of Sosa's appearance have popped up throughout social media, where he has garnered comparisons to Michael Jackson, as well as a wide variety of inanimate objects and cartoon characters, including the Pink Panther, Pepto Bismol, a boneless chicken breast, the "thing under a scab," "chewed-up bubble gum," a pink crayon, Princess Poppy (from the 2016 animated *Trolls* movie), an "unwrapped pink starburst," and "Neapolitan ice cream" (which progresses from chocolate to vanilla to strawberry).[103] In 2018, after Sosa was photographed wearing western attire for his wife's "cowboy-themed birthday party," Twitter users joked that he looked like a "Norteño singer" (a singer of regional music from northern Mexico) or a "*Toy Story* character" (from the Disney film franchise, which features a comical [white] talking cowboy action figure).[104] These criticisms imagine Sosa's racial presentation as a spectacle comparable to fictionalized entertainment figures, none of which are properly "Black," and one of which is not even human.

Many social media posts and sports news outlets remarked upon Sosa's appearance as unbelievable, or even unreal. Reposting tweets related to one of Sosa's interviews on ESPN in 2017, NBC Sports described how the "internet [was] freaking out" over Sosa's looks. One of the tweets featured side-by-side images of Sosa, one from the 1990s and one from 2017, with accompanying commentary (fig. 4.7). The tweet read, "They need to do a #30for30 [the ESPN documentary series] on Sammy Sosa and not even talk about baseball. What if I told you that this guy . . . was also *this* guy."[105] Similarly, the sports section of the *Chicago Tribune* described Sosa's face as "roughly

50 shades lighter than it appeared during his playing days." The commentator then joked,

> A recent Comcast SportsNet [CSN] poll asked viewers whether the Cubs should ask Sammy Sosa to return next season. The choices:
>
> A. Yes, he's an all-time great
> B. Yes if he admits to cheating
> C. No way
>
> Missing was D: Only if he tells what the heck is happening to his face. . . . As for the CSN poll, the electorate appears split. With His Samminess, things are rarely black and white. [106]

In these and other media assaults, Sosa's race is framed as both a farce and a nonreality. And yet, on some level, it is obvious that "this guy" *is* "also this guy" and, moreover, that everyone actually knows "what the heck . . . happen[ed] to his face." In other words, no one is actually questioning whether both images portray Sosa, or whether he has been abducted and replaced by a doppelganger; instead, it is obvious that all of the images portray the same man, and that he clearly used some technique to alter his skin color.

At the same time, however, the requirement that Sosa verify his identity, his skin tone, and his relationship to both suggests a form of racial

Figure 4.7. Twitter post about Sammy Sosa, reposted by the NBC Sports account, 2017.

disciplining that assumes three things: (1) that racial identity is fixed and undeniable; (2) that there is something "wrong"—odd, incorrect, unreal, inauthentic—about the transformation of his complexion; and (3) that such a transformation necessarily casts aspersions on Sosa's character and mental stability.[107] These kinds of discourses exist as an extension of the long-held expectation that people of color must in some way "prove" the veracity and authenticity of their racial identity. As Simone Browne has documented, the continual burden placed upon Black people to self-illuminate—what she calls "black luminosity"—conscripts them in the process of their own panoptic surveillance.[108] Relatedly, Natasha Howard has noted how African Americans and Afro-Latin Americans are often perceived to be "inauthentic" subjects who are "viewed as culturally deficient" because their "cultural heritage is thought to be simply an outcome of enslavement—making it relatively new."[109]

Perhaps because of the obvious racism implied by the critique of Sosa's appearance, a few commentators were more sympathetic to his story. Understanding Sosa as a "victim of [Latin American] colorism," some connected his changing skin tone to the geopolitics of race, noting that he was born and raised in the Dominican Republic, where "dark-skinned [people] are urged to marry light . . . so their children don't inherit their complexion, a practice known as *mejorar la raza* or *blanqueamiento*, that can be traced to histories of European colonialism."[110] (Perhaps it was meaningful, then, that the only explanatory statement he ever gave regarding the change in his skin color was performed in Spanish on a Spanish-language television show.) In response to queries from US press agents, Sosa has continually sidestepped the issue. When questioned about it during a 2018 interview with *People* magazine, he responded, "Look at what I am today. This is my life, and I don't take garbage from nobody. I do whatever I want." *People* then attempted to get a clearer answer from his son, Sammy Sosa Jr., who also responded in similarly indirect terms: "It doesn't affect him, but I'm sure he feels a certain way. . . . Like, 'Man, I gave so many years and so much hard work for you guys, and now you want to undermine all that because of some decisions I'm making—some personal decisions that don't affect you all?'"[111]

Other press stories that mention Sosa's earlier confession on *Primer Impacto* continually link the use of skin lightening creams to non-US contexts. Writers report on how "skin whitening is a booming business in countries where lighter skin tones are hailed as a beauty must-have sparked by years of colorism, racism, and ideals of lighter complexions being more attractive."[112] Afflicted areas are cited as western Africa and South Africa, where "billboard ads [are] tagged with ways for women to achieve 'perfect white' skin";

Asia, where "the skin whitening industry is worth over $13 billion . . . [and] historically, milky white skin . . . has been a symbol of nobility, wealth, and an aristocratic lifestyle";[113] the African diaspora more broadly;[114] India;[115] Latin America in general; and the Dominican Republic specifically, where "people are overwhelmingly black: 90 percent have African ancestry. Yet only 11 percent identify themselves as black."[116] Writing about Sammy Sosa's birthplace, one commentator noted,

> The Dominican Republic is a nation whose hairdressers are known for their hair-straightening prowess and most Dominican women get their hair straightened. Although dark folks are the overwhelming majority, black skin, wide noses, and "pelo malo" (bad hair) do not fit the standard of beauty. So, hair relaxers and skin whiteners are in, and people will call themselves a number of things, such as Indian, burned Indian, Moreno and cinnamon—anything but negro (the Spanish word), or black. This is what years of submerging your culture will do.[117]

Although a few media reports mention previous controversies surrounding skin whitening among US-based celebrities of color (including Michael Jackson, Nicki Minaj, and Azealia Banks), none of the writing concerning Sosa's skin color attributes it to US-based racism or acknowledges the prevalence of skin whitening in the US context. Instead, the desire and means to lighten one's skin are understood as foreign imports, and Sosa's use of such products becomes legible only through his Dominican heritage.

All of these accounts strangely ignore the fact that skin whitening in the United States is a centuries-old practice. Scholars have demonstrated that the US skin-whitening industry is rooted in anti-Black sentiment produced through the history of racialized slavery and, further, that it must be understood as inseparable from the rise of the modern cosmetics industry that ascended at the turn of the twentieth century. During this time period, as Amoaba Gooden has documented, advertisements for skin-lightening products could be found throughout the African American popular press, in such news publications as the *Chicago Defender*, the *Crusader*, the *Crisis*, the *New York Amsterdam*, and *Ebony*, among others.[118] According to Jacob S. Dorman, skin bleaching in the early twentieth century "was far more than merely cosmetic: it was a profoundly micro-political form of self-masking and identity shifting mediated by the new mass market. . . . [S]kin bleaching represented part of a 'Great White Hope' that lightskinned 'New Negroes' might actually be able to escape their 'Negro' past."[119] For this reason, skin bleaching and hair straightening were also hotly contested in African American political journals and eventually became the subject matter for George Schuyler's significant novel, *Black No More* (1931), "whose title was the trade name of an actual skin bleach."[120]

The story of skin lightening in the US context is further complicated by the fact that the beauty industry was also a hub of African American entrepreneurial enterprise, emblematized by the success of figures such as Madam C. J. Walker, whose cosmetic and hair-care manufacturing company was founded in 1906, and who became the wealthiest American businesswoman in the United States to that date. Walker and her contemporaries found success in marketing a wide variety of products to African Americans, including skin creams such as "Tan-Off," which was "recommended for brightening sallow or dark skin, for the treatment of tan, freckle, skin-blotch and for clearing the complexion," as well as hair-care products that offered smoothing, straightening effects.[121] While fraught attitudes toward skin lightening in the United States have persisted from the industry's origins, the popularity of such products has expanded over time with the rise of consumer capitalism. To this day, skin-bleaching products continue to be widely sold across the United States and are available in greater quantity and variety in areas with larger African American populations. More troubling still is the fact that these products are packaged with labels presenting "derogatory images" that "devalue black skin" and convey that lightening "black physicality is socially acceptable because white skin is the superior and sought after ideal."[122]

In the United States, the entanglements of skin color, hair texture, and African ancestry have also been critical to legal categorizations of racial difference that produced (dis)enfranchisement through the Black/white binary.[123] As scholars have documented, policies based in slave law, such as the "one drop" rule (whereby any African lineage legally relegated a person to the status of Black) and the doctrine of *partus sequitur ventrem* (in which children of mixed racial parentage took the legal status of the mother, thereby erasing sexual violence under slavery), produced a racial caste system that imagined Blackness as a devaluing and degrading force that threatened whiteness.[124] Race in this calculation is understood to be essential and unchanging, even as the proximity to or imitation of whiteness is tied to greater rights and opportunities. Centuries later, colorism remains a very real issue for communities of color, a point well made by the ever-growing popularity of cosmetic products and procedures aimed at lightening skin and refining features according to Anglo-American beauty standards. For example, patient requests for intravenous drips of glutathione, an antioxidant that lightens skin by deactivating the enzyme that produces melanin, are on the rise.

Neither the treatment nor the drip are regulated by the Food and Drug Administration, and both have been linked to "serious skin rashes, thyroid issues, and kidney failure," among other problems.[125]

At the same time, debate continues to swirl around the use of more traditional types of skin lighteners, as well as hair straighteners and plastic surgeries, all of which serve to Anglicize nonwhite features. These procedures remain widely available and ever popular but have also become sources of criticism for celebrities who are known to make use of them, including the entertainment figures Blac Chyna, Nicki Minaj, Azealia Banks, Lil' Kim, and Keri Hilson, among others. Yet while these and other figures have been accused at various times of setting a "bad example" for African American youth (i.e., by selling out to a mainstream culture that prioritizes whiteness), the response to their actions has been nowhere near as scathing as the critiques that have circulated surrounding Sammy Sosa and Michael Jackson. Gender is clearly at work in the public's reaction to these celebrities, both because cosmetic practices are traditionally feminized and because their transformations seemed to move them further away from normative standards of masculinity.[126]

Looking at the conversations surrounding public discomfort with both Sosa and Jackson, it is clear that the ridicule they have inspired is as much about the (willful, self-chosen) feminization of their appearance as it is about the whitening of their skin. While this fact has been more plainly stated in the case of Jackson's transformation (and is well documented in the media and in academic writing), it has not been as overt in the case of Sosa.[127] Instead, this concern is evident with respect to Sosa through the media's continual recirculation of and commentary on two images: his 2017 ESPN appearance, in which he wore a pink hat and shirt (see fig. 4.7), and his wife's 2018 birthday party, at which he wore a red cowboy hat, a coordinating western-style shirt embroidered with red roses, and a red ribbon cravat (fig. 4.8). In both images, the color and type of clothing worn by Sosa are a far cry from earlier media representations that typically portrayed him in his baseball uniform or a traditional men's suit. Media conversation surrounding these images link Sosa's skin tone to his clothing as mutually fortifying evidence that something is "wrong" with him.

Critiques of Sosa's skin color and clothing are further compounded by commentary surrounding his obvious weight gain since his days as a high-profile athlete, all of which is mirrored through repeated comparisons made between Sosa and soft, sweet things (e.g., bubblegum, ice cream, and Starburst candy). Sander Gilman and others have argued that excess weight exists in complicated relationship to normative standards of masculinity; while

Figure 4.8.
Image of Sammy
Sosa dressed in
western wear. From
"Sammy Sosa As a
Cowboy? Sure, Why
Not," NBC Sports,
February 11, 2018.
© Equipo Films,
Luis Duarte.

it may be more tolerable for a "man" than a "woman" to be overweight in contemporary US society, a surplus of fatty tissue is associated with a lack of self-control and strength, a feminine or feminized form, and a lack of authenticity (i.e., it should not be present within the body of a "real" man).[128] In chapter 2, I argued that John Bobbitt's masculinity was put into question not only because his penis was forcibly removed but also because he chose to spectacularize his body, and, further, that this spectacularization has contributed to an understanding of his racial identity as not fully or properly "white." In Sosa's case, the interlocution of whiteness and masculinity functions in similarly complicated ways.

While it is without question that nonwhite men are subject to a variety of discursive and institutional forms of prejudice that distance them from the masculine ideal (represented in universal/white form), it is also the case that white masculinity has often been understood to be insufficient in comparison with nonwhite masculinity. Discourses of scientific racism have long identified certain nonwhite men—particularly those from the African and Latin American diasporas—as hypermasculine (i.e., as more muscle-bound and virile than their white colonial counterparts). As Richard Dyer writes, "The white insistence on spirit, on a transcendent relation to the body, has also led to a view that perhaps non-whites have better bodies, run faster, reproduce more easily, have bigger muscles, that perhaps indeed 'white men can't jump,' a film title that has both a literal, basketball reference and an appropriately heterosexual, reproductive connotation."[129] Similarly, Isabel Molina-Guzmán and Angharad Valdivia write that "Whiteness is associated with a disembodied intellectual tradition free from the everyday desires of the body, and non-Whiteness is associated with nature and the everyday needs of the body to consume food, excrete waste, and reproduce sexually."[130]

Thus, the category of whiteness, the desire to become white, and the practice of "whitening" oneself are in an inevitably fraught relationship with the project of normative masculinity. There is, in a sense, an implicit feminization in becoming white. This is not only because white men are often perceived to be less masculine than nonwhite men but also, as feminists of color have observed, because skin tone operates as a barometer of proper femininity that prioritizes white women over nonwhite women, and nonwhite women with lighter skin tones over nonwhite women with darker skin tones. For all of these reasons, the project of skin whitening—as a concept and a literal process—cannot be understood apart from the disciplinary regulations of normative gender, which is itself racialized. As Molina-Guzmán describes, "gendering is particularly interconnected with racialization as both work together to create a media discourse of Latinidad as Other. A white Latina, for example, may be read as nonwhite because of her national origin . . . or because of her accent." Thus, unlike other ethnoracial populations, Latinxs may be phenotypically white while at the same time they are "gendered and racialized outside whiteness by the media because of ethnic markers that are commonly associated with US Latin[x]s or Latin America as foreign or exotic."[131]

Yet, even as the discourse surrounding Sosa's changing skin tone seems to imply that racial identity is fixed, and that any attempt to alter it is surely cause for ridicule, it also suggests a discomfort with the possibility that Sosa may have succeeded in changing *something* that he shouldn't be able to change in the first place (i.e., he "looks like a white man"). But if this is true—if he "looks" white—does this mean that whiteness is something transitive, and further, does it also mean that he *was*, at one point, something other than white? (And here, we could think of a parallel with respect to the scholarship on nineteenth-century blackface minstrelsy, which posits that the whiteness of the performers—themselves recent immigrants from undesirable parts of Europe—was produced through the contrast of blackening their faces.)[132] Ironically, then, if Sosa was attempting to escape his Blackness, his journey toward lighter skin only seems to have shored up his Black identity; and yet, at the same time, because he is so often understood as a "foreigner," his Blackness remains liminal. Thus, the spectacularization of Sosa's body, his ethnicity, and his race are simultaneously hypervisible and mystified through racist forms of humor that discount his identity and personhood.

Section VII. "Rachel said I didn't look Hispanic": Latinx Ambiguity and the Arbitration of Racial Authenticity

As the totality of the facts surrounding Rachel Dolezal's deception came to light in 2015—including everything from her tanning practices to her leadership in organizations designated specifically for African Americans—one story emerged that received little attention but is significant for the purposes of this chapter. When reporters sought interviewees who had taken some of Dolezal's courses in the Africana Studies Program at Eastern Washington University, one student came forward anonymously to describe a peculiar "fishbowl" game. In this exercise, a single "student sat in front of the class as others were invited to ask them questions about their racial and cultural experiences. In the first round . . . Dolezal sought out a volunteer of Hispanic background to be questioned." Identifying as "Hispanic," the student raised her hand. But Dolezal refused to call on her, explaining, "'I think we should ask another student.' . . . Rachel said I didn't look Hispanic . . . [and she] doubted that I could share experiences of racial or ethnic discrimination because I didn't have the appearance of looking Hispanic."[133] News outlets that picked up the story used it as further evidence of Dolezal's fraudulence, wherein she falsely positioned herself as an arbiter of Black experience by redirecting suspicion onto someone else whom she deemed inauthentic.

While we cannot know whether such an incident happened to other students, it is important to think about how and why Dolezal chose *this* student to publicly doubt. For the student in question, growing up in a Spanish-speaking country and speaking fluent Spanish were enough to render her authentically "Hispanic," yet she suspected that Dolezal rejected her because of her "light" complexion. In this anecdote, geographic origin, language of origin, and phenotype are mobilized in telltale ways to (dis)prove ethnic and racial identity. And yet, at the same time, the fact that such markers can be questioned in some cases and not others—namely, in those involving Latinx subjects, from Uchis to Guerrero to Sosa to the anonymous student in Dolezal's class—speaks to the ways in which the production of Latinidad as inherently ambiguous, as part race, part ethnicity, is not without consequence.

When thinking about the debates surrounding the (in)authenticity of Latinx public figures, particularly with regard to their proximity to brownness and Blackness, it is important to observe how Latinx ambiguity is weaponized as a way of policing nonwhite identity while disavowing anti-Black sentiment. From the anecdote shared by Dolezal's student, and from everything that Dolezal has said in relation to her purported transracial identity, it is clear that Dolezal's understanding of the malleability of race goes beyond the typical forms of deconstructionism that seek to de-essentialize difference. Much like Sealey's assessment that "a comportment that claims to be able to fully opt out of racially-constituted privilege seems bound to the privilege upon which this comportment rests," and Blow's understanding that "a person like Rachel has the privilege to present and perform blackness because we are conditioned in America to accept those presentations" as a part of white hegemony, the "proper" whiteness of Dolezal becomes evident in the way she continually positioned herself as an arbiter of racial authenticity.[134]

In the years since the scandal first broke, Dolezal has doubled down on her identification as transracial, changing her name to Nkechi (Nkechinyere) Amare Diallo, taking her first name from the Igbo of Nigeria and her last name from the Fulani of Guinea and Senegal.[135] But she has also given interviews explaining that race is simply a "worldview" or "state of mind." As the sociologist Ann Morning has observed, Dolezal's 2017 autobiography, *In Full Color: Finding My Place in a Black and White World*, at times "sounds like an Intro Soc textbook on race" that details "the flaws in the traditional American belief in discrete, biologically grounded race."[136] In Morning's estimation, Dolezal "is *not* a passer—someone who seeks to turn existing racial categories to their advantage—so much as a person who rejects widespread beliefs about the criteria for racial categorization."[137] If this is true, however, it raises the question of who among us has the right and the ability to "reject" dominant frames of categorization, and at what cost. When contextualized within ongoing conversations about (Afro) Latinx authenticity, it also becomes clear that there are no certain "criteria for racial categorization" in the case of Latinx subjects. Instead, "Latinx" remains a transient category that is applied at will in different times and places.

CONCLUSION

"Feeling brown":
Conjuring Latinidad, Here and Now

One can feel very brown and perhaps not register as brown as the dark-skinned person standing next to one who is involved in the endeavor of trying to feel white.

JOSÉ ESTÉBAN MUÑOZ, "'CHICO, WHAT DOES IT FEEL LIKE TO BE A PROBLEM?': THE TRANSMISSION OF BROWNNESS"

In the preceding chapters, I have argued that the ambiguous construction of Latinx subjectivity and embodiment has been critical to the production of Latinidad in the late twentieth and early twenty-first centuries. Produced as a fungible semiotic category, Latinidad has simultaneously become a hyperbolic presence and an invisibilized backdrop upon which broader cultural and sociopolitical issues have become debated. I demonstrated how this phenomenon can be seen in the treatment of specific Latinx figures by the US media and juridical systems. In doing so, I have sought to call attention to the ways in which stereotypical ethnoracial, gendered, and sexual representations have material consequences, not just for those whom they are aimed at but also for the discursive and imaginary frameworks that we use to conceptualize difference.

While the examples I have provided understand Latinx ambiguity as a predominantly damaging and dangerous ideological space that intensifies the precarity of marginalized subjects, recent scholarship in queer and Latinx studies has imagined the matter differently. In particular, the concept of "brownness," as theorized by José Estéban Muñoz, has become a pivot point in conversations surrounding the futurity of Latinidad.

Prior to Muñoz's work, the term "brown" was linked to Latinidad through the history of activism (the Brown Berets, Brown Pride, and so on), and through the work of Richard Rodriguez (who imagines "brown" as a symbol for all of the ways Latinxs are imagined as impure, dirty, and shameful).[1] Unlike these conceptualizations, Muñoz's approach centers on the idea of racial performativity. Just as gender theorists such as Judith Butler, Monique Wittig, and Simone de Beauvoir have argued against essentialist constructions of sex or gender, Muñoz contends that race is not simply a matter of "being" but rather a matter of "doing":

> The inquiry I am undertaking here suggests that we move beyond notions of ethnicity as fixed (something that people are) and instead understand it as performative (what people do), providing a reinvigorated and nuanced understanding of ethnicity. . . . In lieu of viewing racial or ethnic difference as solely cultural, I aim to describe how race and ethnicity can be understood as "affective difference," by which I mean the ways in which various historically coherent groups "feel" differently and navigate the material world on a different emotional register.[2]

Muñoz thus pushes against dichotomies that locate Latinidad as "excess" in relation to the "norms" of whiteness. If "we look at whiteness from a racialized perspective," he posits, "the affective performance of normative whiteness is minimalist to the point of emotional impoverishment" and underdevelopment.[3] For Muñoz, this shift is critical to reconceptualizing Latinidad in a way that moves away from the "toxic language of shame" that impacts marginalized identities, reformulates the boundaries of acceptable ethnic/racial affective modes of being, and thus produces liberatory possibilities.[4]

At the same time, Muñoz asserts that this reformulation will help to undo hegemonic classifications of race and ethnicity, for which Latinidad has always posed a difficulty (as it is composed of "groups who do not cohere along lines of race, nation, language, or any other conventional demarcation of difference").[5] Here, he draws from canonical writing in Latinx studies on the fundamental ambiguity, hybridity, and plurality evidenced in the figuration of mestizaje. As Gloria Anzaldúa has written, mestiza identity "has always been inner, and is played out in the outer terrains. . . . Nothing happens in the 'real' world unless it first happens in the images in our heads."[6] Similarly, scholarship that draws upon Muñoz's theorization of brownness often conceives of Latinidad according to increasingly vague terms. For example, in his assessment of the Supreme Court justice Sonia Sotomayor, Josh Takano Chambers-Letson notes that although

> Sotomayor describes herself as having a "Latina identity," the actual portrait that she paints is less as a singular identity than a range of embodied practices and affective attachments.

Identity [here] . . . occurs in and on the body. It occurs through strategic cultural affiliations that are neither permanent nor entirely immaterial. . . . [T]he experience of *latinidad* as an embodied practice occurs through a range of performances and feelings that cannot be reduced to an essential subject position. . . . Put otherwise, racial difference and *latinidad* emerge as performative constructions, rather than constative definitions.[7]

But can this type of theorization of Latinidad as "neither permanent nor entirely immaterial" apply to all Latinx subjects whose phenotype and skin tone marks them as Other? Muñoz suggests that yes, "feeling brown" as an affective mode of identification and belonging may exist independently from "looking brown":

Feeling brown refers to what I describe earlier as a *manera de ser*, a way of being in the world. This is not the same as being seen or perceived as brown. Similarly to the field of visual ethnic recognition, within the affective register there are indeed varied affective shadings of brownness, whether it be different national experiences among Latina/os or types of colorism that are akin to the physical biases that exist within blackness. The visual and the affective are different identificatory routes: *one can feel very brown and perhaps not register as brown as the dark-skinned person standing next to one who is involved in the endeavor of trying to feel white.*[8]

Here, Muñoz seems to suggest that affective identity with respect to brownness as an ethnoracial identity can, and does, contradict phenotype. What does it mean to "feel very brown" but not "register as brown"? Is brownness being understood as affective status, a depressive structure of feeling that all Latinxs experience and may access independent of physical appearance, lived experience, and state-sanctioned processes of ethnoracial interpellation? And, perhaps more provocatively, if Latinx subjectivity produces brown feelings, can the experience of brown feelings produce Latinx subjects? If so, this logic moves uncomfortably close to the type of reasoning employed by advocates of transracialism: I feel, therefore I am. At the same time, what does it mean to juxtapose the person who "can feel very brown and perhaps not register as brown" (i.e., who is white passing) with "the dark-skinned person" who is "trying to feel white" (i.e., whose brownness is legible but who may, for various reasons, seek to identify or align with the dominant racial group)?

In a white-supremacist world where proximity to whiteness confers basic humanity as well as access to care, protection, and material benefit, non-white subjects are required to mimic, feel, and desire whiteness for the sheer purpose of survival. Importantly, this demand does not go both ways. As Zahira Kelly explains, for people whose nonwhite racial identity is legible,

> code-switching becomes a means of survival in the most visceral way. It's a matter of life and death, of being housed and fed or homeless and hungry. And as immigrants of color or their children, code-switching can even be the difference between being picked up by ICE and sent to hellish detention centers to face deportation or not. Unfortunately, the less attuned we appear to be with our non-white culture, the more access to safety and humanity we are granted, even if we are only ever dealt scraps in the end. . . . Hiding parts of ourselves society hates is both a privilege and a burden, as some cannot hide who they are no matter how hard they try and will not be able to escape consequences for it.[9]

At the same time, Kelly laments that the appropriation of Afro-Latinx culture by white Latinxs disturbingly mirrors Anglo European appropriations of Blackness: "Now it's latina chicks with hair everybody already calls pelo bueno, wearing nappyhead girls 'pelo bueno' tees."[10]

In her own artwork depicting Afro-Latinidad, Kelly often reframes popular images from dominant culture. In her "Virgen Negra" collection, Kelly portrays Afro-Latina women as the Virgin Mary, an iconic representation typically reserved for white women (figs. 5.1 and 5.2). For Kelly, switching the identity of "Mary" becomes a way to interrogate dominant power structures. "For me," she explains, "depicting La Virgen as a Negra is fusing our African ancestry with Catholicism like many in our country [the Dominican Republic] have done before with spiritual figures. It is also a question: Can you see lower class Black women as the Holy Mother in such a classist, anti-Black misogynist postcolonial landscape?"[11]

Similarly, for the sociologist Agustín Laó-Montes, the promise of Afro-Latinx critique resides in the capacity to think in precise and nuanced ways about intersectional identity:

> If elaborated as a category for post-colonial critique and as an oppositional form of political identity, Afro-Latina/o difference could reveal and recognize hidden histories and subalternized knowledges, while unsettling and challenging dominant (essentialist, nationalist, imperial, patriarchal) notions of African-ness, American-ness, and Latinidad, along with the forms of power/knowledge that are embedded in these categories.[12]

Here, radical potential is found in the enumeration of the specificities of oppression, in the revelation of ever more "hidden" pasts that might shed light

Figures 5.1–2. "Virgen Negra" series, Zahira Kelly, 2017. © Zahira Kelly.

on the present. What does it mean that such a theorization operates to directly contradict the expansive vision of brownness? Further, what does it mean that brownness bears such a striking resemblance to foundational theorizations of mestizaje as a "cosmic mix" that gloss over issues of colonialism, slavery, and genocide?

In many ways, the call to brownness as affective connection poses a problem for the very thing it seeks to correct—namely, the production of identity categories that are insufficient and exclusionary and that overlook difference in the name of solidarity. Paulla Ebron and Anna Lowenhaupt Tsing have observed that when it comes to intersectional social justice movements, we often seek to "build alliances with a rhetoric of solidarity, but we have few tools with which to create critical and reflexive conversations that recognize our differences as well as our common stakes."[13] This is especially true in the case of the coalescence of Latinidad, which has been envisioned as a site of broad-based plurality in myriad ways.

In his critique of the recent popularization of "Latinx" (over "Latina/o/@" and so on)—a trend that claims to produce *greater* inclusivity—Richard T. Rodríguez asserts that advocates of the *x* run "the risk of eclipsing the particular politics of recognition for which they purport to be advocating. . . . To insist that everyone identify as Latinx . . . seems to me one way *not* to be respected but subsumed under a letter that anyone can claim."[14] Comparing the x to the use of "queer," Rodríguez quotes the feminist theorist Teresa de Lauretis, who, despite coining the term "queer theory" in 1991, "would soon distance herself from [it] . . . opting instead to hold on to the category lesbian given that queer theory, as she put it, had 'become a conceptually vacuous creature of the publishing industry.'"[15] Rodríguez suggests that "if Latinx is going to be handed over as a user-friendly identity, then we need to recognize its complicity with a politics of diversity that need not draw attention to the hierarchical order reinforcing its structural foundations."[16] In other words, the forcible application of the x may, at times, make certain historically meaningful identities unavailable, casting aspersions on those who continue to claim them. Calling attention to the politics of class, gender, and generational differences, Rodríguez cautions that far from representing marginalized factions, the x is often most rigidly asserted by those who hail from positions of privilege.

Similarly, Juana María Rodríguez contends that the universalizing impulse behind the utopian thread in queer theory often overlooks the varying degrees of precarity that are experienced along lines of gender and sexuality. Pointing to the celebration of public spaces as sites for queer sexual engagement (including sex clubs, bathhouses, and so on), she explains that such places "can prove deadly to female-bodied people, female-presenting people, and others perceived as physically vulnerable."[17] Thus, while a framework of "queer" may be used to celebrate sex in spaces presumably untouched by the coercive dictates of heteronormativity and heteropatriarchy, such utopian fantasies also disavow those for whom these spaces are also sites of imperilment. As Juana María Rodríguez writes, the marginalization of the vulnerable serves not only to further obscure their endangerment but also to severely circumscribe their capacity to produce their own visions of queer futurity, or of a life lived otherwise.

At the same time, the broad-based form of identification offered through the medium of brownness also exists in strange relation to another contemporary use of brownness: namely, the xenophobic rhetoric that speaks of the nation's "browning."[18] In recent years, this discourse has been employed by the conservative right, in the works of political pundits and ideologues such as Samuel Huntington, Victor Davis Hanson, Pat Buchanan, and Mark Steyn. For these men and their ilk, the United States is "browning" not simply because of demographic shifts that will soon produce a "Hispanic society" but also because, as they protest, the border somehow appears to be "moving north."[19] With a "Reconquista" under way (i.e., a long-term strategic revenge enacted upon the United States by a group of people attempting to recapture the territories taken by the United States from Mexico following the Treaty of Guadalupe Hidalgo in 1848), the nation must prepare to mourn its "bleeding Southern border."[20] As Leo R. Chavez argues in his work on the "Latino threat," the perceived unassimilability of Latinx people as an "immigrant group" leads to paranoia over the ever-impending "destruction" of the "American way of life."[21] These challenges to and against "American-ness" undergird what the *New York Times* opinion columnist Charles Blow has dubbed "white extinction anxiety," itself a recapitulation of the nation's long-held concern over changing demographic patterns.

At the same time, such an extinction anxiety only proves true if the na-tion is indeed becoming less white. Indeed, statistics regarding the expan-sion of the Latinx population as effecting a "majority minority" shift in the nation's demographic only play out *if Latinxs are not considered white*. This suggests that the statistics are meaningful in the service of an "extinction" narrative only if they are read from a particular vantage point. Thus, it must be asked, what does it mean that the "largest" and ever-expanding minor-ity group in the United States will "brown" the nation only if, in a sense, we allow it to do so? There are already myriad examples of the ways in which Latinxs are often counted as white in both official and unofficial ways. What does it mean for this whiteness not to be factored into the broader paranoia about white extinction anxiety? What would it look like to address this is-sue through the lens of brownness, where Latinidad need not be sutured in any clear way to a particular skin color or phenotype? This is not a question about the types of "honorary" whiteness that might be projected onto cer-tain "exceptional" minority subjects. Rather, it is a question that gets to the heart of the political use value of conjuring Latinidad.

The mythology that we are, in the end, a "nation of immigrants" pro-duces the United States as distinct from others. Ours is a country riddled with centuries-old anxieties about the nation's ethnic and racial composure and about the rising tides of "new" immigrants whose beliefs, cultures, and practices may upend "America" as we know it. As a result, our racial cate-gorizations have become a way through which to catalog, rank, and nego-tiate difference. And even though Latinidad is a product of such catalog-ing, ranking, and negotiating, its unique ambivalence and manipulability means that it will never properly perform its function. The apparent ambi-guity of Latinidad is thus fundamental to the production of what Eduardo Bonilla-Silva terms "color-blind racism," an ideology that has risen in the twenty-first-century United States and is the "norm all over Latin America, den[ying] the salience of race, scorn[ing] those who talk about race, and in-creasingly proclaim[ing] that 'We are all Americans.'"[22]

In this way, just as the nation conjures Latinidad, so too does Latinidad hold up a mirror to the nation; each appears as a specter of the other, two imagined communities forged across and between persons of diverse ethnoracial backgrounds and varying degrees of citizenship. And yet, just like the United States, Latinidad is unequally structured. This unequal structuring is not accomplished in radical ways. Rather, it draws upon and recapitulates the logics of settler colonialism, cultural imperialism, racism, colorism, and xenophobia. All of this suggests that the stakes are too high to continue to advocate for any conceptualization of Latinx identity that expands or further ambiguates the parameters of inclusion without stopping to think in nuanced ways about the differences that are so often silenced along the way.

Notes

Introduction

1. Ezra Klein, "White Threat in a Browning America," *Vox*, July 30, 2018, https://www.vox.com/policy-and-politics/2018/7/30/17505406/trump-obama-race-politics -immigration.

2. Given that this work sits at the intersection of Latino studies and queer studies, I have opted to use the word "Latinx." As Lourdes Torres writes, "'Latinx' is used to "represent the variety of possible genders as well as those who may identify as non-gender-binary or transgender" (Torres 284). I also share concerns with other scholars over the use of this term in lieu of "Latina/o" and discuss this in the conclusion.

3. Cacho, *Social Death*, 43.

4. As Meenakshi Gigi Durham and Douglas M. Kellner note, "the idea that all cultural representations are political is one of the major themes of media and cultural theory of the past several decades." In particular, stereotypical and biased images of minoritized groups "can serve pernicious interests of cultural oppression by positioning certain groups as inferior, thus pointing to the superiority of dominant social groups." Durham and Kellner, introduction to *Media and Cultural Studies*, xxxii.

5. C. Rodríguez, *Changing Race*, 5.

6. On the politics of self-identification and the use of the term "Hispanic," see Newby and Dowling, "Black and Hispanic," 343–366; Gimenez, "Latino/'Hispanic,'" 557–571.

7. Mora, *Making Hispanics*, 117–118; Dávila, *Latinos, Inc.*, 1–3; Rúa, *Grounded Identidad*, 90; Oboler, *Ethnic Labels, Latino Lives*. On the more recent use of "Latinx" over "Latina/o/@" specifically, see Torres, "Latinx?," 283–285.

8. Molina-Guzmán, *Dangerous Curves*, 6. On this point, see also Canclini, *Hybrid Cultures*; Lugones, *Pilgrimages/Peregrinajes*; Bebout, *Whiteness on the Border*; Valdivia, *Latina/os and the Media*.

9. Anzaldúa, *Borderlands / La Frontera*; Cherríe Moraga and Gloria Anzaldúa, "Entering the Lives of Others: Theory in the Flesh," in Moraga and Anzaldúa, *This Bridge Called My Back*; Arrizón, "Latina Subjectivity, Sexuality, and Sensuality," 191–192; María P. Figueroa, "Resisting 'Beauty' and *Real Women Have Curves*," in Gaspar de Alba, *Velvet Barrios*, 265–282.

10. Anzaldúa, *Borderlands / La Frontera*, 99, 103, 101; emphasis in the original.

11. Anzaldúa, 102–103.

12. Viego, *Dead Subjects*, 21.

13. J. Rodríguez, *Sexual Futures, Queer Gestures*, 2, 6.

14. Muñoz, "Feeling Brown"; Muñoz, "Chico"; Alvarado, *Abject Performances*; Pérez, *Taste for Brown Bodies*; Vargas, "Ruminations on Lo Sucio," 715.

15. Muñoz, "Feeling Brown," 70.

16. Muñoz, "Chico," 444.

17. Alvarado, *Abject Performances*, 9; Pérez, *Taste for Brown Bodies*, 104.

18. Derrida, *Specters of Marx*, 6. On the spectral turn, see Blanco and Peeren, introduction to *Spectralities Reader*, 1; Jeffrey Andrew Weinstock, "Introduction: The Spectral Turn," in Blanco and Peeren, *Spectralities Reader*, 62.

19. Butler, *Precarious Life*, 33–34; my emphasis.

20. "Occult presence" is Marriott's term; see Marriott, *Haunted Life*, xxi. On racial spectrality, see also Marriott, "Spooks/Postmortem TV," 308; Bergland, *National Uncanny*, 21; McClintock, "Imperial Ghosting and National Tragedy," 821, 827; A. Gordon, *Ghostly Matters*, xvi; Ramírez, *Colonial Phantoms*, 3.

21. Mbembe, "Necropolitics," 40; Cacho, *Social Death*, 7.

22. García, "Illegalities of Brownness," 145. See also Menjívar, "Liminal Legality," 999–1037; Zilberg, *Spaces of Detention*; Coutin, *Legalizing Moves*.

23. Peeren, *Spectral Metaphor*, 4–5. See also León, *La Llorona's Children*, 262. Liam Connell also refers to undocumented laborers as "revenants"; see Connell, "Worker as Revenant," 13.

24. Mendible, introduction to *From Bananas to Buttocks*, 6.

25. William A. Calvo-Quirós, "Liberanos de Todo Mal / But Deliver Us from Evil: Latina/o Monsters Theory and the Outlining of Our Phantasmagoric Landscapes," in Aldama, *Companion to Latina/o Popular Culture*, 382; Pérez, *Taste for Brown Bodies*, 104.

26. Chavez, *Latino Threat*, 2.

27. Chavez, 6.

28. Molina-Guzmán, "Gendering Latinidad," 181–182. On the relationship between media representation and journalistic reporting, see also Bird, "Facing the Distracted Audience," 29–33. As Bird observes, "journalism emerges from and responds to cultural specificities" (30). On the construction of ideology through journalistic discourse, see Allan, "News from NowHere," 105–141; Hall et al., *Policing the Crisis*. Hall et al. write, "The media do not simply and transparently report events which are 'naturally' newsworthy in themselves. 'News' is the end-product of a complex process which begins with a systematic sorting and selecting of events and topics according to a socially constructed set of categories" (54).

29. Zelizer, introduction to *Changing Faces of Journalism*, 6–7.

30. Ouellette, introduction to *Media Studies Reader*, 2.

31. Marriott, *Haunted Life*, 110. On this point, see also Marriott, "Waiting to Fall," 163–240.

32. Marriott, *Haunted Life*, 17.

33. Pérez-Melgosa, "Low Intensity Necropolitics," 218.

34. Pérez-Melgosa, 231.

35. Pérez-Melgosa, 231.

36. Mbembe, "Necropolitics," 40; Smith-Nonini, "Illegal and the Dead," 454–474; Puar, "Cost of Getting Better," 152.

Chapter 1: "This could be Satanic-related"

1. When referring to the San Antonio Four, I use "Latina," as all of the women identify as such. Later on in the chapter, I use the term "Latinx" as a gender neutral and nonbinary version of "Latina/o." On the use of these terms as they pertain to racial and imperial politics, see de Onís, "What's in an 'X'?," 56–86.

2. *Kristie Mayhugh et al. v. State of Texas*, 175th District Court, Bexar County, nos. WR-84, 700-01; WR-84, 700-02.

3. See, for example, Laura Berger, "'Southwest of Salem' Helps Exonerate Four Wrongfully Convicted Women," *Women and Hollywood*, November 28, 2016, https://womenandhollywood.com/southwest-of-salem-helps-exonerate-four-wrongfully-convicted-women-b2784885e457/#.aouoomlhj.

4. Michael Barajas, "The San Antonio Four Are Finally Declared 'Actually Innocent,'" *San Antonio Current*, November 23, 2016, https://www.sacurrent.com/the-daily/archives/2016/11/23/the-san-antonio-four-are-finally-declared-actually-innocent; Jeff Truesdell, "New Documentary Examines Controversial Conviction of 'San Antonio Four' Amidst Satanic Ritual Panic," *People*, October 13, 2016, https://people.com/crime/new-documentary-examines-controversial-conviction-of-san-antonio-four-amidst-satanic-ritual-panic/.

5. Maurice Chammah, "The Mystery of the San Antonio Four," *Texas Observer*, January 7, 2014, https://www.texasobserver.org/mystery-san-antonio-four/.

6. The case was one of the first to benefit from Texas Senate Bill 344, which mandates the court to reexamine cases that relied upon scientific evidence since proved to be incorrect. See Michael Hall, "The San Antonio Four Are Finally Free," *Texas Monthly*, November 19, 2016, http://www.texasmonthly.com/the-daily-post/the-san-antonio-4-are-finally-free/.

7. Linda Rodriguez McRobbie, "How Junk Science and Anti-lesbian Prejudice Got Four Women Sent to Prison for More Than a Decade," *Slate*, December 4, 2013, http://www.slate.com/blogs/outward/2013/12/04/san_antonio_four_junk_science_and_anti_lesbian_prejudice_sent_them_to_prison.html.

8. Esquenazi, *Southwest of Salem*.

9. Chammah, "Mystery of the San Antonio Four."

10. Victor, *Satanic Panic*; Nathan and Snedecker, *Satan's Silence*; Poole, *Satan in America*; Beck, *We Believe the Children*.

11. Daniel Goleman, "Proof Lacking for Ritual Abuse by Satanists," *New York Times*, October 31, 1994, http://www.nytimes.com/1994/10/31/us/proof-lacking-for-ritual-abuse-by-satanists.html. Similarly, a 1992 study by the FBI found no credible evidence linking satanic ritual with child abuse or any other violent crime. See Kenneth V. Lanning, "Investigator's Guide to Allegations of 'Ritual' Child Abuse," Behavioral Science Unit, National Center for the Analysis of Violent Crime (Quantico, VA: Federal Bureau of Investigation, 1992), https://www.ncjrs.gov/pdffiles1/Digitization/136592NCJRS.pdf.

12. Jenkins, *Moral Panics*; Victor, *Satanic Panic*; Nathan and Snedecker, *Satan's Silence*; Poole, *Satan in America*; Beck, *We Believe the Children*.

13. As Seth McCloud explains, third-wave Christian literature asserts that alcoholism in certain Indigenous communities is caused by "ancient spiritual pacts" made with demonic spirits. Similarly, noted Christian Right figurehead Pat Rob-

ertson claimed that the 2010 earthquake that devastated Haiti was divine retribution for a pact that enslaved Haitians made with the devil to gain liberation from the French centuries ago. See McCloud, *American Possessions*, 102; "Pat Robertson Says Haiti Is Paying for 'Pact to the Devil,'" CNN, January 13, 2010, http://www.cnn.com /2010/US/01/13/haiti.pat.robertson/.

14. Brownmiller, *Against Our Will*, 14–15.

15. For more on recovered memory / false memory, see Conway, *Recovered Memories and False Memories*; Loftus and Ketcham, *Myth of Repressed Memory*.

16. Bass and Davis, *Courage to Heal*, 22.

17. McHugh, *Try to Remember*, 52.

18. Jonathan Schooler, Miriam Bendiksen, and Zara Amabadar, "Taking the Middle Line," in Conway, *Recovered Memories and False Memories*, 257.

19. Jianjian Qin et al., "Repressed Memories," in Lynn and McConkey, *Truth in Memory*, 264; Ofshe and Watters, *Making Monsters*, 181–182.

20. Poole includes such examples as the musicians AC/DC, Black Sabbath, and Ozzy Osbourne; the comic book *The Dark Night Returns* (1986); the tabletop game *Dungeons and Dragons*; and television features such as *20/20*'s "The Devil Worshippers" (1985) and Geraldo Rivera's NBC special *Devil Worship* (1988). See Poole, *Satan in America*, 156, 176–180.

21. By pointing to the timeline here, I mean to suggest that the Four's intersectional marginalization made possible the mobilization of anachronistic and erroneous evidence.

22. See, for example, Glick, "Of Sodomy and Cannibalism," 266–282.

23. Treichler, "AIDS, Homophobia, and Biomedical Discourse," 35, 37.

24. See, for example, Ordover, *American Eugenics*.

25. For instance, Anita Bryant famously declared that "the male homosexual eats another man's sperm. Sperm is the most concentrated form of blood. The homosexual is eating life." See Bryant quoted in Poole, *Monsters in America*, 206.

26. Anzaldúa, *Borderlands / La Frontera*, 19; Carla Trujillo, "Chicana Lesbians: Fear and Loathing in the Chicano Community," in Trujillo, *Chicana Lesbians*, 187; Cherríe Moraga, "La Güera," in Moraga and Anzaldúa, *This Bridge Called My Back*. See also Esquibel, *With Her Machete in Her Hand*, for an overview of Chicana lesbian experience and intersectional feminism.

27. William A. Calvo-Quirós, "Liberarnos de Todo Mal / But Deliver Us from Evil: Latina/o Monsters Theory and the Outlining of Our Phantasmagoric Landscapes," in Aldama, *Companion to Latina/o Popular Culture*, 382.

28. Jillian Hernandez, "'You Look Like a Bratz Doll,'" 66.

29. Jillian Hernandez quoted in Collins-White et al., "Disruptions in Respectability," 463–475.

30. Jillian Hernandez, "'You Look Like a Bratz Doll,'" 64.

31. As Jillian Hernandez writes, "The chonga . . . is in many ways a younger version of the chusma, or the chusma-as-teenager." See "'You Look Like a Bratz Doll,'" 67–68. See also Muñoz, *Disidentifications*, 182.

32. Muñoz, *Disidentifications*, 191.

33. Vargas, "Ruminations on Lo Sucio," 715.

34. Vargas, 715.

35. Vargas, 716; my emphasis.

36. Muñoz, *Cruising Utopia*, 9.

37. Edelman, *No Future*.

38. Vargas, "Ruminations on Lo Sucio," 723.

39. Esquenazi quoted in Cuevas, *Post-Borderlandia*, 138.

40. Mendoza, "States of Dismemberment," 23, 28.

41. Mendoza, 25, 53.

42. Cuevas, *Post-Borderlandia*, 138.

43. Cuevas, 17, 138.

44. Cuevas, 4.

45. Bebout, *Whiteness on the Border*, 9, 15–16.

46. Madeline Messick and Claire Bergeron, "Temporary Protected Status in the United States: A Grant of Humanitarian Relief That Is Less Than Permanent," Migration Policy Institute, July 2, 2014, https://www.migrationpolicy.org /article/temporary-protected-status-united-states-grant-humanitarian-relief-less -permanent; Atticus Lee, "Sexual Deviants Need Not Apply: LGBTQ Oppression in the 1965 Immigration Amendments," in Chin and Villazor, *Immigration and Nationality Act of 1965*, 250.

47. US Customs and Border Protection, "Border Patrol History," US Department of Homeland Security, October 5, 2018, https://www.cbp.gov/border-security /along-us-borders/history; Alden, "Is Border Enforcement Effective?," 481–490; Bob Herber, "In America; NAFTA and the Elite," *New York Times*, November 19, 1993, https://www.nytimes.com/1993/11/10/opinion/in-america-nafta-and-the-elite.html.

48. Guy Garcia, "The Believers: Cult Murders in Mexico," *Rolling Stone*, June 29, 1989, http://www.rollingstone.com/culture/features/the-believers-19890629.

49. Mayra Santos-Febres, Hal Barton, and Judy Rosenthal, "Border Murders Stir Harmful Stereotypes," *New York Times*, May 15, 1989, http://www.nytimes.com /1989/05/15/opinion/l-border-murders-stir-harmful-stereotypes-065289.html.

50. Peter Applebome, "13th Victim Is Found on Ranch Where Drugs and Occult Mixed," *New York Times*, April 14, 1989, http://www.nytimes.com/1989/04/14 /us/13th-victim-is-found-on-ranch-where-drugs-and-occult-mixed.html.

51. Garcia, "The Believers."

52. Chavez, *Latino Threat*, 2.

53. Santos-Febres, Barton, and Rosenthal, "Border Murders."

54. Hampton interviewed in Esquenazi, *Southwest of Salem*, 33:08.

55. Vasquez quoted in Michelle Mondo, "Woman Recants Accusation of Sex Assault," *My San Antonio*, September 17, 2012, https://www.mysanantonio.com /news/local_news/article/Woman-recants-accusation-of-sex-assault-3868974.php #ixzz279UMQrM5.

56. Cassandra Rivera, "Four Lives Lost," case narratives, *Four Lives Lost* (blog), July 3, 2000, http://fourliveslost.com/case-narratives.

57. Tom Dart, "Texas Clings to Unconstitutional, Homophobic Laws—and It's Not Alone," *Guardian*, June 1, 2019, https://www.theguardian.com/world/2019/jun /01/texas-homophobic-laws-lgbt-unconstitutional.

58. Shah, "Policing Privacy," 277.

59. Shah, 276.

60. Shah also points to age and class status as primary determinants in the history of the prosecution of sodomy and other "public morals" cases. See Shah, 277.

61. In *Southwest*, Vasquez's mother explains that she tried to reach out to lesbian and gay rights groups for support but was unsuccessful.

62. Rodriguez McRobbie, "Junk Science and Anti-lesbian Prejudice."

63. Mendoza, *States of Dismemberment*, 91, 39–40.

64. *Southwest of Salem*; *Häxan* (dir. Benjamin Christensen, 1922).

65. On the dates of the women's releases, see "Timeline," *Southwest of Salem* website, accessed January 3, 2019, http://www.southwestofsalem.com/timeline-1/. On Vasquez's screenwriting, see Andrew Lapin, "'I Helped Four Women Get Out of Prison': Deborah Esquenazi on Her True-Crime Doc 'Southwest of Salem,'" No Film School, April 14, 2016, https://nofilmschool.com/2016/04/i-helped-four -women-get-out-prison-deborah-esquenazi-her-tribeca-doc-southwest-salem.

66. *Southwest of Salem* website, press materials, accessed January 15, 2019, https:// drive.google.com/drive/folders/0B7EnaZVAgr1RVTFzRWYxZEZiUnM.

67. Esquenazi interviewed by Yvonne S. Marquez, "Southwest of Salem: How Four Wrongfully Convicted Latina Lesbians Survived a Witch-Hunt," Autostrad-dle, November 18, 2016, https://www.autostraddle.com/southwest-of-salem-how -four-wrongfully-convicted-latina-lesbians-survived-a-witch-hunt-356648/; empha-sis in the original.

68. Esquenazi quoted in Claire Landsbaum, "Director Deborah Esquenazi on What Drew Her to a Satanic-Ritual Abuse Trial in Texas," *The Cut*, April 17, 2016, https://www.thecut.com/2016/04/deborah-esquenazi-on-her-doc-southwest-of -salem.html.

69. Rebecca Sharpless, "'Immigrants Are Not Criminals': Respectability, Im-migration Reform, and Hyperincarceration," *Houston Law Review* 53, no. 3 (2016): 727, 711.

70. Cacho, *Social Death*, 43.

71. "DA Disbarred for Sending Texas Man to Death Row," CBS News, June 12, 2015, https://www.cbsnews.com/news/charles-sebasta-prosecutor-of-wrongfully-con victed-man-anthony-graves-loses-law-license/; Amanda Holpuch, "Texas Prosecu-tor Officially Disbarred for Sending Innocent Man to Death Row," *Guardian*, Feb-ruary 9, 2016, https://www.theguardian.com/us-news/2016/feb/09/texas-prosecutor -charles-sebasta-disbarred-anthony-graves-innocent-death-row.

72. "Anthony Graves on Overcoming a Wrongful Conviction," Legal Talk Net-work, June 20, 2018, https://legaltalknetwork.com/podcasts/state-bar-texas/2018/06 /anthony-graves-on-overcoming-a-wrongful-conviction/; "Anthony Graves," ACLU, accessed March 11, 2019, https://www.aclu.org/bio/anthony-graves.

73. "Anthony Graves," ACLU.

74. Sarah Chu, "Houston Chronicle Op-Ed: Keep Houston Forensic Science Cen-ter Independent," June 2, 2016, https://www.innocenceproject.org/houston-chronicle -op-ed-keep-houston-forensic-science-center-independent/.

75. "Houston Forensic Science Center: Past, Present, Future," Houston Foren-sic Science Center, accessed March 1, 2019, http://www.houstonforensicscience.org /faq.php; my emphasis. It is also important to note that elsewhere in the FAQ, it is explained that while the center desires to be financially independent, it still pres-ently relies on government funding (i.e., the same source of funding that the HPD crime lab used).

76. "IPTX's Anna Vasquez Appointed to Houston Forensic Science Center

Board," Innocence Project of Texas, June 18, 2019, https://innocencetexas.org/news/iptx-director; my emphasis.

77. Lisa Duggan, "The New Homonormativity: The Sexual Politics of Neoliberalism," in Castranovo and Nelson, *Materializing Democracy*, 188–189.

78. Puar, *Terrorist Assemblages*, 4.

79. Salvador Zamora quoted in Brittny Mejia, "Many Latinos Answer Call of the Border Patrol in the Age of Trump," *Los Angeles Times*, April 23, 2018, https://www.latimes.com/local/lanow/la-me-ln-citizens-academy-20180323-htmlstory.html.

80. For a history of Latinx subjects in the US military and Border Patrol, see K. Hernández, *Migra!* As Kelly Lytle Hernández and others have attested, military service has long been mobilized as a site for marginalized groups to demonstrate their loyalty to the nation. At the same time, as Suzanne Oboler has noted, twenty-first-century attitudes toward the carceral state have been shaped by 9/11, a date after which the "actual *practice* of racism in daily life . . . changed. . . . Racial profiling, for example, has again acquired a new acceptance—even by some sectors within minority groups." See Oboler, "Citizenship and Belonging," 116.

81. As of July 2019, the US Border Patrol employed 19,555 agents. See "Snapshot: A Summary of CBP Facts and Figures," US Customs and Border Protection, July 1, 2019, https://www.cbp.gov/sites/default/files/assets/documents/2019-Aug/CBP_Snapshot_07032019.pdf.

82. Garrett M. Graff, "The Border Patrol Hits a Breaking Point," *Politico*, July 15, 2019, https://www.politico.com/magazine/story/2019/07/15/border-patrol-trump-administration-227357.

83. Tal Kopan, "Border Patrol Has Thousands of Openings It Can't Fill," CNN, April 6, 2018, https://www.cnn.com/2018/04/06/politics/border-patrol-hiring-difficulties/index.html.

84. Correa and Thomas, "Rebirth of the U.S.-Mexico Border," 241.

85. "The Ray E. Helfer Society Recognizes Dr. Nancy Kellogg for Outstanding Teaching," Ray E. Helfer Society, accessed March 30, 2019, https://www.helfersociety.org/nancy-kellogg.

Chapter 2: "A life is worth more than a penis"

1. John Christl quoted in "Woman Found Guilty of Cutting Off Ex-Husband's Penis, Throwing It in Garbage Disposal," *New York Daily News*, April 29, 2013, https://www.nydailynews.com/news/crime/woman-guilty-cutting-man-penis-article-1.1330678.

2. Denisse Salazar, "Woman Accused in Penis-Slicing Hides Face in Court," *Orange County Register*, July 13, 2011, https://www.ocregister.com/2011/07/13/woman-accused-in-penis-slicing-hides-face-in-court/.

3. "'You Deserve It': Woman on Trial in Severed Penis Case," *Daily Beast*, April 21, 2017, https://www.thedailybeast.com/woman-on-trial-in-severed-penis-case.

4. "Woman Who Cut Off Husband's Penis Was Vengeful, Prosecutors Say," *Los Angeles Times*, April 30, 2013, https://www.latimes.com/local/lanow/la-xpm-2013-apr-30-la-me-ln-woman-who-cut-off-husbands-penis-was-vengeful-prosecutor-says-20130430-story.html.

5. "Woman Who Cut Off Husband's Penis."

6. Kieu Becker also received a sentencing enhancement for the "personal use of a knife." See Michael Martinez, "California Ex-wife Sentenced for Cutting Off Husband's Penis," CNN, June 29, 2013, https://www.cnn.com/2013/06/28/justice /california-penis-knifing/index.html.

7. Salazar, "Woman Accused in Penis-Slicing"; Martinez, "California Ex-wife Sentenced."

8. "Catherine Kieu Becker May Have Poisoned Husband's Tofu Soup," *Huffington Post*, September 21, 2011, https://www.huffpost.com/entry/catherine-kieu-becker -tofu-soup_n_907018; Salazar, "Woman Accused in Penis-Slicing."

9. Kim Masters, "Lorena Bobbitt: Sex, Lies, and an 8-Inch Carving Knife," *Vanity Fair*, November 1, 1993, https://www.vanityfair.com/style/1993/11/lorena-bobbitt -interview-sex-lies-carving-knife.

10. "Lorena Bobbitt: I Just Went Insane," *Steve Harvey*, season 4, episode 68, December 28, 2015.

11. Amelia McDonell-Parry, "John and Lorena Bobbitt, 25 Years Post-Castration," *Rolling Stone*, July 6, 2016, https://www.rollingstone.com/culture/cul ture-news/lorena-bobbitt-john-bobbitt-25-years-696573/.

12. Olivia B. Waxman, "'He Could Have Killed Me': Lorena Bobbitt on Domestic Abuse and What She Wants You to Know about Her Case 25 Years Later, *Time*, June 22, 2018, https://time.com/5317979/lorena-bobbitt-today-anniversary-interview/.

13. Peele quoted in Olivia A. Waxman, "How Lorena Bobbitt's Place in the Conversation about Domestic Violence Has Evolved," *Time*, February 15, 2019, http://time.com/5528544/lorena-bobbitt-domestic-violence/.

14. Katie Rife, "Enraging and Enlightening, *Lorena* Finally Puts Lorena Bobbitt at the Center of Her Own Story," *AV Club*, February 15, 2019, https://tv.avclub .com/enraging-and-enlightening-lorena-finally-puts-lorena-b-1832605826; Waxman, "Lorena Bobbitt's Place."

15. Coulter, *¡Adios America!*, 297.

16. Richard Bonnie, "Does the Law Treat the Insane Differently Than the Retarded?," *Slate*, June 27, 2001, https://slate.com/news-and-politics/2001/06/does-the -law-treat-the-insane-differently-than-the-retarded.html.

17. Gandy quoted in David Margolick, "Lorena Bobbitt Acquitted in Mutilation of Husband," *New York Times*, January 22, 1994, https://www.nytimes.com/1994 /01/22/us/lorena-bobbitt-acquitted-in-mutilation-of-husband.html.

18. Pollitt, *Reasonable Creatures*, 148.

19. Although the preference in contemporary domestic violence literature and activism is to refer to individuals who have experienced domestic violence as "survivors" rather than "victims," my use of the term "victim" here is intended to conjure the juridical category of the injured party and to use language that is historically accurate. This choice also follows the chapter's argument, which is that the conceptualization of the "victim" is central to the ascent of domestic violence policy.

20. Scott, *Only Paradoxes to Offer*.

21. Mehra and Ahmed, "Sara Ahmed," *Guernica*, July 17, 2017, https://www .guernicamag.com/sara-ahmed-the-personal-is-institutional/.

22. Lorena Gallo quoted in Lili Anolik, "Lorena Bobbitt's American Dream," *Vanity Fair*, June 28, 2018, https://www.vanityfair.com/style/2018/06/lorena-bobbitt -john-wayne-bobbitt-25-years.

23. Marylou Tousignant and Bill Miller, "Lorena Bobbitt Details Demise of Marriage," *Washington Post*, January 13, 1994, https://www.washingtonpost.com /archive/politics/1994/01/13/lorena-bobbitt-details-demise-of-marriage/1b1487f0 -769f-4d13-a85e-4670b722f1b0/?noredirect=on.

24. Masters, "Lorena Bobbitt."

25. Gallo quoted in Anolik, "Lorena Bobbitt's American Dream."

26. Bobbitt quoted in Anolik.

27. Bobbitt quoted in Anolik.

28. Masters, "Lorena Bobbitt."

29. Anolik, "Lorena Bobbitt's American Dream."

30. David A. Kaplan and Ellen Ladowsky, "Bobbitt Fever," *Newsweek* 123, no. 4 (1994): 52.

31. Debra Haffner quoted in Kaplan and Ladowsky, "Bobbitt Fever," 52.

32. Masters, "Lorena Bobbitt."

33. Pershing, "'His Wife Seized His Prize,'" 5–6. Although it is beyond the scope of this chapter to address how the trial was perceived outside of the United States, it is important to note that Lorena received considerable support from Ecuadorians.

34. Bill Miller and Marylou Tousignant, "'Just So Many Pictures in My Head': Lorena Bobbitt Recalls Rage before Mutilation but Not Act Itself," *Washington Post*, January 15, 1994.

35. Cynthia Heimel, "Sure, Women Are Angry," *Newsweek* 123, no. 4 (1994): 58.

36. Heimel, 58.

37. Barbara Ehrenreich, "Feminism Confronts Bobbittry," *Time* 143, no. 4 (1994): 74.

38. Ehrenreich, 74. Pollitt also wrote that Lorena's supporters were those who had to struggle with "female-ghetto jobs, too much housework, too little respect, too many men like John Bobbitt." See Pollitt, *Reasonable Creatures*, 147.

39. Filetti, "From Lizzie Borden to Lorena Bobbitt," 475, 476–477.

40. In making this point, Filetti compares Bobbitt's actions to the earlier crime of Lizzie Borden, which neither the courts nor the public could "comprehend." In both cases, the "butcherlike method [of the women's] . . . brutality seemed to have nothing feminine about it." See Filetti, 471.

41. Lakoff, "Cries and Whispers," 39.

42. Priest, Jenefsky, and Swenson, "Phallocentric Slicing," 101, 102.

43. See, for example, Elizabeth Stephens, "The Spectacularized Penis: Contemporary Representations of the Phallic Male Body," *Men and Masculinities* 10, no. 1 (2007): 85–98; Filetti, "From Lizzie Borden to Lorena Bobbitt"; Lakoff, "Cries and Whispers"; Priest, Jenefsky, and Swenson, "Phallocentric Slicing."

44. Deem, "From Bobbitt to SCUM," 516.

45. Stephens, "Spectacularized Penis," 90.

46. Dervin, "Bobbitt Case," 249; see also Grindstaff and McCaughey, "John Bobbitt's Missing Manhood," 172–192. For uses of "castration complex" in the media, see, for example, T. J. Edwards, "Grin and Bobbitt: What We Men Learned from Lorena & Co.," *Washington Post*, January 2, 1994, C5; McDonell-Parry, "John and Lorena Bobbitt."

47. D. Davis, "'Breaking Up' [at] Phallocracy," 127.

48. On this point, see also Lakoff, "Cries and Whispers," 39–40.

49. Frye, "Necessity of Differences," 996.

50. On Lorena as a "hot-blooded Latina," see Deem, "From Bobbitt to SCUM," 514; Rife, "Enraging and Enlightening." On Lorena as a "Latin firecracker," see Pershing, "'His Wife Seized His Prize,'" 5.

51. Pershing, "'His Wife Seized His Prize,'" 5. Pershing also describes how Lorena was supported by Latinas/os in the United States.

52. Charla Ogaz, "On the Semiotics of Lorena Bobbitt," in Mendible, *From Bananas to Buttocks*, 209.

53. Ogaz, "On the Semiotics of Lorena Bobbitt," 209.

54. Sawyer, "Bobbittizing Texaco," 151.

55. S. Berger, "(Un)Worthy," 200. Linda Kelly notes that the IMFA was "driven by stereotypical images of devious male aliens, rather than a realistic portrayal of the female aliens affected by this legislation." See L. Kelly, "Stories from the Front," 670.

56. Anderson, "A License to Abuse," 1401.

57. S. Berger, "(Un)Worthy," 203. On the evolution of VAWA, see Kandel, "Immigration Provisions," 1–34.

58. F. Franco, "Unconditional Safety," 109.

59. NOW LDEF member quoted in Meisel, "'Something on Women,'" 95.

60. Meisel, 95.

61. Bernstein, "Sexual Politics of the New Abolitionism," 128–143; Bernstein, "Militarized Humanitarianism Meets Carceral Feminism," 45–71. Meisel also notes that feminist support for VAWA "seems in hindsight to implicate legal feminists in the creation of the carceral state, but it is nowhere evident that those working on VAWA twenty-five years ago could have foreseen the extent to which it would push the movement . . . one step closer to co-optation by those bent on pursuing law and order. Instead . . . [it] is a reminder that even actions taken with the best of intentions can have very ugly consequences" (Meisel, "'Something on Women,'" 20). I do not agree with Meisel's assertion that feminist participation in the carceral state was an "ugly" side effect; rather, there is no way to separate out a desire to protect (certain) women from violence without knowingly criminalizing potential offenders. On this point, see also Halley, *Split Decisions*, where she argues,

> It would be a mistake to think that governance issues only from that combination of courts, legislatures, and police which constitutes the everyday image of "the state." Employers, schools, health care institutions, and a whole range of entities, often formally "private," govern too—and feminism has substantial parts of them under its control. . . . Feminists have learned how to participate in what is often called "the new governance." . . . By positioning themselves as experts on women, sexuality, motherhood, and so on, feminists walk the hall of power. . . . The 1990s was the decade par excellence of the emergence of governance feminism . . . a time of intense theoretical productivity among feminists. (20–21, 32)

62. The Violence Against Women Act quoted in DeCasas, "Protecting Hispanic Women," 75–76.

63. Silver, "Evaluation and Legal Standards," 44, 46. Between 1996 and 2000, more than 6,500 individuals, mostly women, have become legal residents through VAWA provisions.

64. Collopy, "Thwarting the Intent," 4.

65. Collopy, 4–5. While the Immigration and Nationality Act states that a "petitioner's admissibility *shall not* [be barred] . . . if the [court] finds that the act or conviction was connected to the alien's having been battered or subject to extreme cruelty," Collopy notes that the ambiguity present in the language is more often than not used as a basis for exclusion rather than inclusion (8).

66. Linda Kelly notes that "by incorporating the doctrines of coverture and chastisement, immigration law has been recognized to perpetuate the no longer viable assumption that a wife belongs to her husband." See L. Kelly, "Stories from the Front," 667. Sarah M. Wood also notes that VAWA legislation has been "constrained by the historical roots of immigration law in coverture," producing a "rigid structure of family-based immigration." See Wood, "VAWA's Unfinished Business," 154.

67. Coulter, *¡Adios, America!*, 294–295.

68. Donald Trump quoted in David Jackson, "Video: Trump Planned to Describe Some Mexican Migrants 'Rapists,'" *USA Today*, September 30, 2016, https://www.usatoday.com/story/news/politics/elections/2016/2016/09/30/donald-trump-mexico-restaurant-deposition-washington-dc/91331486/. Trump remarked, "When Mexico sends its people, they're not sending their best. . . . They're bringing drugs. They're bringing crime. They're rapists. And some, I assume, are good people."

69. Abu-Lughod, "Do Muslim Women Really Need Saving?," 783–790; Kwok Pui-lan, "Unbinding Our Feet: Saving Brown Women and Feminist Religious Discourse," in Donaldson and Kwok, *Postcolonialism, Feminism, and Religious Discourse*, 62–81; Puar, *Terrorist Assemblages*, 37–78.

70. Domestic violence has only been understood as a human rights issue since the early 2000s. See Yáñez, "From Asylum to VAWA," 418.

71. In theory, cultural competency is defined as

effective verbal and nonverbal interactions between individuals or groups, with a mutual understanding and respect of each other's values, beliefs, preferences and culture, to promote equity in healthcare with the goal of providing culturally sensitive care . . . [where] culture is defined as "the sum total of the ideas, beliefs, customs, values, knowledge, and material artefacts that are handed down from one generation to the next in a society" . . . [and] cultural sensitivity is defined as "the ability to recognize, understand, and react appropriately to behaviors of persons who belong to a cultural or ethnic group that differs substantially from one's own."

Cultural competency seeks to move away from models of clinician-patient communication that are "paternalistic, authoritarian, and hierarchical," toward a model that is "more collaborative and patient-centered" in the interest of better treatment compliance rates. Brooks, Manias, and Bloomer, "Culturally Sensitive Communication," 384–385.

72. Mark Bixler, "Domestic Abuse Often Culturally Acceptable," *Atlanta Journal and Constitution*, September 25, 2000, 1B. On this point, see also Tini Tran, "California and the West Asians, Latinos Now Find Refuge from Domestic Violence Services," *Los Angeles Times*, May 4, 1998, A3.

73. DeCasas, "Protecting Hispanic Women," 70.

74. Perilla, "Domestic Violence," 108.

75. See Crenshaw, "Demarginalizing the Intersection," 139–167.

76. Bixler, "Domestic Abuse," 1B.

77. Rivera, "Domestic Violence against Latinas," 9–10.

78. L. Kelly, "Stories from the Front," 681–682.

79. In the United States, the first battered women's shelter opened in 1964 in Pasadena, California; by 1979, 79 shelters were open nationwide; in 1985, there were 700; in 1993, there were 1,200. See "Historical Growth of Domestic Violence Shelters in US," Across Walls, accessed June 10, 2018, http://www.acrosswalls.org/statistics/history-domestic-violence-shelters/.

80. Nanasi, "U Visa's Failed Promise," 280.

81. Wrangle, Fisher, and Paranjape, "Ha Sentido Sola?," 262. Importantly, use of available statistics also often does not differentiate between undocumented women and women who are US citizens. For an example of how these figures appear, see Espenoza, "No Relief for the Weary," where the author cites two studies—one targeting undocumented women in the San Francisco Bay area and the other targeting general "Latinas" in the Washington, DC, area—to draw conclusions about the "prevalence of domestic violence in the Latino community" (207).

82. Perilla, "Domestic Violence," 114. There is also a strange phenomenon identified in, and/or created by, the domestic violence literature, in which it appears that Latina immigrants are more likely to be victims of abuse once they arrive in the United States, than during their past experiences in their countries of origin. On this point, see Zachary et al., "Domestic Abuse in the Emergency Department," 801.

83. DeCasas, "Protecting Hispanic Women," 61. Public health, legal, and social-science literature frequently uses the term "Hispanic women" as interchangeable with "Latina women." While this terminology is problematic, it has yet to be resolved in academic or public policy discourse. Therefore, when quoting, I do my best to remain faithful to the original author's wording choice—even when the author does not explain the terminology.

84. Rivera, "Domestic Violence against Latinas," 3.

85. L. Kelly, "Stories from the Front," 681.

86. Perilla, "Domestic Violence," 115.

87. Perilla, 120.

88. Perilla, 123.

89. Hernández-Truyol, "Sex, Culture, and Rights," 626. Kiran Hussain, S. Gisela Leija, Florence Lewis, and Bridget Sanchez have also explained that "because self-sacrifice is a core characteristic of marianismo, the tolerance of pain and suffering may be rendered as a symbol of strength." See Hussain et al., "Unveiling Sexual Identity," 75.

90. Rivera, "Domestic Violence against Latinas," 1. More recent scholarship continues to note the dearth of relevant statistics on domestic violence within Latina populations. See, for example, Adames and Campbell, "Immigrant Latinas' Conceptualizations," 1341; Levine and Peffer, "Quiet Casualties," 641.

91. Hernández-Truyol, "Sex, Culture, and Rights," 625. She also writes, "Latinas in this country are the poorest of any group in all of the United States. . . . Latinas are the least educated and the least represented in any body politic" (625).

92. Perilla, "Domestic Violence," 120. DeCasas also notes that the "literature on

domestic violence has given little attention to the specific issue of violence against Hispanic women." See DeCasas, "Protecting Hispanic Women," 61.

93. See, for example, Rivera, "Domestic Violence against Latinas"; Adames and Campbell, "Immigrant Latinas' Conceptualizations"; Levine and Peffer, "Quiet Casualties."

94. DeCasas, "Protecting Hispanic Women," 62.

95. Throughout my reading of scholarship on the issue of Latina women's experiences of domestic violence, I have noticed that authors often identify Latina women as the "most" disadvantaged population in the United States, typically by way of poverty and educational standing. These comparisons are either directly or obliquely made in relation to white and Black women. No mention of other ethnicities or races is given. While it is not within the scope of this work to speculate on why this is the case, it is important to note that these conclusions often do not differentiate between Latinas who are US citizens and those who are considered noncitizens, nor between those for whom English is a first or second language. While the position of noncitizens in the United States is certainly precarious and is necessarily correlated with poverty and a lack of access to education, it is also the case that analyses that prioritize these factors often gloss over issues of citizenship and ethnicity, while also overlooking the vast states of inequality experienced by other non-Latina noncitizens, other nonwhite groups, and especially Native American peoples. See, for example, Espenoza, "No Relief for the Weary," 207; Rivera, "Domestic Violence against Latinas," 3.

96. Natasha Frost, "Lorena Bobbitt's 12-Inch Knife Changed Awareness about Spousal Abuse," History Channel, August 22, 2018, https://www.history.com/news/lorena-bobbitt-case-cut-husband-john-bobbitt-spousal-abuse.

97. Marylou Tousignant and Bill Miller, "A Tale of Two Lorenas: Bobbitt Trial Doctors Detail States of Mind," *Washington Post*, January 19, 1994, D1.

98. See, for example, Margolick, "Lorena Bobbitt Acquitted."

99. Blair Howard quoted in Peele, *Lorena*, part 1.

100. Stern, *Eugenic Nation*, 18; Molina, "Medicalizing the Mexican," 22–37.

101. On the history of intelligence testing, see Gould, *Mismeasure of Man*, 176–203.

102. Hester Lacey, "The Hester Lacey Interview: He Could Easily Pass for Another of the Walton Brothers, Though Long-Lost, Disowned and Surgically Enhanced," *Independent*, September 8, 1996, https://www.independent.co.uk/life-style/john-wayne-bobbitt-1362268.html; Allan Fotheringham, "The Sweet Mystery of Manhood," *Maclean's*, January 24, 1994, http://archive.macleans.ca/article/1994/1/24/the-sweet-mystery-of-manhood.

103. Anna Silman, "The Bobbitt Penis Doctor on the Surgery He'll Never Forget," *The Cut*, February 13, 2019, https://www.thecut.com/2019/02/lorena-bobbitt-penis-surgery-john-wayne.html.

104. Gregory Murphy quoted in Peele, *Lorena*, part 1.

105. Murphy quoted in Masters, "Lorena Bobbitt." On John's intelligence, see also Frost, "Lorena Bobbitt's 12-Inch Knife."

106. Anolik, "Lorena Bobbitt's American Dream."

107. Jordan Peele quoted in Waxman, "Lorena Bobbitt's Place."

108. Peele, *Lorena*. On John's upbringing, see also Sharon Lynn Pruitt, "John

Bobbitt Opens Up about Dark Childhood, Molestation, and Abuse in New Amazon Doc," *Oxygen*, February 21, 2019, https://www.oxygen.com/martinis-murder/john-bobbitt-claims-childhood-sexual-abuse-domestic-violence-lorena.

109. Peele, *Lorena.*

110. John Wayne Bobbitt quoted in Rife, "Enraging and Enlightening." While some press coverage of *Lorena* represents John's childhood abuse as coming to light through the documentary, his mother's alleged rapes were noted in a nonchalant fashion in 1990s accounts. See, for example, Lacey, "Hester Lacey Interview."

111. Anolik, "Lorena Bobbitt's American Dream." The plot of the movie is a "takeoff on the Bobbitts' story, with a 'Lorena' character re-enacting the kitchen-knife incident. Bobbitt, playing himself, goes to the hospital for reattachment and is shown soon after the operation having intercourse with the nurses. Later, he has sex with women in a beauty parlor and on a pool table." See Fern Shen, "In a Huff over Bobbitt in Buff: Plan to Show X-Rated Film Riles Some GW Students," *Washington Post*, February 19, 1995. On the popularity of the film, see Joyce Chen, "Fine, We Can (Briefly) Talk about John Wayne Bobbitt's Porn Career," Refinery 29, February 16, 2019, https://www.refinery29.com/en-us/2019/02/224500/john-wayne-bobbitt-porn-movies-career.

112. Patricia O'Connell, "Miss Howard Stern New Year's Eve Pageant," *Variety*, January 2, 1994, https://variety.com/1994/tv/reviews/miss-howard-stern-new-year-s-eve-pageant-1200435431/.

113. McDonell-Parry, "John and Lorena Bobbitt." IMDb describes the film's plot as focusing on "a man who was castrated by his undersexed wife. Seeking the ability to have sex once again, he has a bizarre surgery in which a large, castrated penis is sewn onto him. It works, but brings the consequences of being endangered by the oversexed, ultimate pleasure master, The Bride of Frankenpenis, who has more stamina than any man alive." See "Frankenpenis, 1996," IMDb, accessed February 9, 2019, https://www.imdb.com/title/tt0140058/.

114. See, for example, classic works in visual theory, such as J. Berger, *Ways of Seeing*; Mulvey, "Visual Pleasure and Narrative Cinema," 6–18.

115. Dyer, *White*, 145–183. Relatedly, a 2019 article in *Rolling Stone* asks, "Is the photograph of John Wayne Bobbitt's severed penis one of the original dick pics? The beginning of a long tradition of phalluses in the public eye? Copious coverage of the 1993 Bobbitt scandal . . . kicked off two decades of penises inserting their way into the national discourse." Claire Hoffman, "'Lorena' Shines a Light on the Ugly Truth of the Bobbitt Scandal," *Rolling Stone*, February 15, 2019, https://www.rollingstone.com/tv/tv-features/lorena-bobbitt-amazon-793659/.

116. Stephens, "Spectacularized Penis," 95.

117. Brown, *Body and Society*, 10; Bersani, *Is the Rectum a Grave?*, 30; Grosz, *Volatile Bodies*, 200. On this point, see also Elizabeth Stephens, "Redefining Sexual Excess as a Medical Disorder: Fin-de-siècle Representations of Hysteria and Spermatorrhoea," in Evans and Griffiths, *Pleasure and Pain*, 209.

118. Grosz, *Volatile Bodies*, 200.

119. Lisa Kemler quoted in Arthur Hirsch, "Lorena Bobbitt Goes on Trial before 200 Reporters," *Baltimore Sun*, January 11, 1994, https://www.baltimoresun.com/news/bs-xpm-1994-01-11-1994011015-story.html.

120. Lisa Miller, "John Hinckley Left the Mental Hospital Seven Months Ago,"

New York, March 20, 2017, http://nymag.com/intelligencer/2017/03/john-hinckley-is -out-of-the-mental-hospital.html. Hinckley was obsessed with the actor Jodie Foster and claimed that she would be impressed by his actions, which he felt bore some similarity to those of a character in the film *Taxi Driver* (1976) who ends up rescuing Foster's character.

121. Natalie Jacewicz, "After Hinckley, States Tightened Use of the Insanity Plea," NPR, July 28, 2016, https://www.npr.org/sections/health-shots/2016/07/28 /486607183/after-hinckley-states-tightened-use-of-the-insanity-plea.

122. "Insanity Defense," Legal Information Institute, Cornell University, accessed May 2, 2019, https://www.law.cornell.edu/wex/insanity_defense. On the historical use of the insanity defense in the case of domestic abuse victims, see also Frost, "Lorena Bobbitt's 12-Inch Knife."

123. On insanity as a medical versus legal concept, see Bonnie, "Does the Law Treat the Insane Differently."

124. IQ level and other forms of standardized testing are used to prove a lack of capacity. Although these tests are highly problematic and are wed to histories of biological essentialism, they are understood by the courts as providing "objective" data that can be used to substantiate an insanity defense. By contrast, no empirical test can quantify impulse control.

125. Interestingly, however, the concept of impulsivity continues to be debated because of the nature of its vagueness and its inability to be concretely demonstrated. Comprehensive Crime Control Act language quoted in "Insanity Defense," Legal Information Institute, Cornell University, accessed May 2, 2019, https://www.law .cornell.edu/wex/insanity_defense.

126. Walker, "Battered Woman Syndrome," 142.

127. "Violence Prevention: Timeline," Centers for Disease Control and Prevention, January 16, 2019, https://www.cdc.gov/violenceprevention/publichealthissue /timeline.html. The term "intimate partner violence" (IPV) was introduced in the early 2000s and is intended to provide a gender-neutral replacement for the typically feminized terms "domestic violence" or "spousal abuse." IPV also expands the context beyond the institution of marriage and allows for the inclusion of different types of sexual partners beyond the boundaries of normative heterosexuality. On the change to IPV, see Dutton, "Complexity of Women's Response," 1277–1282.

128. Walker, *Battered Woman*.

129. Walker, "Battered Woman Syndrome," 143, 146. The mid-1970s marks the beginning of widespread research and publication on the subject of spousal abuse and domestic violence. Prior to this period, sparse and indirect references can be found in literature on topics of "morbid or paranoid jealousy, homicide," "sado-masochistic couples," and "conjugal homicide." See Okun, *Woman Abuse*, 11–12.

130. Walker, "Battered Woman Syndrome," 144–145; emphasis in the original.

131. Walker, 144.

132. Walker, 153.

133. Dimock, "Reasonable Women in the Law," 161–162.

134. Dimock, 162.

135. Dimock, 166. On this point, Kevin Jon Heller also writes, "It only makes sense to use a 'reasonable battered woman' or a 'reasonable battered child' standard instead of a 'reasonable person' standard if being battered prevents women and chil-

dren from perceiving and acting as reasonable persons." See Heller, "Beyond the Reasonable Man?," 83.

136. To be clear, I am not glorifying the position of the normative reasonable subject here. Instead, I am suggesting, along the lines of the legal theorists quoted in this chapter, that under US law, legal autonomy and personal agency are inseparable from conceptions of the reasonable subject. Thus, it is of great consequence that not every person is imagined to be able to meet the threshold of reasonability.

137. Pateman, *Sexual Contract*. On this point, see also Nussbuam, *Sex and Social Justice*; Mills, *Racial Contract*.

138. Similarly, in her critique of the lasting imprint of religious doctrine on sexual inequality, Gloria Anzaldúa describes how Christian rhetoric has long projected "all the evils onto children, third world people, animals, and women. . . . Men were supposed to be the ones with the soul; they were supposed to be spiritual, and women carnal." See Anzaldúa, "Spirituality, Sexuality, and the Body: An Interview with Linda Smuckler," in Keating, *Gloria Anzaldúa Reader*, 87–88.

139. Denno, "Gender, Crime, and the Criminal Law Defenses," 86–87.

140. Denno, 87.

141. Denno, 90.

142. Wolfe quoted in Pershing, "'His Wife Seized His Prize,'" 9.

143. Estrich quoted in Pershing, 8.

144. Simon and Young quoted in Pershing, 8.

145. Fiester quoted in Tousignant and Miller, "A Tale of Two Lorenas," D1.

146. Tousignant and Miller, "A Tale of Two Lorenas," D1.

147. Even as the state's expert witnesses came to change their opinions over the course of the trial, they never fully agreed with Fiester's diagnosis of a "psychotic episode." Instead, they were willing to agree that BWS had inspired an "irresistible impulse."

148. Gwaltney quoted in David Margolick, "Witness Says Lorena Bobbitt Earlier Threatened to Maim Husband," *New York Times*, January 20, 1994, A12.

149. Ryans quoted in Tousignant and Miller, "A Tale of Two Lorenas," D1.

150. Lorena Bobbitt quoted in Margolick, "Lorena Bobbitt Acquitted."

151. Margolick, "Witness Says Lorena Bobbitt Earlier Threatened," A12.

152. Strangely, Ryans also had a private conversation with Keegan at the recommendation of the prosecutor on the case, Paul Ebert; Ryans then used this conversation in his second testimony. At the time of the trial, this would not have been public knowledge. It was, however, the case that Keegan repeated the information she provided to Dr. Ryans over the phone in her testimony in open court.

153. Keegan quoted in Peele, *Lorena*, part 3.

154. Ryans quoted in Peele, *Lorena*, part 3. As explained earlier, BWS is clinically defined as a type of PTSD.

155. Juror quoted in Peele *Lorena*, part 3.

156. Whitaker and Howard quoted in Bill Miller and Marylou Tousignant, "Bobbitt Liked Rough Sex, Jury Told: Husband Denies Defense Claim, Says He Never Abused Wife," *Washington Post*, January 12, 1994.

157. Beth Ann Wilson quoted in Tousignant and Miller, "Lorena Bobbitt Details Demise."

158. This is a gloss on Gayatri Spivak's important turn of phrase, "white men

saving brown women from brown men," which she uses to articulate the intersections of race, gender, sexuality, and imperialism. See G. Spivak, "Can the Subaltern Speak?" Subsequently, other scholars have added to Spivak's theorization by considering the important role that white women have played in regulating brown women, brown men, and white men. See, for example, Coloma, "White Gazes, Brown Breasts," 243–261; Syed and Ali, "White Woman's Burden," 349–365; Frye, *Willful Virgin*, 147–169; Chandra Talpade Mohanty, "Under Western Eyes," in Mohanty, Russo, and Torres, *Third World Women*.

159. Mehra and Ahmed, "Sara Ahmed," *Guernica*, July 17, 2017, https://www
.guernicamag.com/sara-ahmed-the-personal-is-institutional/. As Ahmed explains,

> Gayatri Spivak's diagnosis of the imperial mission [in her 1988 essay "Can the Subaltern Speak?"] as "white men saving brown women from brown men" remains precise. Additionally, imperial feminism can take the form of "white women saving brown women from brown men." We still witness all around us how feminism is narrated as an imperial project. Even anti-racism can become a discourse of white feminist pride: what white women can give us by overcoming their whiteness. As we know too well, Muslim women are assumed as passive, oppressed, and in need of being saved by feminists who seem curiously more concerned with other women's liberation than their own. . . . The assumption that feminism travels from the West to the rest can mean that you do not notice the transit that moves in the other direction. We have to interrupt the feminist story by changing how we start a conversation, by starting with those who found feminism in a different way.

160. Masters, "Lorena Bobbitt"; my emphasis.

161. Torry, "Multicultural Jurisprudence," 128–129.

162. These specific scholars were chosen based on the frequency of cross-citation within prevailing literature, and are thus suggestive of broader ideological paradigms.

163. Gomez, "Dilemma of Difference," 361.

164. Gomez, 367.

165. See, for example, Renteln, "Justification of the Cultural Defense," 437–526.

166. Volpp, "(Mis)Identifying Culture," 61.

167. Torry, "Multicultural Jurisprudence," 131, 127; emphasis in the original.

168. Torry, 142–146.

169. Maguigan, "Cultural Evidence and Male Violence," 36–37.

170. Gallin, "Cultural Defense," 724, 725.

171. Gallin, 735.

172. Gallin, 736.

173. Gallin, 741, 743.

174. Holmquist, "Cultural Defense or False Stereotype?," 65.

175. Holmquist, 65.

176. Holmquist, 46.

177. Masters, "Lorena Bobbitt"; Margolick, "Lorena Bobbitt Acquitted"; Tousignant and Miller, "Lorena Bobbitt Details Demise."

178. Lorena quoted in Masters, "Lorena Bobbitt."

179. Lorena quoted in Waxman, "'He Could Have Killed Me.'"

180. Dennis Romero, "Catherine Kieu Becker's Penis Cutting Incident Could

Bring Life behind Bars," *LA Weekly*, January 6, 2012, https://www.laweekly.com
/catherine-kieu-beckers-penis-cutting-indictment-could-bring-life-behind-bars/.

181. McDonell-Parry, "John and Lorena Bobbitt."

Chapter 3: "A troubled, battered mind"

1. "NFL Lockout Aside, Patriots Aaron Hernandez Leads Latino Mental
Health Awareness Day," Fox News, May 1, 2011, https://www.foxnews.com/world
/nfl-lockout-aside-patriots-aaron-hernandez-leads-latino-mental-health-awareness
-day.

2. Gardner Pilot Academy home page, accessed March 1, 2019, http://stage
.gardnerpilotacademy.org.

3. The Lucero Program website states that training occurs through a process of
"intensive immersion in Spanish language and Hispanic cultures" in the interest of
preparing "culturally sensitive clinicians." See Massachusetts School of Professional
Psychology, "Professional Athlete, Aaron Hernandez, Scores Touchdown with Latino Children during Awareness Day for Improved Latino Mental Health," PR
Newswire, May 26, 2011, https://www.prnewswire.com/news-releases/professional
-athlete-aaron-hernandez-scores-touchdown-with-latino-children-during-aware
ness-day-for-improved-latino-mental-health-122659348.html; "Dr. Cynthia Lucero Center for Latino Mental Health (LMHP)," William James College, accessed
March 2, 2019, https://www.williamjames.edu/academics/centers-of-excellence/la
tino-mental-health/index.cfm. It is unclear what "culturally and linguistically appropriate mental health services" would look like here. They are not defined by the
author but seem to revolve around a similarity with respect to familial values and
community standards. Certainly, this is complicated in the case of Hernandez, who
grew up as one of only a few Latinx kids in his school system; by contrast, Gardner
Pilot Academy is located in a predominantly Latinx area.

4. Karen Guregian, "Past Leads Aaron Hernandez to Share Love, Lessons
in Latino Community," *Boston Herald*, April 24, 2011, https://www.bostonherald
.com/2011/04/24/past-leads-aaron-hernandez-to-share-love-lessons-in-latino-com
munity/; Gardner Pilot Academy, "Latino Patriots Star Helps Out Community
Center," https://www.gardnerpilotacademy.org/wp-content/uploads/2011/05/Aaron
-Hernandez-El-Mundo.pdf.

5. Guregian, "Past Leads Hernandez to Share Love."

6. Mbembe, "Necropolitics," 11–40.

7. Pérez-Melgosa, "Low Intensity Necropolitics," 217–236; Berlant, "Slow Death,"
754–780.

8. Cacho, *Social Death*, 150.

9. Cacho, 149. On this point, see also Cacho, "'How Much He Meant,'" 182–208.

10. Beth Healy, "Part 5 of 6: Prison; A Room of His Own," *Boston Globe*, October 18, 2018, https://apps.bostonglobe.com/spotlight/gladiator/prison/.

11. Richard Lapchick, "The 2018 Racial and Gender Report Card: National Football League," Institute for Diversity and Ethics in Sport, 2019, https://43530132-36e9
-4f52-811a-182c7a91933b.filesusr.com/ugd/7d86e5_4a7afdf9bf414bffa46b3a099bf8c9f5
.pdf. In their recent work on the history of Latinos' participation in the NFL, Fred-

erick Luis Aldama and Christopher González suggest that these numbers may invisibilize the presence of Latinos without traditionally Spanish-sounding names. They also argue that even in light of statistical disparities, the publicity surrounding a few well-known Latino players suggests that we rethink the place of Latinos in the sport. See Aldama and González, *Latinos in the End Zone*.

12. Sam Farmer, "Report: Police Probe Aaron Hernandez's Possible Role in 2007 Shooting," *Los Angeles Times*, July 3, 2013, https://www.latimes.com/sports/la -xpm-2013-jul-03-la-sp-sn-aaron-hernandez-2007-20130703-story.html.

13. I make this distinction because it remains unclear how Hernandez chose to identify himself. Mainstream media sources have referred to him as both gay and bisexual. One of his attorneys, George Leontire, claims that he spoke with Hernandez about his sexuality and that "this man was clearly gay [and] acknowledged it, acknowledged the immense pain it had caused him . . . [because] he had also came out of a culture that was so negative about gay people that he exhibited some self-hatred." Leontire quoted in *Aaron Hernandez Uncovered* (Oxygen, 2018). By contrast, Hernandez's brother, Jonathan "DJ" Hernandez, claims that when he asked Aaron if he was "gay," he was met with a strong refusal. See Hernandez and Anderson, *Truth about Aaron*, 78.

14. Shayanna Jenkins-Hernandez, foreword to Baez and Willis, *Unnecessary Roughness*, xi.

15. Charles Bethea, "The Worrisome Reporting on Aaron Hernandez's Sexuality," *New Yorker*, April 30, 2017, https://www.newyorker.com/sports/sporting-scene /the-worrisome-reporting-on-aaron-hernandezs-sexuality.

16. Michele McPhee, Kirk Minihane, and Gerry Callahan quoted in Bethea, "Worrisome Reporting on Hernandez's Sexuality."

17. McPhee quoted in Bethea, "Worrisome Reporting on Hernandez's Sexuality."

18. The first piece details his relationship with his "prison boyfriend," Kyle Kennedy; his intimacy with another boy while he was in high school; and the use of the terms "smoocher" and "limp wrist" by Odin Lloyd and Ernest Wallace, respectively, in reference to Aaron. The second piece describes the content of one of three suicide notes left by Hernandez and uses the letter as "proof" of Aaron's gay identity, which in turn is used to identify his alleged motive in the Odin Lloyd case. See Michele McPhee, "Aaron Hernandez's Sex Life Probed as Murder Motive, Police Source Says," *Newsweek*, April 21, 2017, https://www.newsweek.com/aaron-hernandez -hidden-sexuality-murder-police-587879; McPhee, "'I Think I'm Going to Hang It Up, LOL': Aaron Hernandez Note to Prison Boyfriend," *Newsweek*, April 26, 2017, https://www.newsweek.com/aaron-hernandez-aaron-hernandez-suicide-aaron-her nandez-boyfriend-aaron-590582.

19. Harrison, "First Concussion Crisis," 822–833.

20. Sacha Pfeiffer, "Part 6 of 6: CTE; A Terrible Thing to Waste," *Boston Globe*, October 18, 2016, https://apps.bostonglobe.com/spotlight/gladiator/cte/.

21. R. Spivak, "Not Guilty by Reason of CTE," 1283. In response to the publication of these findings, the NFL funded and published its own study attempting to discredit Omalu's assertion that football caused CTE. Backed by a group of prominent physicians, Omalu refused to retract his findings; in 2006, he found similar signs of the disease in former NFL player Terry Long (R. Spivak, 1284).

22. In a 2017 study conducted by Boston University on 111 brains of ex-football

players, 110 were diagnosed with CTE. See J. Amy Dillard and Lisa A. Tucker, "Is C.T.E. a Defense for Murder?," *New York Times*, September 22, 2017, https://www.nytimes.com/2017/09/22/opinion/aaron-hernandez-cte.html. Similarly, a 2018 study found that 98 percent of NFL wives reported having witnessed a behavior associated with concussion symptoms. See Faure and Casanova, "Fall of the Gladiators," 1–16.

23. Pfeiffer, "Part 6 of 6."

24. Pfeiffer, "Part 6 of 6."

25. Faure and Casanova, "Fall of the Gladiators," 1. Conflicting information exists on this figure. Baez states that the payout was $765 million; see Baez and Willis, *Unnecessary Roughness*, 249–250.

26. Faure and Casanova, "Fall of the Gladiators," 14.

27. Alana Semuels, "The White Flight from Football," *Atlantic*, February 1, 2019, https://www.theatlantic.com/health/archive/2019/02/football-white-flight-racial-divide/581623/.

28. Andrew Ryan, "Lost in 'The Swamp,'" *Boston Globe*, October 14, 2018, https://apps.bostonglobe.com/spotlight/gladiator/florida.

29. My point in providing these statistics is not to reify essentialized racial categories but rather to give an overall picture of racial disparities in the sport. For NFL statistics, see Lapchick, "2018 Report Card: National Football League"; for college-level statistics, see Richard Lapchick, "The 2018 Racial and Gender Report Card: College Sport," Institute for Diversity and Ethics in Sport, 2019, https://43530132-36e9-4f52-811a-182c7a91933b.filesusr.com/ugd/7d86e5_05a980a149c24e69baa5265abc63c3b2.pdf.

30. Semuels, "White Flight from Football."

31. Albert Samaha, "The Kids Who Still Need Football," *New York Times*, September 12, 2018, https://www.nytimes.com/2018/09/08/opinion/sunday/football-kids-brain-damage.html.

32. Branch quoted in Diane Roberts, "College Football's Big Problem with Race," *Time*, November 12, 2015, https://www.time.com/4110443/college-football-race-problem/. Branch identifies an amount of $3.5 billion; $4.2 billion reflects the revenue as of 2018. See Ryan, "Lost in 'The Swamp.'"

33. Ryan, "Lost in 'The Swamp.'" In order to keep up with college-level coursework, many of these players take additional classes at local community colleges, although these courses do not count toward their graduation requirements, and it is not uncommon for them to not graduate.

34. From this point forward, I will often refer to Aaron Hernandez by his first name, to avoid confusion with references to his brother, DJ Hernandez, and his father, Dennis Hernandez.

35. Eric Levenson, "Aaron Hernandez Was Beaten and Sexually Abused as a Child," CNN, October 18, 2018, https://www.cnn.com/2018/10/15/us/aaron-hernandez-spotlight/index.html. Many sources, including those that quote directly from interviews with Aaron, observe that he had a difficult time coping with his father's death.

36. Ron Borges and Paul Solotaroff, "The Gangster in the Huddle: Aaron Hernandez; Inside Dark, Tragic Life of Former Patriots Star," *Rolling Stone*, September 12, 2013, https://www.rollingstone.com/culture/culture-sports/aaron-hernandez-inside-dark-tragic-life-of-former-patriots-star-118525/.

37. Pfeiffer, "Part 6 of 6." His attorney George Leontire describes the following: "He had been molested fairly intensely as a very young kid. . . . Hernandez seemed to think the sexual abuse had made him gay. . . . He saw it as a way to control his self-hatred, because it wasn't his fault." Leontire quoted in Healy, "Part 5 of 6."

38. Historians of sexuality and queer theorists have demonstrated ongoing linkages between practices of criminalization and antiqueer sentiment. See, for example, Kunzel, *Criminal Intimacy*.

39. Notably, sources disagree on the results of Hernandez's drug tests. For example, University of Florida coach Urban Meyer was reportedly unhappy with Aaron's "chronic marijuana use" but also noted that "the tests would come back that he was not smoking and he [Aaron] denied it all the time." Here, as elsewhere, it is unclear what the "truth" may be—that is, whether Meyer was lying, whether Aaron was using masking agents, or whether Aaron might not have been using as much marijuana as was speculated. Since Meyer was known publicly to want Aaron off the team, it seems unlikely he would have lied in his favor to keep him at Florida. See Meyer quoted in Ryan, "Lost in 'The Swamp.'"

40. This language was used in multiple sources. See, for example, Amy Laskowski, "Was Patriots' Hernandez a Time Bomb?," *Boston University Today*, July 2, 2013, https://www.bu.edu/today/2013/was-patriots-aaron-hernandez-a-time-bomb/; Justin Peters, "Aaron Hernandez's Unsavory Past Has No Bearing on His Unsavory Present," *Slate*, June 21, 2013, https://slate.com/news-and-politics/2013/06/aaron-hernandez-the-patriots-tight-end-s-unsavory-past-has-no-bearing-on-his-unsavory-present.html; "Hot-Headed Hernandez," *New York Post*, July 4, 2013, https://nypost.com/2013/07/04/hot-headed-hernandez/.

41. Amna Nawaz, "How 'Football Inc' Missed Warning Signs around Aaron Hernandez," *PBS News Hour*, October 18, 2018, https://www.pbs.org/newshour/show/how-football-inc-missed-warning-signs-around-aaron-hernandez. See also K. Belson, "Debilitated Players Accuse N.F.L. of Stalling on Settlement Payments," *New York Times*, November 13, 2017, https://www.nytimes.com/2017/11/13/sports/football/nfl-concussion-lawsuit.html.

42. Michele McPhee quoted in *Aaron Hernandez Uncovered*.

43. David Whitley, "Commentary: Aaron Hernandez Had a Criminal Mind before CTE," *Orlando Sentinel*, September 21, 2017, https://www.orlandosentinel.com/opinion/david-whitley/os-sp-aaron-hernandez-david-whitley-blog-20170921-story.html. On the ambiguous link between CTE and violence, see Ken Belson, "Aaron Hernandez Had Severe CTE When He Died at Age 27, *New York Times* September 21, 2017, https://www.nytimes.com/2017/09/21/sports/aaron-hernandez-cte-brain.html.

44. Patterson, Abramovich, and Harvkey, *All-American Murder*, 172–173.

45. Patterson, Abramovich, and Harvkey, 99–100.

46. Brian Murphy quoted in Patterson, Abramovich, and Harvkey, 355–356.

47. Borges and Solotaroff, "Gangster in the Huddle."

48. Dave Altimari quoted in *Aaron Hernandez Uncovered*.

49. Baez and Willis, *Unnecessary Roughness*, 95–96.

50. Hernandez and Anderson, *Truth about Aaron*, iii.

51. Hohler quoted in Nawaz, "How 'Football Inc' Missed Signs." After Aaron's death, Dennis SanSoucie, a high school friend and teammate of Aaron's, came for-

ward and acknowledged an "on again off again relationship" that began in middle school and that the boys kept hidden from their families and other friends. See Hohler et al., "The Secrets behind the Smile," *Boston Globe*, October 13, 2018, https://www.bostonglobe.com/metro/2018/10/13/bristol/tPEm7cOM36yOoeTvmf5RoH/story.html.

52. Hernandez and Anderson, *Truth about Aaron*, 9.

53. Hohler et al., "Secrets behind the Smile."

54. Hernandez and Anderson, *Truth about Aaron*, 78.

55. Here, I am not making a judgment call about "acceptable" practices of crying in public or private, or their rightful correlation with particular gender identities. Rather, I am explaining that this behavior was frequently noted by teammates and journalists who found it cause for concern, described it in gendered terms, and labeled it as "abnormal." See, for example, Nawaz, "How 'Football Inc' Missed Signs"; Lia Eustachewich, "It Was Really Awkward Being Aaron Hernandez's Teammate," *New York Post*, October 16, 2018, https://nypost.com/2018/10/16/it-was-really-awkward-being-aaron-hernandezs-teammate/; Ian Rappaport quoted in Patterson, Abramovich, and Harvkey, *All-American Murder*, 115. It is of course also the case that the years of Hernandez's decline coincided with the rise of the Trump administration, which ushered in an era of prized hypermasculinity. Reading Hernandez's behavior in this context is meaningful because it suggests just how high the stakes were (and are) for nonnormative gender presentations.

56. Lloyd quoted in Nawaz, "How 'Football Inc' Missed Signs."

57. Eustachewich, "It Was Really Awkward."

58. Ian Rappaport quoted in Patterson, Abramovich, and Harvkey, *All-American Murder*, 115.

59. On Hernandez's psychological assessment, see Ryan, "Lost in 'The Swamp.'" While this information has been described in retrospect as an unheeded "warning sign" of the violence to come, it is also true that Aaron, then twenty years old, was one of the youngest NFL draft picks and that much of his "immaturity" (which appears in different reports to be a synonym for poor self-esteem, maladjustment, depression, moodiness, and general instability) was read in relation to his father's death, which coincided with his departure from home to play college football. See, for example, Patterson, Abramovich, and Harvkey, *All-American Murder*, 98.

60. Baez and Willis, *Unnecessary Roughness*, 192–195.

61. Patterson, Abramovich, and Harvkey, *All-American Murder*, 307–308.

62. As Khalil Gibran Muhammad has argued, statistics linking African Americans to crime must be treated with circumspection. Not only are these rates linked to complicated processes of criminalization that involve the production of structural inequalities and disproportionate policing policies, but so too does the very project of "crime statistics" have a historical root in anti-Black segregationist rhetoric. See Muhammad, *Condemnation of Blackness*.

63. On the racial dynamics of the US criminal justice system and incarceration patterns, see Alexander, *New Jim Crow*.

64. Ian Crouch, "Judging Aaron Hernandez," *New Yorker*, June 24, 2013, https://www.newyorker.com/sports/sporting-scene/judging-aaron-hernandez; my emphasis.

65. Besnier, Brownell, and Carter, *Anthropology of Sport*, 117–118.

66. Martin, Fasching-Varner, and Hartlep, *Pay to Play*, 7. This study, like many

others, asks players to identify their race and/or ethnicity, separating out Blackness and whiteness from Hispanic/non-Hispanic. The authors also use the terms "Hispanic" and "Latino" interchangeably throughout the book.

67. Martin, Fasching-Varner, and Hartlep, 7–8.

68. Martin, Fasching-Varner, and Hartlep, 83–88.

69. Leonard, "Jumping the Gun," 254. Notably this is not the case for white athletes, who are typically associated with the positive attributes of the game and with more "intellectualized" roles (e.g., quarterback). On this point see Leonard, *Playing While White*.

70. Baez and Willis, *Unnecessary Roughness*, 151–152.

71. Borges and Solotaroff, "Gangster in the Huddle."

72. Borges and Solotaroff, "Gangster in the Huddle."

73. I am not offering a reading or interpretation of Hernandez's tattoos as revelatory about his experience, views, or consciousness. Rather, because there is very little explanation provided by Hernandez himself regarding his tattoos, this chapter focuses on media representations and interpretations of the tattoos.

74. Baez and Willis, *Unnecessary Roughness*, 4, 5. Versions of this description can be found in numerous media reports. See, for example, John Breech, "Police Release Full, Detailed Report on Prison Suicide of Aaron Hernandez," *CBS Sports*, May 5, 2017, https://www.cbssports.com/nfl/news/police-release-full-detailed-report-on-prison-suicide-of-aaron-hernandez/; Jessica A. Botelho, "Report: Aaron Hernandez Was Naked When Found Hanged, NBC News 10, May 4, 2017, https://turnto10.com/news/local/report-aaron-hernandez-was-naked-when-found-hanged.

75. "Tattoos as Evidence: Aaron Hernandez's Far from the First," *Hartford Courant*, January 12, 2017, https://www.courant.com/news/connecticut/hc-hernandez-tattoos-0113-20170112-story.html.

76. See, for example, Yaron Steinbuch, "Aaron Hernandez's Prison Records Reveal a Nightmare Inmate," *New York Post*, May 5, 2017, https://nypost.com/2017/05/05/hernandez-had-a-lengthy-discipline-record-in-prison/; Andy Rosen and John R. Ellement, "Does Aaron Hernandez's Body Ink Mean He Did It?," *Boston Globe*, December 27, 2016, https://www.bostonglobe.com/metro/2016/12/27/aaron-hernandez-case-back-boston-court/SFrS6SWksAubVUouhLT7OO/story.html.

77. Butler, "Endangered/Endangering," 20–21.

78. On the phenomenon of memes and the portrayal of problematic content, see Peters and Allan, "Weaponizing Memes."

79. Brisman, "'Are You Serious?'"

80. On the history of criminology as a racialized discipline, see Simon A. Cole, *Suspect Identities: A History of Fingerprinting and Criminal Identification* (Cambridge, MA: Harvard University Press, 2001).

81. Simpson, known as one of the best running backs in football history, has faced various legal troubles, beginning with the double murder of Nicole Brown and Ron Goldman in 1995. Although he was acquitted in that case, he was later incarcerated "for armed robbery after attempting to steal sports memorabilia that he said belonged to him." See "Dr. Bennet Omalu 'Would Bet My Medical License' that O.J. Simpson Has CTE," ESPN, January 30, 2016, http://www.espn.com/nfl/story/_/id/14677428/dr-bennet-omalu-bet-my-medical-license-oj-simpson-cte.

82. R. Spivak, "Not Guilty by Reason of CTE," 1290.

83. R. Spivak, 1292.

84. Bruce Y. Lee, "Could Concussions Become a Legal Defense?," *Forbes*, February 4, 2016, https://www.forbes.com/sites/brucelee/2016/02/05/concussions-as-a-legal-defense/#40c840a83984.

85. R. Spivak, "Not Guilty by Reason of CTE," 1293.

86. Wailoo, *Pain*, 4.

87. Wailoo, 59.

88. Wailoo, 81–84.

89. Wailoo, 98, 194.

90. Faure and Casanova, "Fall of the Gladiators," 14.

91. Faure and Casanova, "Fall of the Gladiators," 9. To be clear, neither Rodgers nor Faure and Casanova make an argument about CTE as a form of closeting or as being connected to nonnormative sexuality. See also Katie Rodgers, "I Was a Gladiator: Pain, Injury, and Masculinity in the NFL," in Oates and Furness, *NFL*, 142–159.

92. Pérez-Melgosa, "Low Intensity Necropolitics," 219.

93. Pérez-Melgosa, 231.

94. Currently, a CTE diagnosis is obtained through injecting sliced brain tissue with chemicals to reveal the clumps of tau proteins associated with the disease. The procedure can take several months and is not a part of standard autopsies. In recent years, researchers have worked to find different ways of measuring protein buildup in the brain and blood, but it remains inconclusive with respect to CTE diagnosis. See, for example, Kevin Hrusovsky, "FDA Approves First Blood Test for Concussions," *Medical Laboratory Observer*, August 22, 2018, 42.

95. "What Is CTE?," Concussion Legacy Foundation, accessed April 30, 2019, https://concussionfoundation.org/CTE-resources/what-is-CTE.

96. Richard Sherman, "We Chose This Profession," *Sports Illustrated*, October 23, 2013, https://www.si.com/2013/10/23/richard-sherman-seahawks-concussions-in-the-nfl.

97. Associated Press, "Players Still Willing to Hide Head Injuries," ESPN, December 26, 2011, http://www.espn.com/nfl/story/_/id/7388074/nfl-players-say-hiding-concussions-option; my emphasis.

98. Rick Maese, "NFL Abuse of Painkillers and Other Drugs Described in Court Filings," *Washington Post*, March 9, 2017, https://www.washingtonpost.com/sports/redskins/nfl-abuse-of-painkillers-and-other-drugs-described-in-court-filings/2017/03/09/be1a71d8-035a-11e7-ad5b-d22680e18d10_story.html?utm_term=.741f2f8c84b7.

99. Eugene Monroe, "Getting off the T Train," *The Players' Tribune*, May 21, 2016, https://www.theplayerstribune.com/en-us/articles/2016-5-23-eugene-monroe-ravens-marijuana-opioids-toradol-nfl.

100. Andrew Ryan and Bob Hohler, "In Jail Calls, Hernandez Talked about Painkillers," *Boston Globe*, November 13, 2018, https://www.bostonglobe.com/metro/2018/11/12/jail-calls-hernandez-discussed-nfl-reliance-painkillers-with-former-teammates/mHETD8Ea7XXZagrGQXxiSN/story.html. In addition, Toradol can cause internal bleeding and kidney damage.

101. Transcript of Hernandez's phone call with teammate "Spikes" quoted in Ryan and Hohler, "In Jail Calls."

102. Ryan and Hohler, "In Jail Calls." While medicinal and recreational use of marijuana has been banned by the NFL, it remains a widely used pain remedy by players across the league. At the time of his death, Hernandez's postmortem toxicology report came back negative, but speculation remains surrounding his use of K2 while incarcerated, given that the drug "can be difficult to detect in routine drug tests." On Hernandez's alleged use of K2, see Matt Bonesteel, "Aaron Hernandez Was Smoking K2 before His Suicide, Fellow Inmate Told Investigators," *Washington Post*, October 30, 2018, https://www.washingtonpost.com/sports/2018/10/30/aaron -hernandez-was-smoking-k-before-his-suicide-fellow-inmate-told-investigators /?utm_term=.31aaff985d50.

103. Borges and Solotaroff, "Gangster in the Huddle."

104. Berlant, "Slow Death," 754, 757.

105. Berlant, 759.

106. Berlant, 759, 761.

107. Berlant, 763, 761. Disability studies theorists have also called attention to the ways in which time operates in differential and oppressive modes for those whose bodies are not coded as normative. See, for example, Samuels, "Six Ways of Looking at Crip Time."

108. Berlant, "Slow Death," 759.

109. Puar, "Coda," 152.

110. Puar, 152–153.

111. Puar, 153; my emphasis.

112. John Branch, "On the Table, the Brain Appeared Normal," *New York Times*, November 9, 2017, https://www.nytimes.com/2017/11/09/sports/aaron-hernandez -brain-cte.html.

113. Ann McKee quoted in Rich Barlow, "Aaron Hernandez's CTE Worst Seen by BU Experts in a Young Person," Boston University Research, November 10, 2017, http://www.bu.edu/research/articles/aaron-hernandez-cte-worst-seen-in-young -person/; my emphasis. See also Adam Kilgore, "Aaron Hernandez Suffered from Most Severe CTE Ever Found in a Person of His Age," *Washington Post*, November 9, 2017, http://www.washingtonpost.com/sports/aaron-hernandez-suffered-from -most-severe-cte-ever-found-in-a-person-his-age/2017/11/09/fa7cd204-c57b-11e7 -afe9-4f60b5a6c4a0_story.html. Here McKee is quoted as stating, "In this age group, he's clearly at the severe end of the spectrum. . . . There is a concern that we're seeing an accelerated disease in young athletes. Whether or not that's because they're playing more aggressively or if they're starting at younger ages, we don't know. But we are seeing ravages of this disease, in this specific example, of a young person."

114. Branch, "On the Table"; my emphasis.

115. Baez quoted in *Aaron Hernandez Uncovered*.

Chapter 4: "Who's going to tell Sammy Sosa he is Afro-Latino?"

1. Etienne Rodriguez, "The Problem with Kali Uchis / White Latinxs; And Why We Need to Have This Conversation," *Medium*, June 3, 2017, https://medium.com /@Etinni_/the-problem-with-kali-uchis-white-latinxs-ea76b39372e5; my emphasis.

2. Esperanz Aguilera Fuentes quoted in Jaquira Diaz, "Who Is the Real Kali

Uchis?," *The Fader*, July 13, 2017, https://www.thefader.com/2017/07/13/kali-uchis-cover-story-album-tyrant-interview.

3. Fuentes quoted in Diaz, "Who Is the Real Kali Uchis?" As Isabel Molina-Guzmán writes, "Even as the ideology of racial mixture and democracy is celebrated among many Latina/os, whiteness and white notions of beauty (*blanqueamiento*) still reign supreme, as most clearly exemplified in the representational privileging of lighter-skinned Latinas on television programs" produced in Latin America. See Molina-Guzmán, *Dangerous Curves*, 5–6.

4. Diaz, "Who Is the Real Kali Uchis?"

5. Zahira Kelly quoted in Diaz, "Who Is the Real Kali Uchis?"

6. Uchis quoted in Diaz, "Who Is the Real Kali Uchis?"

7. bell hooks, *Black Looks*, 21.

8. Kelly quoted in Diaz, "Who Is the Real Kali Uchis?"

9. The *Oxford English Dictionary* dates the term "transracial" to as early as 1971, but quotes the earliest source as stating that it already exists in "sociologists' jargon." The dictionary does not provide a definition of "transracial" in the sense this chapter addresses. *Oxford English Dictionary Online*, s.v. "transracial, adj.," accessed August 3, 2021, https://www-oed-com.ezproxy.wesleyan.edu/view/Entry/205049?redirectedFrom=transracial. A user-written entry in the Urban Dictionary defines the term as follows: "When a person who is born of one race, makes the decision to become or represent themselves as another race. This is often done by persons who are mixed or biracial and can hence pass for multiple races. In more extreme circumstances, persons will change their outward appearance (through tanning etc.) to appear to be of one race and not another." See DuanCulo, "Transracial," *Urban Dictionary*, June 13, 2015, https://www.urbandictionary.com/define.php?term=transracial. As addressed in this chapter, many balk at the concept itself in this secondary usage, and so it is by no means a settled definition.

10. Snorton, *Black on Both Sides*, 8.

11. Tuvel, "In Defense of Transracialism," 264. Some critics have objected to the use of the word "transracial" to denote a person who chooses to reject the racial identity they have been assigned or have inherited, noting that the term has also already been in use to represent interracial adoptees. See, for example, Ellie Freeman, "Transracial Doesn't Mean What Rachel Dolezal Thinks It Means," Media Diversified, June 15, 2015, https://mediadiversified.org/2015/06/15/transracial-doesnt-mean-what-rachel-dolezal-thinks-it-means/; Lisa Marie Rollins, "Transracial Lives Matter: Rachel Dolezal and the Privilege of Racial Manipulation," Lost Daughters, June 14, 2015, http://www.thelostdaughters.com/2015/06/transracial-lives-matter-rachel-dolezal.html.

12. Rachel Dolezal interviewed on *Melissa Harris-Perry*, MSNBC, June 16, 2015.

13. Nora Berenstain, "Nora Berenstain on Rebecca Tuvel and *Hypatia*," *GenderTrender*, April 29, 2017, https://gendertrender.wordpress.com/nora-berenstain-on-rebecca-tuvel-and-hypatia/.

14. Elise Springer et al., "Open Letter to Hypatia," archive.today, April 30, 2017, https://archive.is/lUeR4.

15. The original letter is now removed but is quoted and summarized in Kelly Oliver, "If This Is Feminism . . . ," *The Philosophical Salon*, May 8, 2017, https://

thephilosophicalsalon.com/if-this-is-feminism-its-been-hijacked-by-the-thought
-police/.

16. Brubaker, *Trans*, xi.

17. Most of the criticism surrounding Brubaker's book highlighted his analysis's lack of intersectionality, which, as Tey Meadow notes, "conditions trans discourse as white discourse." See Meadow, "Whose Chosenness Counts?," 1309. For
other similar critiques of Brubaker, see Ray, "Logic of *Trans*," 479; Chauvin, "Comment on Brubaker," 1320–1329. Brubaker even wrote a *New York Times* op-ed piece
criticizing the backlash against Tuvel once the controversy surrounding her essay
spread to mainstream news sources, where he applauds her "impeccable . . . cultural-
left credentials." See Rogers Brubaker, "The Uproar over 'Transracialism,'" *New York
Times*, May 18, 2017, https://www.nytimes.com/2017/05/18/opinion/the-uproar-over
-transracialism.html.

18. Jones, "Rachel Dolezal Is Really Queer."

19. Raymond, *Transsexual Empire*.

20. Jeffreys, *Gender Hurts*, 36, 41.

21. Serano, *Whipping Girl*, 242–243.

22. Emi Koyama, "Whose Feminism Is It Anyway? The Unspoken Racism of
the Trans Inclusion Debate," in Stryker and Whittle, *Transgender Studies Reader*,
698–705.

23. Bobby Noble, "Trans. Panic: Some Thoughts toward a Theory of Feminist
Fundamentalism," in Enke, *Transfeminist Perspectives*, 47.

24. Aja Romano also notes that the terms "transracial" and "transethnic" might
have gained currency on Tumblr in the context of parodic posts that "mock Tumblr's
efforts to be respectful of people's self-identifying terms by taking them to illogi-
cal extremes" (e.g., a user posting as a "transracial unicorn"). Romano observes that
just as Tumblr provides a forum for the expression of diverse, nonnormative forms
of identification, so too has it produced a corollary troll culture that is often politically conservative, derisive of certain identities, and deeply transphobic. See Aja Romano, "The Trollish Tumblr Roots of the Term 'Transracial,'" Daily Dot, June 12,
2015, https://www.dailydot.com/irl/rachel-dolezai-transracial-transethnic-trolling/.

25. Bloodsucker-unanimous (user handle), "Transethnicity," accessed November 12, 2018, https://www.tumblr.com/search/Transethnicity.

26. Sistahintransit (user handle), "I Am Who I Say I Am," *The No. 1 Place for
Transracial/ethnic Thought* (blog), accessed November 12, 2018, https://sistahintransit
.tumblr.com/.

27. Somnipath (user handle), "Dear 'Transethnic' People," Tumblr, 2015, http://
marisanora.tumblr.com/post/115048936055/dear-transethnic-people.

28. Nakamura, *Digitizing Race*, 3.

29. See, for example, Lott, *Love and Theft*; Deloria, *Playing Indian*.

30. Sealey, "Transracialism and White Allyship," 21–29.

31. Charles Blow quoted in Connor Williams, "CNN Guest: Dolezal Represents
'White Privilege at a Spectacular Level," NewsBusters, June 16, 2015, https://www
.newsbusters.org/blogs/connor-williams/2015/06/16/cnn-guest-dolezal-represents
-white-privilege-spectacular-level.

32. Bey and Sakellarides, "When We Enter," 34.

33. Sealey, "Transracialism and White Allyship."

34. Heyes, "Changing Race, Changing Sex," 267.

35. Heyes, 273.

36. Heyes quoted in Jesse Singal, "This Is What a Modern-Day Witch Hunt Looks Like," *New York*, May 2, 2017, http://nymag.com/intelligencer/2017/05/trans racialism-article-controversy.html.

37. Raymond, *Transsexual Empire*, xv–xvi.

38. Ray, "Logic of *Trans*," 479.

39. Snorton, *Black on Both Sides*, 8.

40. Snorton, 56–58.

41. Snorton, 108.

42. Snorton, 157.

43. Meadow, "Whose Chosenness Counts?," 1307.

44. C. Riley Snorton and Jin Haritaworn, "Trans Necropolitics: A Transnational Reflection on Violence, Death, and the Trans of Color Afterlife," in Stryker and Aizura, *Transgender Studies Reader 2*, 47.

45. Rodríguez, "X Marks the Spot," 210, 212.

46. Miller, *Rise and Fall of the Cosmic Race*, 40.

47. José Martí, "Our America; Published in *El Partido Liberal* (Mexico City), March 5, 1892," History of Cuba, accessed June 10, 2019, http://www.historyofcuba .com/history/marti/America.htm. Hiram Pérez has noted, "Although Martí argues that the emergence of '*nuestra América mestiza*' hails the end of racial difference and consequently the end of 'racial hate,' his utopic (paradoxically deracialized) vision requires the cooption of the very real, racialized body of the mestizo." See Pérez, *Taste for Brown Bodies*, 86.

48. Vasconcelos, *Cosmic Race*, 9.

49. Vasconcelos, 20; my emphasis.

50. Vasconcelos quoted in Miller, *Rise and Fall of the Cosmic Race*, 40.

51. Pérez-Torres, *Mestizaje*, 16.

52. Saldaña-Portillo, *Indian Given*, 13–14.

53. Paz, *Labyrinth of Solitude*, 87.

54. Miller, *Rise and Fall of the Cosmic Race*, 23.

55. Paz, *Labyrinth of Solitude*, 85.

56. Soto, *Reading Chican@ Like a Queer*, 66.

57. Anzaldúa, *Borderlands*, 102–103.

58. Soto, *Reading Chican@ Like a Queer*, 68.

59. Pérez, *Taste for Brown Bodies*, 87.

60. Arrizón, *Queering Mestizaje*, 85.

61. Arrizón, 84.

62. T. Hernández, "'Too Black to Be Latino/a,'" 152. See also Silvio Torres-Saillant, "Problematic Paradigms: Racial Diversity and Corporate Identity in the Latino Community," in Suárez-Orozco and Páez, *Latinos*, 435–455.

63. T. Hernández, "'Too Black to Be Latino/a,'" 156.

64. Molina-Guzmán, *Dangerous Curves*, 5–6.

65. Goin, "Marginal Latinidad," 347.

66. Kelly quoted in "Zahira Kelly Discusses Accountability & Asserting Afro-Latina Existence in 2017," YouTube video, uploaded by Ain't I Latina?, August 4, 2017, https://www.youtube.com/watch?v=JfuK7uluVYc&t=1s.

67. Kelly quoted in Jamila Johnson, "'Bad Dominicana' Zahira Kelly Is an Afro-Latina You Should Know," *Al Día*, March 16, 2017, https://aldianews.com/articles/culture/visual-arts/bad-dominicana-zahira-kelly-afro-latina-you-should-know/46695.

68. Kelly quoted in "Zahira Kelly Discusses Accountability."

69. Ana M. Lara, "Uncovering Mirrors: Afro-Latina Lesbian Subjects," in Román and Flores, *Afro-Latin@ Reader*, 303.

70. Suzanne Oboler and Anani Dzidzienyo, "Flows and Counterflows: Latina/os, Blackness, and Racialization in Hemispheric Perspective," in Dzidzienyo and Oboler, *Neither Enemies nor Friends*, 18–19.

71. Frances Negrón-Muntaner, "Barbie's Hair: Selling Out Puerto Rican Identity in the Global Market," in Habell-Pallán and Romero, *Latina/o Popular Culture*, 42. On the production of Latina dolls, see also Angharad Valdivia, "The Gendered Face of Latinidad: Global Circulation of Hybridity," in Hegde, *Circuits of Visibility*, 53–67; Karen Goldman, "La Princesa Plastica: Hegemonic and Oppositional Representations of Latinidad in Hispanic Barbie," in Mendible, *From Bananas to Buttocks*, 263–278.

72. Negrón-Muntaner, "Barbie's Hair," 45.

73. Torii Hunter quoted in Joshua Reese, "The MLB Imposters," *Bleacher Report*, March 20, 2010, https://bleacherreport.com/articles/366024-torii-hunter-and-the-mlb-imposters.

74. Hunter quoted in "Hunter Talks about Race," ESPN, March 11, 2010, https://www.espn.com/los-angeles/mlb/news/story?id=4983236.

75. Marcus Vanderberg, "Torii Hunter Is Right about Blacks in Baseball," *The Grio*, March 11, 2010, https://thegrio.com/2010/03/11/why-torii-hunter-was-right-about-blacks-in-baseball/.

76. "Torii Hunter: Black Latinos Are 'Imposters,'" *Huffington Post*, May 10, 2010, https://www.huffpost.com/entry/torii-hunter-black-latino_n_493652.

77. Reggie Jackson quoted in Mark Feinsand, "Former New York Yankee Reggie Jackson Defends Torii Hunter's 'Imposter' Comment," *New York Daily News*, March 12, 2010, https://www.nydailynews.com/sports/baseball/yankees/new-york-yankee-reggie-jackson-defends-torii-hunter-imposter-comment-article-1.177162.

78. Guillén quoted in "Hunter Talks about Race."

79. Guillén quoted in "Hunter Talks about Race."

80. Tommy Craggs, "Black Hispanic Ballplayers Aren't Black Enough for Torii Hunter," *Deadspin*, March 10, 2010, https://deadspin.com/black-hispanic-ballplayers-arent-black-enough-for-torii-5490095.

81. Craig Calcaterra, "Torii Hunter: Black Dominican Players Are 'Imposters,'" NBC Sports, March 10, 2010, https://mlb.nbcsports.com/2010/03/10/torii-hunter-black-dominican-players-are-imposters/.

82. Tony Menendez, "Torii Hunter: Latinos Want an Apology after 'Imposter' Comments," *Bleacher Report*, March 11, 2010, https://bleacherreport.com/articles/360812-torii-hunter-latinos-want-an-apology.

83. Adrian Burgos Jr., "What Chris Rock Got Wrong: Black Latinos and Race in Baseball," *Sporting News*, May 10, 2015, https://www.sportingnews.com/us/mlb/news/arfrican-americans-baseball-chris-rock-latinos/1spqgzamfumih1eprzkmlfpki7.

84. Menendez, "Torii Hunter."

85. Burgos, "What Chris Rock Got Wrong."

86. Burgos, *Playing America's Game*, 88.

87. Burgos, "What Chris Rock Got Wrong."

88. Rudolph, *Baseball as Mediated Latinidad*, 10.

89. Steven Golman, "The BP Broadside: The Latino," *Baseball Prospectus*, February 10, 2012, https://legacy.baseballprospectus.com/article_legacy.php?articleid =16013.

90. J. C. Bradbury, "Repeat: What Caused the Decline of African-Americans in Baseball?" Sabernomics, March 17, 2010, http://www.sabernomics.com/sabernomics /index.php/2010/03/repeat-what-caused-the-decline-of-african-americans-in -baseball/index.html. As Jane Juffer writes, "Latin American ballplayers are signed by US scouts for small sums and often languish for years in the minors, sometimes ending up as undocumented workers in US cities." See Juffer, "Who's the Man?," 341.

91. Feinsand, "Torii Hunter's 'Imposter' Comment." While the percentage of foreign-born players in the MLB is typically reported as 28 percent, this is because the MLB has included players from Puerto Rico and the Virgin Islands within this figure. When players from Puerto Rico and the Virgin Islands are not counted, the percentage drops a point, to 27 percent. Foreign-born players most represented in the MLB roster include players from the Dominican Republic, Venezuela, Cuba, and Mexico. On the distinction between percentage points and the nationalities of foreign-born players, see Stuart Anderson, "27 Percent of Major League Baseball Players Are Foreign-Born," *Forbes*, April 27, 2018, https://www.forbes.com/sites /stuartanderson/2018/04/27/27-of-major-league-baseball-players-are-foreign-born /?sh=5bd569807712.

92. Deron Snyder, "Torii Hunter Was Right about Baseball," *The Root*, March 15, 2010, https://www.theroot.com/torii-hunter-was-right-about-baseball-1790878914.

93. Torii Hunter, "A Hurtful, Unfortunate Episode," *Torii's Storiis* (blog), March 10, 2010, http://toriihunter.mlblogs.com/2010/03/10/a-hurtful-unfortunate -episode/.

94. As Jennifer Domino Rudolph notes, sports must be taken as serious social and economic phenomena when considering the fates of "Latinos and other men of color in the US, from youth to adulthood, [who] continue to be denied equal access to institutions such as higher education that would provide them with the economic status associated primarily with white masculinity." Thus, she writes, "sociostructural forces funnel them into professions that rely more on physical than mental performance." See Rudolph, *Baseball as Mediated Latinidad*, 12.

95. To be clear, I am seeking not to justify or excuse Hunter's remarks but rather to think about their structural context and the political use value of imagining their content as solely linked to an individual (Black) speaker. It is also true that Hunter has found himself in other debacles surrounding intolerance. In 2014, he recorded an advertisement for the Arkansas gubernatorial race supporting Republican Asa Hutchinson, in which he applauded the candidate's interest in keeping marriage "between one man and one woman." See Kevin Draper, "Torii Hunter Doubles Down on His Anti-gay Beliefs," *Deadspin*, October 29, 2014, https://deadspin.com /torii-hunter-doubles-down-on-his-anti-gay-beliefs-1652553533.

96. Bradbury, "What Caused the Decline?"

97. Daniel Cubias, "Is Torii Hunter Right to Call Latin Americans 'Imposters'?," *Huffington Post*, May 10, 2010, https://www.huffpost.com/entry/is-torii-hunter-right-to_b_494365.

98. Cubias, "Is Torii Hunter Right?"; my emphasis.

99. Yesha Callahan, "Sammy Sosa's Brown Skin No Longer Exists," *The Root*, November 11, 2017, https://www.theroot.com/1820406720.

100. Janice Williams, "From Black to White: Why Sammy Sosa and Others Are Bleaching Their Skin," *Newsweek*, July 13, 2017, https://www.newsweek.com/sammy-sosa-skin-bleaching-lightening-636516.

101. "Sammy Sosa's Skin Tone Raises Questions," NPR, November 12, 2009, https://www.npr.org/templates/story/story.php?storyId=120340650.

102. Sosa quoted in Williams, "From Black to White."

103. Williams, "From Black to White"; Shirley Gómez, "Sammy Sosa White? Baseball Legend Looks Unrecognizable, Fans React [MEMES]," *Latin Times*, July 13, 2017, https://www.latintimes.com/sammy-sosa-white-baseball-legend-looks-unrecognizable-fans-react-memes-420580.

104. Nadra Nittle, "Samy Sosa Is a Victim of Colorism," *Racked*, February 15, 2018, https://www.racked.com/2018/2/15/17013740/sammy-sosa-bleached-skin-colorism-amara-la-negra. While a western-themed birthday party might conjure the idea of "Indians" versus cowboys, which has been a popular mode of cultural appropriation throughout much of US history, I do not provide an analysis of this here, since no evidence exists that Sosa's party included any representation or co-optation of Indigenous culture.

105. "Sammy Sosa Made an Appearance," NBC Sports, July 20, 2017, https://www.nbcsports.com/chicago/chicago-cubs/sammy-sosa-has-changed-his-appearance-yet-again-and-internet-freaking-out.

106. Teddy Greenstein, "The Lighter, Lighter, Lighter Side of Sammy Sosa," *Chicago Tribune*, July 13, 2017, https://www.chicagotribune.com/sports/cubs/ct-sammy-sosa-lighter-skin-20170713-column.html.

107. On Sosa's skin bleaching as a sign of mental illness, see Laura Rodriguez, "Sammy Sosa, from Black to 'White,'" *Chicago Tribune*, July 13, 2017, https://www.chicagotribune.com/hoy/ct-hoy-sammy-sosa-from-black-to-white-20170713-story.html.

108. Browne, "Everybody's Got a Little Light," 546.

109. Howard, "Spatializing Blackness in New Mexico," 38.

110. Nittle, "Sammy Sosa Is a Victim of Colorism."

111. Sammy Sosa and Sammy Sosa Jr. quoted in "Sammy Sosa Says He Doesn't Care What People Say about His Lighter Skin Tone: 'This Is My Life,'" *People*, June 27, 2018, https://people.com/sports/sammy-sosa-addresses-lighter-skin-tone/.

112. Ny MaGee, "Fans React to Sammy Sosa's Whiter, Er, Pink-er(?) Complexion Transition—Look!" *Electronic Urban Report*, July 14, 2017, https://eurweb.com/2017/07/14/fans-react-to-sammy-sosas-whiter-complexion-transition/.

113. Williams, "From Black to White."

114. W. Bill Smith, "What Is Sammy Sosa's Problem?," *African American–Latino World* (blog), July 30, 2011, http://ahorasecreto.blogspot.com/2011/07/what-is-sammy-sosas-problem.html.

115. King Sukii, "The Unbearable Whiteness of Sammy Sosa," *Cassius*, July 13,

2017, https://cassiuslife.com/12651/the-unbearable-whiteness-of-sammy-sosa/; "Exploring Race: Is Sammy Sosa Whitening His Skin?" *Chicago Tribune*, November 9, 2011, https://newsblogs.chicagotribune.com/race/2009/11/is-sammy-sosa-whitening -his-skin.html; Liz Dwyer, "The Skin Bleaching Industry Is Laughing at Sammy Sosa's Face All the Way to the Bank," *Good*, July 14, 2017, https://www.good.is/sports /sammy-sosa-skin-lightening-big-business; Steve Sailer, "Jim Webb, the GOP, and the Sammy Sosa Solution," VDARE, July 25, 2010, https://vdare.com/articles/jim -webb-the-gop-and-the-sammy-sosa-solution.

116. David A. Love, "Sammy Sosa's New Skin Reflects an Ugly Mentality," *The Grio*, November 9, 2009, https://thegrio.com/2009/11/09/sammy-sosas-new-skin -reflects-an-ugly-mentality/.

117. Love, "Sosa's New Skin Reflects an Ugly Mentality"; my emphasis.

118. Gooden, "Visual Representations of Feminine Beauty," 81.

119. Dorman, "Skin Bleach and Civilization," 47.

120. Peiss, *Hope in a Jar*, 209.

121. Kathy Peiss notes that although the issue of skin whitening and hair straightening remained fraught for Black commentators and consumers, many discerned between manufacturers who displayed a formal commitment to the advancement of African Americans through hiring practices and promotional events and those who did not. See Peiss, *Hope in a Jar*, 210–211.

122. Charles, "Derogatory Representations of the Skin Bleaching Products," 117.

123. López, *White by Law*, esp. chaps. 1 and 4.

124. Morgan, "Partus sequitur ventrem," 1–17; López, *White by Law*, 20, 83.

125. Meirav Devash, "Women Are Taking Extreme Measures to Lighten Their Skin through IV Treatments," *Allure*, March 11, 2019, https://www.allure.com/story /skin-lightening-iv-treatment-glutathione-dangerous-side-effects.

126. For more on this point, see my discussion of John Bobbitt, masculinity, and whiteness in chapter 2.

127. See, for example, Haiken, *Venus Envy*, 175–228.

128. Gilman, *Fat*, 49–55.

129. Dyer, *White*, 147.

130. Molina-Guzmán and Valdivia, "Brain, Brow, and Booty," 211–212. Jack Halberstam also asserts that "masculinity becomes legible as masculinity when and where it leaves the white middle-class body." See Halberstam, *Skin Shows*, 2.

131. Molina-Guzmán, *Dangerous Curves*, 10–11. On the performance of Latino masculinities, see Rudolph, *Embodying Latino Masculinities*.

132. See, for example, Lott, *Love and Theft*.

133. Tamerra Griffin, "Rachel Dolezal Once Told a Student She Did Not Look Hispanic Enough for a Class Activity," *BuzzFeed*, June 12, 2015, https://www .buzzfeednews.com/article/tamerragriffin/rachel-dolezal-once-told-a-student-she -did-not-look-hispanic. On this incident, see also Bey and Sakellarides, "When We Enter," 34.

134. Sealey, "Transracalism and White Allyship"; Blow quoted in Williams, "CNN Guest."

135. Tatiana Tenreyro, "Rachel Dolezal Has a New Name & It's Going to Make You So Mad," *Bustle*, April 25, 2018, https://www.bustle.com/p/what-does-rachel -dolezals-new-name-mean-its-origins-will-make-you-cringe-so-hard-8808492.

136. Ann Morning, "Race and Rachel Dolezal: An Interview," *Contexts*, March 28, 2017, https://contexts.org/articles/race-and-rachel-dolezal-an-interview/.

137. Morning, "Race and Rachel Dolezal."

Conclusion

1. Richard Rodriguez, *Brown*, xi, xii, 133.

2. Muñoz, "Feeling Brown: Ethnicity and Affect," 70.

3. Muñoz, 70.

4. Muñoz, 70.

5. Muñoz, "Chico," 38.

6. Anzaldúa, *Borderlands*, 242.

7. Chambers-Letson, "Embodying Justice," 156.

8. Muñoz, "Chico," 39; my emphasis.

9. Zahira Kelly, "Dear Marooned Alien Princess," *The New Inquiry*, September 1. 2017, https://thenewinquiry.com/dear-marooned-alien-princess-11/.

10. Kelly quoted in Maya Doig-Acuña, "On Claiming Afro-Latinidad," Latino Rebels, August 26, 2019, https://www.latinorebels.com/2018/02/06/on-claiming-afro-latinidad/.

11. Kelly quoted in Juliana Pache, "Meet Zahira Kelly, the Black Latina Artist Painting Black Women as Goddesses," *Fader*, March 9, 2017, https://www.thefader.com/2017/03/09/zahira-kelly-black-latina-art-cardi-b.

12. Laó-Montes, "Afro-Latinidades," 118.

13. Ebron and Tsing, "In Dialogue?," 390.

14. Richard T. Rodríguez, "X Marks the Spot," 204.

15. Richard T. Rodríguez, 204.

16. Richard T. Rodríguez, 207.

17. J. Rodríguez, *Sexual Futures*, 14.

18. Here I do not mean to imply that these are the only two uses of brownness, just that they are currently, within a US context, the most frequently evoked. On alternative frames of brownness, see, for example, Silva, "Brown," 167–182. Arguably, while the "browning" I refer to in this context has to do with immigration from and through Mexico, immigrants from South East Asia and the Middle East are often represented in similar terms—that is, as nonwhite and thus undesirable.

19. Mark Steyn quoted in Ed Mazza, "Fox News Guest Goes off the Rails: 'White Supremacists Are American Citizens,'" *Huffington Post*, January 19, 2018, https://www.huffpost.com/entry/mark-steyn-white-supremacists_n_5a61890ce4b0125fd6356675.

20. See, for example, the essays compiled in Levitt and Whitaker, *Hurricane Katrina*.

21. Chavez, *Latino Threat*, 2.

22. Bonilla-Silva, *Racism without Racists*, 178.

Bibliography

Abu-Lughod, Lila. "Do Muslim Women Really Need Saving? Anthropological Reflections on Cultural Relativism and Its Others." *American Anthropologist* 104, no. 3 (2002): 783–790.

Adames, Sandra Bibiana, and Rebecca Campbell. "Immigrant Latinas' Conceptualizations of Intimate Partner Violence." *Violence against Women* 11, no. 10 (2005): 1341–1364.

Aldama, Frederick Luis, ed. *The Routledge Companion to Latina/o Popular Culture.* New York: Routledge, 2016.

Aldama, Frederick Luis, and Christopher González. *Latinos in the End Zone: Conversations on the Brown Color Line in the NFL.* New York: Palgrave Macmillan, 2014.

Alden, Edward. "Is Border Enforcement Effective? What We Know and What It Means." *Journal on Migration and Human Security* 5, no. 2 (2017): 481–490.

Alexander, Michelle. *The New Jim Crow: Mass Incarceration in the Age of Colorblindness.* New York: New Press, 2010.

Allan, Stuart. "News from NowHere: Televisual News Discourse and the Construction of Hegemony." In *Approaches to Media Discourse*, edited by Allan Bell and Peter Garrett, 105–141. Oxford, UK: Blackwell, 1998.

Allan, Stuart, and Chris Peters. "Weaponizing Memes: The Journalistic Mediation of Visual Politicization." *Digital Journalism* (2021): 1–13.

Alvarado, Leticia. *Abject Performances: Aesthetic Strategies in Latino Cultural Production.* Durham, NC: Duke University Press, 2018.

Anderson, Michelle J. "A License to Abuse: The Impact of Conditional Status on Female Immigrants." *Yale Law Journal* 102 (1993): 1401–1430.

Anzaldúa, Gloria. *Borderlands / La Frontera: The New Mestiza.* San Francisco: Aunt Lute, 1999 [1987].

Aparicio, Frances R. "Jennifer as Selena: Rethinking Latinidad in Media and Popular Culture." *Latino Studies* 1, no. 1 (2003): 90–105.

Aparicio, Frances R., and Susana Chávez-Silverman. *Tropicalizations: Transcultural Representations of Latinidad.* Hanover, NH: Dartmouth College Press, 1997.

Arrizón, Alicia. "Latina Subjectivity, Sexuality, and Sensuality." *Women and Performance* 18, no. 3 (2008): 189–198.

————. *Queering Mestizaje: Transculturation and Performance*. Ann Arbor: University of Michigan Press, 2006.

Baez, Jose, with George Willis. *Unnecessary Roughness: Inside The Trial and Final Days of Aaron Hernandez*. New York: Hachette, 2018.

Bass, Ellen, and Laura Davis. *The Courage to Heal: A Guide for Women Survivors of Child Sexual Abuse*. New York: Harper and Row, 1988.

Bebout, Lee. *Whiteness on the Border: Mapping the U.S. Racial Imagination in Brown and White*. New York: New York University Press, 2016.

Beck, Richard. *We Believe the Children: A Moral Panic in the 1980s*. New York: Public Affairs, 2015.

Bell, Allan, and Peter Garrett, eds. *Approaches to Media Discourse*. Oxford, UK: Blackwell, 1998.

Berger, John. *Ways of Seeing*. London: Penguin, 1977 [1972].

Berger, Susan. "(Un)Worthy: Latina Battered Immigrants under VAWA and the Construction of Neoliberal Subjects." *Citizenship Studies* 13, no. 3 (2009): 201–217.

Bergland, Renée L. *The National Uncanny: Indian Ghosts and American Subjects*. Hanover, NH: University Press of New England, 2000.

Berlant, Lauren. "Slow Death (Sovereignty, Obesity, Lateral Agency)." *Critical Inquiry* 33, no. 4 (2007): 754–780.

Bernstein, Elizabeth. "Militarized Humanitarianism Meets Carceral Feminism: The Politics of Sex, Rights, and Freedom in Contemporary Antitrafficking Campaigns." *Signs* 26, no. 1 (2012): 45–71.

————. "The Sexual Politics of the New Abolitionism." *Differences* 18 (2007): 128–143.

Bersani, Leo. *Is the Rectum a Grave? And Other Essays*. Chicago: University of Chicago Press, 2010.

Besnier, Niko, Susan Brownell, and Thomas F. Carter. *The Anthropology of Sport: Bodies, Borders, Biopolitics*. Oakland: University of California Press, 2018.

Bey, Marquis, and Theodora Sakellarides. "When We Enter: The Blackness of Rachel Dolezal." *Black Scholar* 46, no. 4 (2016): 33–48.

Bird, S. Elizabeth. "Audience Demands in a Murderous Market: Tabloidization in U.S. Television News." In *Tabloid Tales: Global Debates over Media Standards*, edited by Colin Sparks and John Tulloch. New York: Rowman and Littlefield, 2000.

————. "Facing the Distracted Audience: Journalism and Cultural Context." *Journalism* 1, no. 1 (2000): 29–33.

————. "Storytelling on the Far Side: Journalism and the Weekly Tabloid." *Critical Studies in Mass Communication* 7 (1990): 377–389.

Bird, S. Elizabeth, and Robert Dardenne. "Myth, Chronicle and Story: Exploring the Narrative Qualities of News." In *Media, Myths, and Narratives: Television and the Press*, edited by James W. Carey, 67–86. Newbury, NJ: Sage, 1988.

Blanco, María del Pilar. *Ghost-Watching American Modernity: Haunting, Landscape, and the Hemispheric Imagination*. New York: Fordham University Press, 2012.

Blanco, María del Pilar, and Esther Peeren, eds. *Popular Ghosts: The Haunted Spaces of Everyday Culture*. New York: Continuum, 2010.

————, eds. *The Spectralities Reader: Ghosts and Haunting in Contemporary Cultural Theory*. London: Bloomsbury Academic, 2013.

Bonilla-Silva, Eduardo. *Racism without Racists: Color-Blind Racism and the Persistence of Racial Inequality in America.* 3rd ed. New York: Rowman and Littlefield, 2009 [2003].

Bost, Suzanne. *Encarnación: Illness and Body Politics in Chicana Feminist Literature.* New York: Fordham University Press, 2010.

Brisman, Avi. "'Are You Serious'? *Sports Criminology: A Critical Criminology of Sport and Games*: A Review." *Critical Criminology Online* (2018): https://doi.org/10.1007/s10612-018-9424-9.

Brooks, Laura A., Elizabeth Manias, and Melissa J. Bloomer. "Culturally Sensitive Communication in Healthcare: A Concept Analysis." *Collegian* 26, no. 3 (2019): 383–391.

Brown, Peter. *The Body and Society: Men, Women and Sexual Renunciation in Early Christianity.* London: Faber and Faber, 1990.

Browne, Simone. "Everybody's Got a Little Light under the Sun: Black Luminosity and the Visual Culture of Surveillance." *Cultural Studies* 26, no. 4 (2012): 542–564.

Brownmiller, Susan. *Against Our Will: Men, Women and Rape.* New York: Simon and Schuster, 1975.

Brubaker, Rogers. *Trans: Gender and Race in an Age of Unsettled Identities.* Princeton, NJ: Princeton University Press, 2016.

Burgos, Adrian, Jr. *Playing America's Game: Baseball, Latinos, and the Color Line.* Berkeley: University of California Press, 2007.

Buse, Peter, and Andrew Stott, eds. *Ghosts: Deconstruction, Psychoanalysis, History.* New York: St. Martin's, 1999.

Butler, Judith. "Endangered/Endangering: Schematic Racism and White Paranoia." In *Reading Rodney King / Reading Urban Uprising*, edited by Robert Gooding-Williams. New York: Routledge, 1993.

———. *Precarious Life: The Power of Mourning and Violence.* London: Verso, 2006.

———. *Undoing Gender.* New York: Routledge, 2004.

Cacho, Lisa Marie. *Social Death: Racialized Rightlessness and the Criminalization of the Unprotected.* New York: New York University Press, 2012.

———. "'You Just Don't Know How Much He Meant': Deviancy, Death, and Devaluation." *Latino Studies* 5 (2007): 182–208.

Calafell, Bernadette Marie. "Brownness, Kissing, and US Imperialism: Contextualizing the Orlando Massacre." *Communication and Critical/Cultural Studies* 14, no. 1 (2017): 198–202.

Camacho, Alicia Schmidt. *Migrant Imaginaries: Latino Cultural Politics in the U.S.-Mexico Borderlands.* New York: New York University Press, 2009.

Canclini, Néstor García. *Hybrid Cultures: Strategies for Entering and Leaving Modernity.* Translated by Christopher L. Chiappari and Silvia L. López. Minneapolis: University of Minnesota Press, 2005.

Castranovo, Russ, and Dana D. Nelson. *Materializing Democracy: Toward a Revitalized Cultural Politics.* Durham, NC: Duke University Press, 2002.

Chambers-Letson, Josh Takano. "Embodying Justice: The Making of Justice Sonia Sotomayor." *Women and Performance* 20, no. 2 (2010): 149–172.

Charles, Christopher A. D. "The Derogatory Representations of the Skin Bleaching Products Sold in Harlem." *Journal of Pan African Studies* 4, no. 4 (2011): https://ssrn.com/abstract=2372184.

Chauvin, Sébastien. "Possibility, Legitimacy, and the New Ontologies of Choice: A Comment on Brubaker." *Ethnic and Racial Studies* 40, no. 8 (2017): 1320–1329.

Chavez, Leo R. *The Latino Threat: Constructing Immigrants, Citizens, and the Nation.* Stanford, CA: Stanford University Press, 2008.

Chin, Gabriel J., and Rose Cuison Villazor, eds. *The Immigration and Nationality Act of 1965: Legislating a New America.* Cambridge, UK: Cambridge University Press, 2015.

Collins-White, Mali D., Ariane Cruz, Jillian Hernandez, Xavier Livermon, Kaila Story, and Jennifer Nash. "Disruptions in Respectability: A Roundtable Discussion." *Souls* 18, no. 2 (2016): 463–475.

Collopy, Dree K. "Thwarting the Intent behind VAWA? USCIS' Interpretation of Good Moral Character." *Immigration Briefings* 14, no. 4 (2014): https://content.next.westlaw.com/Document/I91a1a6b1c3a411e39cf4a30083af35de/View/FullText.html?contextData=(sc.Default)&transitionType=Default.

Coloma, Roland Sintos. "White Gazes, Brown Breasts: Imperial Feminism and Disciplining Desires and Bodies in Colonial Encounters." *Paedagogica Historica* 48, no. 2 (2012): 243–261.

Connell, Liam. "The Worker as Revenant: Imagining Embodied Labor in Contemporary Visualizations of Migration." *Social Text* 30, no. 2 (111) (2012): 1–20.

Conway, Martin A., ed. *Recovered Memories and False Memories.* Oxford, UK: Oxford University Press, 1997.

Correa, Jennifer G., and James M. Thomas. "The Rebirth of the U.S.-Mexico Border: Latina/o Enforcement Agents and the Changing Politics of Racial Power." *Sociology of Race and Ethnicity* 1, no. 2 (2015): 239–254.

Coulter, Ann. ¡*Adios, America! The Left's Plan to Turn Our Country into a Third World Hellhole.* Washington, DC: Regnery, 2015.

Coutin, Susan Bibler. *Legalizing Moves: Salvadoran Immigrants' Struggle for U.S. Residency.* Ann Arbor: University of Michigan Press, 2003.

Cowie, Jefferson. "How Labor Scholars Missed the Trump Revolt." *Chronicle of Higher Education*, September 1, 2017. https://www.chronicle.com/article/How-Labor-Scholars-Missed-the/241049.

Crenshaw, Kimberlé. "Demarginalizing the Intersection of Race and Sex: A Black Feminist Critique of Antidiscrimination Doctrine, Feminist Theory and Antiracist Politics." *University of Chicago Legal Forum*, no. 1 (1989): 139–167.

Cuevas, T. Jackie. *Post-Borderlandia: Chicana Literature and Gender Variant Critique.* New Brunswick, NJ: Rutgers University Press, 2018.

Dávila, Arlene. *Culture Works: Space, Value, and Mobility across the Neoliberal Americas.* New York: New York University Press, 2012.

———. *Latino Spin: Public Image and the Whitewashing of Race.* New York: New York University Press, 2008.

———. *Latinos, Inc.: The Marketing and Making of a People.* Berkeley: University of California Press, 2001.

Dávila, Arlene, and Yeidy M. Rivero, eds. *Contemporary Latina/o Media: Production, Circulation, Politics.* New York: New York University Press, 2014.

Davis, Colin. *Haunted Subjects: Deconstruction, Psychoanalysis, and the Return of the Dead.* New York: Palgrave Macmillan, 2007.

———. "Hauntology, Spectres, and Phantoms." *French Studies* 59, no. 3: 373–379.

Davis, Diane. "'Breaking Up' [at] Phallocracy: Postfeminism's Chortling Hammer." *Rhetoric Review* 14, no. 1 (1995): 126–141.

DeCasas, Michelle. "Protecting Hispanic Women: The Inadequacy of Domestic Violence Policy." *Chicano-Latino Law Review* 24, no. 56 (2003): 56–78.

Deem, Melissa D. "From Bobbitt to SCUM: Re-memberment, Scatological Rhetorics, and Feminist Strategies in the Contemporary United States." *Public Culture* 8, no. 5 (1996): 511–537.

De León, Jason. *The Land of Open Graves: Living and Dying on the Migrant Trail.* Oakland: University of California Press, 2015.

Delgado, Richard, and Jean Stefancic, eds. *The Latino/a Condition: A Critical Reader.* New York: New York University Press, 1998.

Deloria, Philip J. *Playing Indian.* New Haven, CT: Yale University Press, 1998.

Denno, Deborah W. "Gender, Crime, and the Criminal Law Defenses." *Journal of Criminal Law and Criminology* 85, no. 1 (1994): 80–180.

de Onís, Catalina M. "What's in an 'X'? An Exchange about the Politics of 'Latinx.'" *Chiricú Journal: Latina/o Literatures, Arts, and Cultures* 1, no. 2 (2017): 56–86.

Derrida, Jacques. *Specters of Marx: The State of the Debt, the Work of Mourning, and the New International.* Translated by Peggy Kamuf. New York: Routledge, 1994.

Dervin, Daniel. "The Bobbitt Case and the Quest for a Good-Enough Penis." *Psychoanalytic Review* 82, no. 2 (1995): 249–256.

DiAngelo, Robin. "White Fragility." *International Journal of Critical Pedagogy* 3, no. 3 (2011): 54–70.

Dimock, Susan. "Reasonable Women in the Law." *Critical Review of International Social and Political Philosophy* 11, no. 2 (2008): 153–175.

Donaldson, Laura E., and Kwok Pui-lan, eds. *Postcolonialism, Feminism, and Religious Discourse.* New York: Routledge, 2002.

Dorman, Jacob S. "Skin Bleach and Civilization: The Racial Formation of Blackness in 1920s Harlem." *Journal of Pan African Studies* 4, no. 4 (2011).

Durham, Meenakshi Gigi, and Douglas M. Kellner, eds. *Media and Cultural Studies: KeyWorks.* Rev. ed. Malden, MA: Blackwell, 2006 [2001].

Dutton, Mary Ann. "Complexity of Women's Response to Violence: Response to Briere and Jordan." *Journal of Interpersonal Violence* 19, no. 11 (2004): 1277–1282.

Dyer, Richard. *White: Twentieth Anniversary Edition.* 2nd ed. New York: Routledge, 2017.

Dzidzienyo, Anani, and Suzanne Oboler, eds. *Neither Enemies nor Friends: Latinos, Blacks, Afro-Latinos.* New York: Palgrave Macmillan, 2005.

Ebron, Paulla, and Anna Lowenhaupt Tsing. "In Dialogue? Reading Across Minority Discourses." In *Women Writing Culture,* edited by Ruth Behar and Deborah A. Gordon, 390–411. Berkeley: University of California Press, 1995.

Edelman, Lee. *No Future: Queer Theory and the Death Drive.* Durham, NC: Duke University Press, 2004.

Enke, Anne, ed. *Transfeminist Perspectives: In and Beyond Transgender and Gender Studies.* Philadelphia, PA: Temple University Press, 2012.

Espenoza, Cecelia M. "No Relief for the Weary: VAWA Relief Denied for Battered Immigrants Lost in the Intersections." *Marquette Law Review* 83, no. 163 (1999): 163–220.

Espiritu, Yen Le. *Asian American Panethnicity: Bridging Institutions and Identities.* Philadelphia, PA: Temple University Press, 1992.

Esquenazi, Deborah, dir. *Southwest of Salem: The Story of the San Antonio Four.* 2016.

Esquibel, Catrióna Rueda. *With Her Machete in Her Hand: Reading Chicana Lesbians.* Austin: University of Texas Press, 2006.

Evans, David, and Kate Griffiths, eds. *Pleasure and Pain in Nineteenth-Century French Literature and Culture.* Amsterdam, Netherlands: Rodopi, 2008.

Faure, Caroline E., and Madeline P. Casanova. "The Fall of the Gladiators: Wives' Tales of Concussion Reporting and (Possible) Progressive Neurogenerative Disease in NFL Players." *Qualitative Report* 24, no. 1 (2019): 1–16.

Fausto-Sterling, Ann. "Race, Gender, and Nation: The Comparative Anatomy of 'Hottentot' Women in Europe, 1815–1817." In *Deviant Bodies: Critical Perspectives on Difference in Science and Popular Culture,* edited by Jennifer Terry and Jacqueline Urla. Bloomington: Indiana University Press, 1995.

Filetti, Jean S. "From Lizzie Borden to Lorena Bobbitt: Violent Women and Gendered Justice." *Journal of American Studies* 35 (2001): 471–484.

Fisher, Mark. "Hauntology?" *Film Quarterly* 66, no. 1 (2012): 16–24.

Flores, Juan, and Renato Rosaldo, eds. *A Companion to Latina/o Studies.* Malden, MA: Wiley-Blackwell, 2011.

Franco, Felicia E. "Unconditional Safety for Conditional Immigrant Women." *Berkeley Women's Law Journal* 96 (1996): 99–141.

Franco, Jean. *Cruel Modernity.* Durham, NC: Duke University Press, 2013.

Frye, Marilyn. "The Necessity of Differences: Constructing a Positive Category of Women." *Signs* 21, no. 4 (1996): 991–1010.

———. *Willful Virgin: Essays in Feminism, 1976–1992.* Freedom, CA: Crossing Press, 1992.

Gallin, Alice J. "The Cultural Defense: Undermining the Policies against Domestic Violence." *Boston College Law Review* 35 (1994): 723–745.

Galvan, R. "EE/UU: Exquisite Expression / Unsettling Utterance." *Cultural Dynamics* 29, no. 3 (2017): https://doi.org/10.1177/0921374017727855.

García, Armando. "The Illegalities of Brownness." *Social Text* 33, no. 2 (2015): 99–120.

Gaspar de Alba, Alicia, ed. *Velvet Barrios: Popular Culture and Chicana/o Sexualities.* New York: Palgrave Macmillan, 2003.

Gilman, Sander L. *Fat: A Cultural History of Obesity.* Cambridge, UK: Polity, 2008.

Gilmore, Ruth Wilson. *Golden Gulag: Prisons, Surplus, and Crisis in Globalizing California.* Berkeley: University of California Press, 2007.

Gimenez, Martha. "Latino/'Hispanic'—Who Needs a Name? The Case against a Standardized Terminology." *International Journal of Health Services* 19, no. 3 (1989): 557–571.

Glick, Megan H. "Of Sodomy and Cannibalism: Dehumanization, Embodiment, and the Rhetorics of Same-Sex and Cross-Species Contagion." *Gender and History* 23, no. 2 (2011): 266–282.

Goin, Keara. "Marginal Latinidad: Afro-Latinas and US Film." *Latino Studies* 14, no. 3 (2016): 344–363.

Gomez, Placido. "The Dilemma of Difference: Race as a Sentencing Factor." *Golden Gate University Law Review* 24 (1994): 357–386.

Gonzales-Day, Ken. "Choloborg; or, The Disappearing Latino Body." *Art Journal* 60, no. 1 (2001): 23–26.

Gooden, Amoaba. "Visual Representations of Feminine Beauty in the Black Press: 1915–1950." *Journal of Pan African Studies* 4, no. 4: 81–100.

Gordon, Avery F. *Ghostly Matters: Haunting and the Sociological Imagination.* Minneapolis: University of Minnesota Press, 2008 [1997].

Gordon, Lewis R. "Thinking through Rejections and Defenses of Transracialism." *Philosophy Today* 62, no. 1 (2018).

Gould, Stephen Jay. *The Mismeasure of Man.* New York: Norton, 1996 [1981].

Grindstaff, Linda, and Martha McCaughey. "Feminism, Psychoanalysis, and (Male) Hysteria over John Bobbitt's Missing Manhood." *Men and Masculinities* 1, no. 2 (1998): 172–192.

Grosz, Elizabeth. *Volatile Bodies: Toward a Corporeal Feminism.* Bloomington: Indiana University Press, 1994.

Habell-Pallán, Michelle, and Mary Romero, eds. *Latina/o Popular Culture.* New York: New York University Press, 2002.

Haiken, Elizabeth. *Venus Envy: A History of Cosmetic Surgery.* Baltimore, MD: Johns Hopkins University Press, 1997.

Halberstam, Jack. *In a Queer Time and Place: Transgender Bodies: Subcultural Lives.* New York: New York University Press, 2005.

———. *Skin Shows: Gothic Horror and the Technology of Monsters.* Durham, NC: Duke University Press, 1995.

Hall, Stuart, ed. *Representation: Cultural Representations and Signifying Practices.* London: Sage, 1997.

Hall, Stuart, Chas Critcher, Tony Jefferson, John Clarke, and Brian Roberts. *Policing the Crisis: Mugging, the State, and Law and Order.* London: Macmillan, 1978.

Halley, Janet. *Split Decisions: How and Why to Take a Break from Feminism.* Princeton, NJ: Princeton University Press, 2006.

Hanson, Victor Davis. *Mexifornia: A State of Becoming.* New York: Encounter Books, 2003.

Harris, Anne, and Stacy Holman Jones. "Feeling Fear, Feeling Queer: The Peril and Potential of Queer Terror." *Qualitative Inquiry* 23, no. 7 (2017): 561–568.

Harrison, Emily A. "The First Concussion Crisis: Head Injury and Evidence in Early American Football." *American Journal of Public Health* 104, no. 5 (2018): 822–833.

Hegde, Radha S., ed. *Circuits of Visibility: Gender and Transnational Media Cultures.* New York: New York University Press, 2011.

Heller, Kevin Jon. "Beyond the Reasonable Man? A Sympathetic but Critical Assessment of the Use of Subjective Standards of Reasonableness in Self-Defense and Provocation Cases." *American Journal of Criminal Law* 26 (1998).

Hernandez, Jillian. "'Miss, You Look Like a Bratz Doll': On Chonga Girls and Sexual Aesthetic Excess." *NWSA Journal* 21, no. 3 (2009): 63–90.

Hernandez, Jonathan, with Lars Anderson. *The Truth about Aaron: My Journey to Understand My Brother.* New York: HarperCollins, 2018.

Hernández, Kelly Lytle. *Migra! A History of the U.S. Border Patrol.* New York: New York University Press, 2010.

Hernández, Tanya Kateri. "'Too Black to Be Latino/a': Blackness and Blacks as Foreigners in Latino Studies." *Latino Studies* 1, no. 1 (2003): 152–159.

Hernández-Truyol, Berta E. "Sex, Culture, and Rights: A Re/Conceptualization of Violence for the Twenty-First Century." *Albany Law Review* 60, no. 607 (1997): 607–635.

Heyes, Cressida. "Changing Race, Changing Sex: The Ethics of Self-Transformation." *Journal of Social Philosophy* 37, no. 2: 266–282.

Holmquist, Kristen L. "Cultural Defense or False Stereotype? What Happens When Latin Defendants Collide with Federal Sentencing Guidelines? *Berkeley Women's Law Journal* 45 (1997): 45–73.

hooks, bell. *Black Looks: Race and Representation.* Boston: South End, 1992.

Howard, Natasha. "Spatializing Blackness in New Mexico." *Africology: The Journal of Pan African Studies* 12, no. 9 (2019).

Hussain, Kiran M., S. Gisela Leija, Florence Lewis, and Bridget Sanchez. "Unveiling Sexual Identity in the Face of Marianismo." *Journal of Feminist Family Therapy* 27, no. 2 (2015): 72–92.

Hyams, Melissa. "Adolescent Latina Bodyspaces: Making Homegirls, Homebodies, and Homeplaces." *Antipode* 35, no. 3 (2003): 536–558.

Jeffreys, Sheila. *Gender Hurts: A Feminist Analysis of the Politics of Transgenderism.* New York: Routledge, 2014.

Jenkins, Philip. *Moral Panics: Changing Concepts of the Child Molester in Modern America.* New Haven, CT: Yale University Press, 1998.

Jones, Angela. "Rachel Dolezal Is Really Queer: Transracial Politics and Queer Futurity." *Social (In)Queery*, June 17, 2015. https://socialinqueery.com/2015/06/17/rachel-dolezal-is-really-queer-transracial-politics-and-queer-futurity.

Juffer, Jane. "Who's the Man? Sammy Sosa, Latinos, and Televisual Redefinitions of the 'American' Pastime." *Journal of Sport and Social Issues* 26, no. 4 (2002): 337–359.

Kandel, William A. "Immigration Provisions of the Violence Against Women Act (VAWA)." Congressional Research Service report no. 7-5700, May 15, 2012, 1–34.

Keating, AnaLouise, ed. *The Gloria Anzaldúa Reader.* Durham, NC: Duke University Press, 2009.

Kelly, Linda. "Stories from the Front: Seeking Refuge for Battered Immigrants in the Violence Against Women Act." *Northwestern University Law Review* 92, no. 2 (1998): 221–269.

Kelly, Zahira. *Baina Colonial.* Vol. 1. Puerto Plata, Dominican Republic: Anacaona, 2016–2017.

Kunzel, Regina. *Criminal Intimacy: Prison and the Uneven History of Modern American Sexuality.* Chicago: University of Chicago Press, 2008.

Lakoff, Robin Tolmach. "Cries and Whispers: The Shattering of the Silence." In *Gender Articulated: Language and the Socially Constructed Self,* edited by Kira Hall and Mary Bucholtz. New York: Routledge, 2012.

Laó-Montes, Agustín. "Afro-Latinidades and the Diasporic Imaginary." *Iberoamericana* 5, no. 17 (2005): 117–130.

León, Luis D. *La Llorona's Children: Religion, Life, and Death in the U.S.-Mexican Borderlands.* Berkeley: University of California Press, 2004.

Leonard, David J. "Jumping the Gun." *Journal of Sport and Social Issues* 24 (2012): 252–262.

———. *Playing While White: Privilege and Power on and off the Field.* Seattle: University of Washington Press, 2017.

Levine, Helisse, and Shelly Peffer. "Quiet Casualties: An Analysis of U Nonimmigrant Status of Undocumented Immigrant Victims of Immigrant Partner Violence." *International Journal of Public Administration* 35 (2012): 634–642.

Levitt, Jeremy I. and Matthew C. Whitaker, eds. *Hurricane Katrina: America's Unnatural Disaster*. Lincoln: University of Nebraska Press, 2009.

Lima, Lázaro. *The Latino Body: Crisis Identities in American Literary and Cultural Memory*. New York: New York University Press, 2007.

Loftus, Elizabeth, and Katherine Ketcham. *The Myth of Repressed Memory: False Memories and Allegations of Sexual Abuse*. New York: St. Martin's, 1994.

López, Ian Haney. *White By Law: The Legal Construction of Race; 10th Anniversary Edition*. New York: New York University Press, 2006 [1995].

Lott, Eric. *Love and Theft: Blackface Minstrelsy and the American Working Class*. New York: Oxford University Press, 1993.

Luckhurst, Roger. "The Contemporary London Gothic and the Limits of the 'Spectral Turn.'" *Textual Practice* 16, no. 3 (2002): 537–546.

Lugones, María. *Pilgrimages/Peregrinajes: Theorizing Coalition against Multiple Oppressions*. New York: Rowman and Littlefield, 2003.

Lynn, Steven Jay, and Kevin M. McConkey, eds. *Truth in Memory*. New York: Guilford Press, 1998.

Maguigan, Holly. "Cultural Evidence and Male Violence: Are Feminist and Multiculturalist Reformers on a Collision Course in Criminal Courts?" *N.Y.U. Law Review* 70, no. 36 (1995): 36–64.

Marriott, David. *Haunted Life: Visual Culture and Black Modernity*. New Brunswick, NJ: Rutgers University Press, 2007.

———. "Spooks/Postmortem TV." *Journal of Visual Culture* 4, no. 3 (2005): 307–327.

———. "Waiting to Fall." *CR: The New Centennial Review* 13, no. 3 (2013): 163–240.

Martin, Lori Latrice, Kenneth J. Fasching-Varner, and Nicholas D. Hartlep. *Pay to Play: Race and the Perils of the College Sports Industrial Complex*. Santa Barbara, CA: Prager, 2017.

Mbembe, Achille. "Necropolitics." *Public Culture* 15, no. 1 (2003): 11–40.

———. *On the Postcolony*. Berkeley: University of California Press, 2003.

McClintock, Anne. "Imperial Ghosting and National Tragedy: Revenants from Hiroshima and Indian Country in the War on Terror." *PMLA* 129, no. 4 (October 2014): 819–829.

McCloud, Seth. *American Possessions: Fighting Demons in the Contemporary United States*. New York: Oxford University Press, 2015.

McHugh, Paul R. *Try to Remember: Psychiatry's Clash over Meaning, Memory, and the Mind*. New York: Dana Press, 2008.

Meadow, Tey. "Whose Chosenness Counts? The Always-Already Racialized Discourse of Trans—Response to Rogers Brubaker." *Ethnic and Racial Studies* 40, no. 8 (2017): 1306–1311.

Mehra, Nishta J., and Sara Ahmed. "Sara Ahmed: Notes from a Feminist Killjoy." *Guernica*, July 17, 2017. https://www.guernicamag.com/sara-ahmed-the-personal-is-institutional/.

Meisel, Irene. "'Something on Women for the Crime Bill': The Construction and Passage of the Violence Against Women Act, 1990–1994." PhD diss., City University of New York, 2016.

Mendible, Myra, ed. *From Bananas to Buttocks: The Latina Body in Popular Film and Culture*. Austin: University of Texas Press, 2007.

Mendoza, Elvia. "States of Dismemberment: State Violence and the Un/making of Queer Subjectivities." PhD diss., University of Texas at Austin, 2016.

Menjívar, Cecilia. "Liminal Legality: Salvadoran and Guatemalan Immigrants' Lives in the United States." *American Journal of Sociology* 111, no. 4 (2006): 999–1037.

Miller, Marilyn Grace. *Rise and Fall of the Cosmic Race: The Cult of Mestizaje in Latin America.* Austin: University of Texas Press, 2004.

Mills, Charles W. *The Racial Contract.* Ithaca, NY: Cornell University Press, 1997.

Mohanty, Chandra Talpade, Ann Russo, and Lourdes Torres, eds. *Third World Women and the Politics of Feminism.* Bloomington: University of Indiana Press, 1991.

Molina, Natalia. "Medicalizing the Mexican: Immigration, Race, and Disability in the Early-Twentieth-Century United States." *Radical History Review* 2006, no. 94 (2006): 22–37.

Molina-Guzmán, Isabel. *Dangerous Curves: Latina Bodies in the Media.* New York: New York University Press, 2010.

———. "Gendering Latinidad through the Elián News Discourse about Cuban Women." *Latino Studies* 3 (2005): 179–204.

Molina-Guzmán, Isabel, and Angharad N. Valdivia. "Brain, Brow, and Booty: Latina Iconicity in U.S. Popular Culture." *Communication Review* 7 (2004): 205–221.

———. "Disciplining the Ethnic Body: Latinidad, Hybridized Bodies, and Transnational Identity." In *Governing the Female Body: Gender, Health, and Networks of Power,* edited by Lori Reed and Paula Saukko, 206–232. Albany: State University of New York Press, 2010.

Mora, G. Cristina. *Making Hispanics: How Activists, Bureaucrats, and Media Constructed a New American.* Chicago: University of Chicago Press, 2014.

Moraga, Cherríe, and Gloria Anzaldúa. *This Bridge Called My Back: Writings by Radical Women of Color.* New York: Kitchen Table / Woman of Color, 1981.

Morgan, Jennifer L. "Partus sequitur ventrem: Law, Race, and Reproduction in Colonial Slavery." *Small Axe* 22, no. 1 (2018): 1–17.

Muhammad, Khalil Gibran. *The Condemnation of Blackness: Race, Crime, and the Making of Modern Urban America.* Cambridge, MA: Harvard University Press, 2011.

Mulvey, Laura. "Visual Pleasure and Narrative Cinema." *Screen* 16, no. 3 (1975): 6–18.

Muñoz, José Estéban. "Chico, What Does It Feel Like to Be a Problem? The Transmission of Brownness." In Muñoz, *The Sense of Brown,* edited by Joshua Chambers-Letson and Tavia Nyong'o. Durham, NC: Duke University Press, 2020.

———. *Cruising Utopia: The Then and There of Queer Futurity.* New York: New York University Press, 2009.

———. *Disidentifications: Queers of Color and the Performance of Politics.* Minneapolis: University of Minnesota Press, 1999.

———. "Feeling Brown: Ethnicity and Affect in Ricardo Bracho's 'The Sweetest Hangover (and Other STDs).'" *Theatre Journal* 5, no. 1 (2000): 67–79.

———. "Feeling Brown, Feeling Down: Latina Affect, the Performativity of Race, and the Depressive Position." *Signs* 31, no. 3 (2006): 675–688.

Nakamura, Lisa. *Digitizing Race: Visual Cultures of the Internet.* Minneapolis: University of Minnesota Press, 2007.

Nanasi, Natalie. "The U Visa's Failed Promise for Survivors of Domestic Violence." *Yale Journal of Law and Feminism* (2018): 373–320.

Nathan, Debbie, and Michael Snedecker. *Satan's Silence: Ritual Abuse and the Making of a Modern American Witch Hunt.* New York: Basic Books, 1995.

Newby, Alison, and Julie A. Dowling. "Black and Hispanic: The Racial Identification of Afro-Cuban Immigrants in the Southwest." *Sociological Perspectives* 50, no. 3 (2007): 343–366.

Nussbaum, Martha C. *Sex and Social Justice.* New York: Oxford University Press, 1999.

Oates, Thomas P., and Zack Furness, eds. *The NFL: Critical and Cultural Perspectives.* Philadelphia, PA: Temple University Press, 2014.

Oboler, Suzanne. "Citizenship and Belonging: The Construction of US Latino Identity Today." *Iberoamericana/Vervuert* 7, no. 25 (2014): 115–127.

———. *Ethnic Labels, Latino Lives: Identity and the Politics of (Re)Presentation in the United States.* Minneapolis: University of Minnesota Press, 1995.

———, ed. *Latinos and Citizenship: The Dilemma of Belonging.* New York: Palgrave Macmillan, 2006.

———. "Reflections on the First Decade of Latino Studies." *Diálogo* 20, no. 2 (2017): 125–134.

Ofshe, Richard, and Ethan Watters. *Making Monsters: False Memories, Psychotherapy, and Sexual Hysteria.* New York: Scribner's, 1996.

Okun, Lewis. *Woman Abuse: Facts Replacing Myths.* Albany: State University of New York Press, 1986.

Ordover, Nancy. *American Eugenics: Race, Queer Anatomy, and the Science of Nationalism.* Minneapolis: University of Minnesota Press, 2003.

Ouellette, Laurie, ed. *The Media Studies Reader.* New York: Routledge, 2013.

Palumbo-Lieu, David, ed. *The Ethnic Cannon: Histories, Institutions, and Interventions.* Minneapolis: University of Minnesota Press, 1995.

Pateman, Carole. *The Sexual Contract.* Oxford, UK: Blackwell, 1988.

Patterson, James, and Alex Abramovich, with Mike Harvkey. *All-American Murder: The Rise and Fall of Aaron Hernandez, the Superstar Whose Life Ended on Murderers' Row.* Boston: Little, Brown, 2018.

Patterson, Orlando. *Slavery and Social Death: A Comparative Study.* Cambridge, MA: Harvard University Press, 1985.

Paz, Octavio. *The Labyrinth of Solitude and Other Writings.* New York: Grove, 1985 [1961].

Peele, Jordan, dir. *Lorena.* Amazon Prime Video, 2019.

Peeren, Esther. *The Spectral Metaphor: Living Ghosts and the Agency of Invisibility.* New York: Palgrave Macmillan, 2014.

Peiss, Kathy. *Hope in a Jar: The Making of America's Beauty Culture.* Philadelphia: University of Pennsylvania Press, 2011.

Pérez, Hiram. *A Taste for Brown Bodies: Gay Modernity and Cosmopolitan Desire.* New York: New York University Press, 2015.

Pérez-Melgosa, Adrián. "Low Intensity Necropolitics: Slow Violence and Migrant Bodies in Latin American Films." *Hispanic Cultural Studies* 20 (2016): 217–236.

Pérez-Torres, Rafael. *Mestizaje: Critical Uses of Race in Chicano Culture.* Minneapolis: University of Minnesota Press, 2006.

Perilla, Julia L. "Domestic Violence as a Human Rights Issue: The Case of Immigrant Latinos." *Hispanic Journal of Behavioral Sciences* 21, no. 2 (1999): 107–133.

Pershing, Linda. "'His Wife Seized His Prize and Cut It to Size': Folk and Popular Commentary on Lorena Bobbitt." *NWSA Journal* 8, no. 3 (1996): 1–35.

Peters, Chris, and Stuart Allan. "Weaponizing Memes: The Journalistic Mediation of Visual Politicization." *Digital Journalism* (2021): 1–10. https://doi.org/10.1080/21670811.2021.1903958.

Pollitt, Katha. *Reasonable Creatures: Essays on Women and Feminism*. New York: Vintage, 1995 [1994].

Poole, W. Scott. *Monsters in America: Our Historical Obsession with the Hideous and the Haunting*. Waco, TX: Baylor University Press, 2014.

———. *Satan in America: The Devil We Know*. Lanham, MD: Rowman and Littlefield, 2009.

Priest, Patricia J., Cindy Jenefsky, and Jill D. Swenson. "Phallocentric Slicing: 20/20's Reporting of Lorena and John Bobbitt." In *No Angels: Women Who Commit Violence*, edited by Alice Meyers and Sarah Wright. San Francisco: HarperCollins, 1996.

Puar, Jasbir K. "Coda: The Cost of Getting Better; Suicide, Sensation, Switchpoints." *GLQ* 18, no. 1 (2012): 149–158.

———. *Terrorist Assemblages: Homonationalism in Queer Times*. Durham, NC: Duke University Press, 2007.

Ramírez, Dixa. *Colonial Phantoms: Belonging and Refusal in the Dominican Americas, from the 19th Century to the Present*. New York: New York University Press, 2018.

Ramos-Zayas, Ana Y. *National Performances: The Politics of Class, Race, and Space in Puerto Rican Chicago*. Chicago: University of Chicago Press, 2003.

Ray, Raka. "The Logic of Trans and the Logic of Place." *European Journal of Sociology* 58, no. 3 (2017): 476–479.

Raymond, Janice. *The Transsexual Empire: The Making of the She-Male*. Boston: Beacon Press, 1979.

Reed, Lori, and Paula Saukko, eds. *Governing the Female Body: Gender, Health, and Networks of Power*. Albany: State University of New York Press, 2010.

Renteln, Alison Dundes. "A Justification for the Cultural Defense as Partial Excuse." *Review of Law and Women's Studies* 2 (1993): 437–526.

Rivera, Jenny. "Domestic Violence against Latinas by Latino Males: An Analysis of Race, National Origin, and Gender Differentials." *Boston College Third World Law Journal* 14, no. 2 (1994): 231–257.

Rodríguez, Clara E. *Changing Race: Latinos, the Census, and the History of Ethnicity in the United States*. New York: New York University Press, 2000.

———, ed. *Latin Looks: Images of Latinas and Latinos in the U.S. Media*. New York: Routledge, 1997.

Rodríguez, Juana María. *Queer Latinidad: Identity Practices, Discursive Spaces*. New York: New York University Press, 2003.

———. *Sexual Futures, Queer Gestures, and Other Latina Longings*. New York: New York University Press, 2014.

Rodriguez, Richard. *Brown: The Last Discovery of America*. New York: Penguin, 2002.

Rodríguez, Richard T. *Next of Kin: The Family in Chicana/o Cultural Politics*. Durham, NC: Duke University Press, 2009.

———. "X Marks the Spot." *Cultural Dynamics* 29, no. 3 (2017): 202–214.

Román, Miriam Jiménez, and Juan Flores, eds. *The Afro-Latin@ Reader: History and Culture in the United States*. Durham, NC: Duke University Press, 2010.

Rosa, Jonathan. *Looking Like a Language, Sounding Like a Race: Raciolinguistic Ideologies and the Learning of Latinidad*. Oxford, UK: Oxford University Press, 2019.

Rúa, Mérida M. *A Grounded Identidad: Making New Lives in Chicago's Puerto Rican Neighborhoods*. New York: Oxford University Press, 2012.

Rudolph, Jennifer Domino. *Baseball as Mediated Latinidad: Race, Masculinity, Nationalism, and Performances of Identity*. Columbus: Ohio State University Press, 2020.

———. *Embodying Latino Masculinities: Producing Masculatinidad*. New York: Palgrave Macmillan, 2012.

Ruiz, Vicki L. *From Out of the Shadows: Mexican Women in Twentieth-Century America*. Oxford, UK: Oxford University Press, 1998.

Saldaña-Portillo, María Josefina. *Indian Given: Racial Geographies across Mexico and the United States*. Durham, NC: Duke University Press, 2016.

Samuels, Ellen. "Six Ways of Looking at Crip Time." *Disability Studies Quarterly* 37, no. 3 (2017): http://dsq-sds.org/article/view/5824/4684.

Sawyer, Suzana. "Bobbittizing Texaco: Dis-membering Corporate Capital and Re-membering the Nation in Ecuador." *Cultural Anthropology* 17, no. 2 (2002): 150–180.

Schooler, Deborah. "Real Women Have Curves: A Longitudinal Investigation of TV and the Body Image Development of Latina Adolescents." *Journal of Adolescent Research* 23, no. 2 (2008): 132–153.

Scott, Joan Wallach. *Only Paradoxes to Offer: French Feminists and the Rights of Man*. Cambridge, MA: Harvard University Press, 1996.

Sealey, Kris. "Transracialism and White Allyship: A Response to Rebecca Tuvel." *Philosophy Today* 62, no. 1 (2018).

Serano, Julia. *Whipping Girl: A Transsexual Woman on Sexism and the Scapegoating of Femininity*. Emeryville, CA: Seal Press, 2007.

Shah, Nayan. "Policing Privacy, Migrants, and the Limits of Freedom." *Social Text* 84–85, nos. 3–4 (2005): 275–284.

Silva, Kumarini. "Brown: From Identity to Identification." *Cultural Studies* 24, no. 2 (2010): 167–182.

Silver, Mark S. "The Evaluation and Legal Standards in Forensic Social Work Immigration Practice: Spousal Abuse, Asylum, Criminal, and Other 'Hardship' Immigration Cases." *Journal of Immigrant and Refugee Services* 3, nos. 3–4 (2005): 43–55.

Smith-Nonini, Sandy. "The Illegal and the Dead: Are Mexicans Renewable Energy?" *Medical Anthropology* 30, no. 5 (2011): 454–474.

Snorton, C. Riley. *Black on Both Sides: A Racial History of Trans Identity*. Minneapolis: University of Minnesota Press, 2017.

Soto, Sandra K. *Reading Chican@ Like a Queer: The De-mastery of Desire*. Austin: University of Texas Press, 2010.

Spivak, Gayatri. "Can the Subaltern Speak?" In *Marxism and the Interpretation of Culture*, edited by Cary Nelson and Lawrence Grossberg. Basingstoke, UK: Macmillan, 1988.

Spivak, Russell. "Not Guilty by Reason of CTE: The Imminent Rise of Football's Foil as a Criminal Defense." *Criminal Law Bulletin* 54, no. 6 (2018): 1279–1310.

Stern, Alexandra Minna. *Eugenic Nation: Faults and Frontiers of Better Breeding in America.* 2nd ed. Berkeley: University of California Press, 2016.

Stevens, Elizabeth. "The Spectacularized Penis: Contemporary Representations of the Phallic Male Body." *Men and Masculinities* 10, no. 1 (2007): 85–98.

Stryker, Susan, and Aren Z. Aizura, eds. *The Transgender Studies Reader 2.* New York: Routledge, 2013.

Stryker, Susan, and Stephen Whittle, eds. *The Transgender Studies Reader.* New York: Routledge, 2006.

Suárez-Orozco, Marcelo M., and Mariela M. Páez, eds. *Latinos: Remaking America.* Berkeley: University of California Press, 2002.

Syed, Jawad, and Fiza Ali. "The White Woman's Burden: From Colonial Civilization to Third World Development." *Third World Quarterly* 32, no. 2 (2011): 349–365.

Terry, Jennifer, and Jacqueline Urla, eds. *Deviant Bodies: Critical Perspectives on Difference in Science and Popular Culture.* Bloomington: Indiana University Press, 1995.

Torres, Lourdes. "Latinx?" *Latino Studies* 16 (2018): 283–285.

Torry, William I. "Multicultural Jurisprudence and the Culture Defense." *Journal of Legal Pluralism and Unofficial Law* 31, no. 44 (1999): 127–161.

Treichler, Paula A. "AIDS, Homophobia, and Biomedical Discourse: An Epidemic of Signification." *October* 43 (Winter 1987): 31–70.

Trujillo, Carla, ed. *Chicana Lesbians: The Girls Our Mothers Warned Us About.* Berkeley: Third World Woman, 1991.

Tuvel, Rebecca. "In Defense of Transracialism." *Hypatia* 32, no. 2 (2017).

Valdivia, Angharad N. *Latina/os and the Media.* New York: Polity, 2010.

Vargas, Deborah R. "Representations of Latina/o Sexuality in Popular Culture." In *Latina/o Sexualities: Probing Powers, Passions, Practices, and Policies*, edited by Marysol Asencio, 117–136. New Brunswick, NJ: Rutgers University Press, 2010.

———. "Ruminations on Lo Sucio as a Latino Queer Analytic." *American Quarterly* 66, no. 3 (2014): 715–726.

Vasconcelos, José. *The Cosmic Race / La raza cósmica.* Translated by Didier T. Jaén. Baltimore, MD: Johns Hopkins University Press, 1997.

Victor, Jeffery S. *Satanic Panic: The Creation of a Contemporary Legend.* Chicago: Open Court, 1993.

Viego, Antonio. *Dead Subjects: Toward a Politics of Loss in Latino Studies.* Durham, NC: Duke University Press, 2007.

———. "The Life of the Undead: Biopower, Latino Anxiety, and the *Epidemiological Paradox.*" *Women and Performance: A Journal of Feminist Theory* 19, no. 2 (2009): 131–147.

Volpp, Leti. "(Mis)Identifying Culture: Asian Women and the 'Cultural Defense.'" *Harvard Women's Law Journal* 17 (1994): 57–103.

Wailoo, Keith. *Pain: A Political History.* Baltimore, MD: Johns Hopkins University Press, 2014.

Walker, Leonore E. *The Battered Woman.* New York: Harper and Row, 1979.

———. "Battered Woman Syndrome: Empirical Findings." *Annals of the New York Academy of Science* 1087 (2006).

Wood, Sarah M. "VAWA's Unfinished Business: The Immigrant Women Who Fall through the Cracks." *Duke Journal of Gender Law and Policy* 11 (2004): 141–156.

Wrangle, John, Josyln W. Fisher, and Anuradha Paranjape. "Ha sentido sola? Culturally Competent Screening for Intimate Partner Violence in Latina Women." *Journal of Women's Health* 17, no. 2 (2008): 261–268.

Yáñez, Jessica. "From Asylum to VAWA: How U.S. Immigration Laws Can Protect Victims of Domestic Violence." *Elon Law Review* 5, no. 415 (2013): 415–425.

Zachary, Mary J., Michael N. Mulvihill, William B. Burton, and Lewis R. Goldfrank. "Domestic Abuse in the Emergency Department: Can a Risk Profile Be Defined?" *Academic Emergency Medicine* 8, no. 8 (2001): 726–803.

Zelizer, Barbie. "Achieving Journalistic Authority through Narrative." *Critical Studies in Mass Communication* 7, no. 4: 336–376.

———, ed. *The Changing Faces of Journalism: Tabloidization, Technology and Truthiness.* New York: Routledge, 2009.

Zilberg, Elana. *Spaces of Detention: The Making of a Transnational Gang Crisis between Los Angeles and San Salvador.* Durham, NC: Duke University Press, 2011.

Index

Page numbers in *italics* refer to figures or tables.

Printed in the USA
CPSIA information can be obtained
at www.ICGtesting.com
JSHW022351180124
55540JS00003B/117